Reflections on the
Revolution in France

Edmund Burke

Reflections on the
Revolution in France

Edited,
with introduction and notes,
by

J. G. A. Pocock

Hackett Publishing Company
Indianapolis/Cambridge

Edmund Burke: 1729–1797

Reflections on the Revolution in France
was originally published in 1790

Cover design by Listenberger Design and Associates

Interior design by Baskerville Book & Editorial Services

For further information, please address

Hackett Publishing Company, Inc.
Box 44937
Indianapolis, Indiana 46204

Library of Congress Cataloging in Publication Data
Burke, Edmund, 1729-1797.
   Reflections on the Revolution in France.

   Originally published 1789-1790.
   Bibliography: p.
   1. France—History—Revolution, 1789-1799—Causes.
2. France—Politics and government—Revolution,
1789-1799.   I. Pocock, J. G. A. (John Greville Agard),
1924-   . II. Title.
DC150.B83 1987   944.04   86-31894
ISBN 0-87220-021-3
ISBN 0-87220-020-5 (pbk.)

Contents

INTRODUCTION

(i)

Edmund Burke's *Reflections on the Revolution in France,* written and published during 1789–90, has become a classic of English conservatism, and that is the reason it is still being read nearly two hundred years later. As soon as one has given that description of it, however, each word has to be explained and qualified. By "conservatism," for example, we do not mean what is meant by the word in the contemporary United States: a blend of American patriotism, evangelical religion and free-enterprise values. Burke's "conservatism" is part of the history of philosophical conservatism, and we shall see in greater detail as we study his text that this is based on the claim that human beings acting in politics always start from within a historically determined context, and that it is morally as well as practically important to remember that they are not absolutely free to wipe away this context and reconstruct human society as they wish. The *Reflections* is an antirevolutionary treatise in the sense that it defines revolutionaries as those who claim that human beings have that freedom and attacks them for making the claim. But it is important to remember that the revolutionary argument may be more complex than this, or than Burke allowed; it may claim either that revolutionaries are free from the constraints of history, or that they are constrained by history to act in a revolutionary way.

In the second place, to say that the *Reflections* is a "classic" of

vii

English conservatism—though Burke himself was not English—is to remind ourselves that it took shape within a context of English politics and political literature; that it was shaped by that context and itself continued to shape it. This must mean, among other things, that its conservatism was of a particularly English kind. It was written in order to defend an English political system—the rule of Britain and Ireland by the monarchy and aristocracy of the eighteenth-century Whigs—and its "conservative" arguments were based on those which that system already used in its own defence. We shall have to analyse the text of the *Reflections* so as to show what these arguments were and how Burke used them, but at the same time we shall have to ask in what ways, if any, he added to these arguments or changed them. This will be especially important if we ask why, and with what results, the *Reflections* has continued to be read after the eighteenth-century Whig order has passed away; either by British readers in the nineteenth and twentieth centuries, or by other readers whose minds have not been formed by specifically "English" experience. To ask such questions must affect our understanding of the *Reflections* as "philosophic conservatism," since the "philosophic" debate between the conservative and revolutionary arguments can take place in many historical contexts and the conservative appeal to history must vary accordingly.[1]

Third, to say that the *Reflections* "has become a classic" is to speak of something that has happened to the text since it was written: to say that it has attained a certain kind of status and authority.[2] This may be ascribed to the rhetorical and philosophical power of the text itself, but it must also be ascribed to the actions of those who read and responded to the text, as distinct from the actions of Burke himself in writing it. There are therefore at least two histories of the *Reflections* to be written. One is the history of what Burke "was doing"[3] in writing the text: of what he intended to do, and of how he came to do what he did. It is unlikely that he "intended" to write "a classic", and therefore it is not certain that he intended to be read exactly as he was by those who made his text a classic. The second history to be written, therefore, is the history of how he was read, as distinct from the history of how he wrote; and the difficulty here is that while the text of the *Reflections* gives us much information about what Burke was doing, the history of what his readers have been doing takes us in a great many directions, towards a great many other texts and in search of information which is not always available

defence

in texts at all. The history of authorship is easier of access than the history of readership, reception and interpretation; and often the best we can do is to take note of our own conventional interpretations of a work such as the *Reflections* and heighten our consciousness by confronting them with what can be discovered about the author's own intentions and achievements.

(ii)

Edmund Burke (1729–1797)[4] was an Irish Protestant by birth, but belonged neither to the Scotch-Irish Presbyterians of the north nor to the Anglo-Irish Protestant landowning class called the Ascendancy. His family name indicates "Old English" or "Norman-Irish" descent, as does that of his wife Jane Nugent, and it is probable that the families of both had only recently converted from Catholicism.[5] It is notable also that he was a strong advocate of the relief of Irish Catholics from some at least of the disabilities imposed on them by the Ascendancy; perhaps this is why he was often caricatured as a Jesuit by political cartoonists. However, he was a baptized member of the Church of Ireland and a vehement defender of the Church of England; he was educated in the Protestant stronghold of Trinity College, Dublin, and afterwards at the Inns of Court, the great law schools in London. He did not become a lawyer, but pursued ambitions as a man of letters and political agent in England, settling in time at Beaconsfield in Buckinghamshire where he died. It is important to understand his career, since it was not unlike those of Hobbes, Locke, Addison or Swift, the great English "political men of letters" before him. As a man dependent on his intellectual and literary talents, he (like them) was obliged to seek the patronage of great independent political aristocrats, whom he served as a writer, adviser, and agent (or "man of business"); but it was possible, and was becoming increasingly common, for the journalistic and literary life to supply a partially independent income. Burke was for many years editor of the *Annual Register,* a leading political review of the time, and a member of Dr. Samuel Johnson's Club of literary men; he had good reason to regard himself as much more than a hired hack. His political connexions brought him a seat in the House of Commons, where for some years he represented Bristol, a large city with an independent electorate; he knew what it was to be more than the dependent of a parliamentary patron, though he represented a pocket borough after losing his Bristol seat. In the House he was a noted though not a popular orator—his long-windedness and Irish intonation caused him to empty the floor—and he rose to an administrative position (Paymaster-General), which entitled him to be called "the Right Honourable Edmund Burke" (probably with a faint sneer by those who did not like him).

In a great many ways, Burke displays the insecurity of the man of talent making a career by his wits in an aristocratic culture. In particular, he displays a deep ambivalence towards the Whig aristocrats of his day (themselves much divided by ideological as well as personal rivalries). At the practical and emotional center of his political career lay his association with the Marquis of Rockingham[6] in the years of the crisis involving the American Revolution; but Rockingham predeceased him in 1782, and in 1789 Burke's political connexions were with Charles James Fox,[7] the rival of the prime minister William Pitt.[8] Fox was an intensely attractive person, and Burke's feelings towards him were highly emotional; but Fox's personal life was disreputable, and he could not be regarded with the veneration commanded by the austere Rockingham. Burke and Fox were to split, in a tearful scene in the House of Commons, over the issue of the French Revolution. Fox was of a recently ennobled family, and it is part of the story that Burke's deep admiration for Whig aristocrats could easily turn into bitter attacks on members of that order whose personal recklessness or ambition seemed to lead them into betraying their order. In this way he attacked the Earl of Shelburne before his breach with Fox and the Duke of Bedford after it, and it is of great interest to see how, in the latter case, his attack grew into something very like an assault on the historical foundations of the Whig nobility's power and wealth.[9] It may be said, then—and it may be read in the text of the *Reflections*—that Burke was ambivalent towards the aristocracy he served and defended; and we may read into this both the fragility of his own personality and the fragility of the aristocracy's political and historical position. Predictably, this has been interpreted as his ambivalence between "aristocracy" and "bourgeoisie",[10] but before hastening to use the latter term, we should remind ourselves that Burke neither belonged to nor feared a class of entrepreneurial capitalists. His theory of revolution, as worked out between 1789 and his death eight years later, stressed not the independent power of men of wealth, but the uncontrolled energy of men of talent; he feared the rise of a revolutionary intelligentsia, made up of the kind of man he might easily have been himself.

(iii)

The foundations of the regime Burke served and defended in Britain lay in the Revolution of 1688–89—still known to Americans as the Glorious Revolution—and to a lesser extent in the Hanoverian Succession of 1714. The *Reflections on the Revolution in France,* despite its title, is to a large extent a continuation of the century-old debate about the true meaning of the Glorious Revolution in England,[11] and this must have puzzled its French readers; only after that does Burke turn to an examination of what the French have been doing to themselves. What may puzzle a modern reader is the limited extent to which the debate about the Whig regime in Britain rested on debate about the English Civil Wars and Commonwealth between 1642 and 1660—the "Puritan Revolution" as we call it. To eighteenth-century Englishmen, this had been neither a stabilising nor a progressive event; it came to be so viewed only with the triumph of the "Whig interpretation of history" in its nineteenth-century version, and this is now under attack once more.[12] They held that the Civil War of 1642 had been a disaster, though it was possible to debate whether the King or his opponents had been the more to blame for it; the execution of the King in 1649, and the temporary abolition of the parliamentary monarchy, had been not so much a disaster as a crime, for which blame rested unequivocally upon the fanatical Puritans and the Army, led by the "great bad man" Oliver Cromwell[13] and wild preachers such as Hugh Peter.[14] 1688–89, however, had been another matter. Whatever had occurred then had come about without civil war, without a dissolution of the government, and without any interlude of rule by plebeian religious fanatics—the three historical memories which most deeply scarred the minds of the English governing classes. There were many reasons why the events of the Glorious Revolution should continue to be bitterly debated; but they included the determination that these three calamities should not be allowed to recur.

An important consequence is that English and Scottish political thought was deeply antirevolutionary; Britain may be described as a political culture in which theories of revolution are invented but never put into practice. What had occurred in 1642 and 1649 was a dissolution of government, the disintegration of a structure of law and government; and most by far of the political treatises of 1640–1660 are based on the assumption that this is the most terrible calamity which can possibly befall a people and must be recognised only in order to confront the supreme necessity that government be restored.[15] Burke, indicting revolution, was writing in the mainstream of English political thought, and the stream was irresistible and at times torrential. What complicates our understanding of this truth is that the greatest (if not the most effective) of English theorists before him had stood out against the mainstream and survived with a high reputation. John Locke's *Second Treatise of Government*[16] had been written before 1688, with the intention of advocating a dissolution of government and an "appeal to heaven", meaning a recourse to civil war; it might well have cost its author his life if he had not hidden the manuscript and gone into exile. When he published it (anonymously) in 1689, the "appeal to heaven" had been made at William of Orange's landing in England and had miraculously ended without civil war; but Locke still seems to have published in order to advocate a dissolution of government, in the sense that the Lords and Commons then sitting at Westminster should become a constituent assembly with freedom to reconstruct the constitution, and not a mere parliament bound by the constitution's normal conventions.

But the Glorious Revolution—glorious because not a civil war, at least in England[17]—had been declared no revolution at all, at least not in this sense. Insofar as any attention had been paid to Locke or those who thought like him, it had been to state that no dissolution of government and no reversion of power to the people had occurred in any of the kingdoms of Great Britain (as, even in Ireland, they never have). In place of the regression of the people to a state of nature, leaving them free to renew the former government or erect a new one, it was insisted that in terminating the kingship of James II and transferring the crown to William and Mary, the nation had acted by the authority and according to the forms of the ancient constitution:[18] of King, Lords and Commons, the common law and its judges, extending back through Magna Carta to the Norman Conquest and beyond. All had been done by precedent and authority, nothing by the *tabula rasa* of the uncommitted intellect. The people had been less free to choose a king or a government than obliged to maintain and preserve a constitution already existing. If (as some of them said) "utmost necessity"[19] had obliged them to dethrone a king and enthrone another, it had also obliged them to preserve the law (and the church, of which more later) by which kings ruled.

The politics of the Whig ruling structure were therefore deeply anti-Lockean, though Locke's more radical current of thought at no time disappeared.[20] Writers as diverse as David Hume in Scotland[21] and Sir William Blackstone in England[22] explicitly stated that Locke's *Second Treatise* was unacceptable as an account of what had happened in 1688–89, and the reading of the Revolution which Burke gives in the *Reflections* was orthodox, not reactionary. What is more remarkable is that Burke does not find it necessary to mention Locke at all. Similarly, the historian Macaulay, writing the greatest nineteenth-century Whig account of the Revolution nearly sixty years after Burke, does not mention Locke's *Treatises* either.[23] Paradoxically, the silence of both men is not unconnected with the survival of Locke's reputation. As a writer on religion and philosophy, he was a towering and widely venerated figure in the thought of the eighteenth century, and it may be that the fact that the *Treatises on Government* were known to be the work of "the great Mr. Locke" helped to conceal their radical character from all but those prepared to recognise it.

Nevertheless, there were always those willing to argue that James II had been deposed, and William III enthroned, by the choice of the English people, who had imposed upon them conditions for their tenure of the monarchy. Burke is retorting to such arguments in the *Reflections,* and the contention (as old as 1689) that the Revolution had been carried out within the framework of the ancient constitution is an important component of his reply. To understand what was happening in 1789–90, however, we have to understand why the members of the Revolution Society saw the early events of the French Revolution in terms of a radical interpretation of the English Revolution a century before. To begin with, the actions of George III in the first thirty years of his reign (which lasted from 1760 to 1820) had set him profoundly at odds with powerful groups of Whig politicians, including the Rockinghamite and Foxite faction to which Burke himself belonged. Some of these—but not Burke or his associates—were prepared to use rhetoric (though never to act upon it) which reminded George III that he owed his throne to the Glorious Revolution and the Hanoverian Succession, and threatened him with the fate of James II (or, if they wished to be particularly shocking, Charles I). It is important that Rockingham, Fox, and Burke had never talked in this way; they had accused the King of making improper use of his influence and governing through hidden means, but had stopped far short of any suggestion that he might forfeit his throne to the people. We should remember, all the same, that the *Reflections on the Revolution in France* was written by an unsuccessful politician in opposition, who mistrusted George III as George mistrusted him, and not by one of the King's Friends. But far to the left of Burke, there were those prepared to talk of the crises of the late eighteenth century as a replay of those of the seventeenth; and this began to matter in 1789.

(iv)

Thirteen years earlier, there had occurred the American Revolution, of which a Lockean reading is certainly possible.[24] The Declaration of Independence indicts the conduct of George III and declares that his power in the American colonies has reverted to the people, and his government is thereby dissolved. We must remember, however, that the effect of the Declaration is not merely to sever a people from its government, but to sever one people (the American) from another (the British), with the result that thirteen "colonies" are declared to be free and independent "states" and the connection between them and "the State of Great Britain" dissolved. It was also part of the Revolutionary assertion that "states", i.e., governments formed by the people and exercising authority over them, had existed in British North America since its settlement. Consequently, power reverted to these states as well as to their peoples, and though the latter found themselves in a Lockean condition of freedom to renew old governments or institute new, they did not necessarily find themselves in a state of nature in which all government had been dissolved. Where we find such arguments used, it is often in areas, like the Connecticut Valley, where rebellion was directed against established colony or state governments as well as the British Crown. It is a question how far the memory of 1776 weighed with Burke and his readers in 1789; but the question is easier to ask than to answer.

Burke had been parliamentary agent for the colony of New York and, in his speeches and actions during the American crisis, had attacked the ministry of Lord North for actions which drove the colonists to rebellion. This has given many readers the impression that he was in sympathy with the American Revolution and has led them to ask how he distinguished between it and the French, which he so utterly opposed.[25] The suggestion has been made—encouraged by Burke's German disciple Friedrich Gentz in 1800[26]—that he saw the American Revolution as made in the name of established rights in a civil society, and not aimed at the revolutionary remodeling of a whole social order. But most of Burke's utterances on the American crisis antedate 1776, and whatever their significance for the structure

xiv

and growth of his thought, are aimed at advancing the Rockingham interest and keeping the colonies within the empire by conciliation. He did not comment at any length on the Declaration of Independence, or at all on the processes leading to the Constitution of the United States. What he thought about the American revolutionary experience we hardly know, and the problem of how he distinguished it from the French may therefore be fictitious. There is nothing to prevent us from constructing a "Burkean" reading of the American Revolution, but whether Burke himself constructed one is another matter.

Perhaps the two most remarkable English commentators on the American Revolution are Richard Price[27] and Josiah Tucker,[28] and the relation of each to Burke is worth study. In 1777 Price published a strongly pro-American work called *Observations on the Nature of Civil Liberty*, which Tucker attacked in 1781 in a *Treatise Concerning Civil Government*. It was, of course, Price's 1789 sermon to the Revolution Society, published as *A Discourse on the Love of Our Country*, whose pro-French language and equation of the Glorious Revolution with the French moved Burke to compose the *Reflections* as we have them; and Tucker in 1781 had very similar motives for his attack on Price.[29] Tucker said that Price's insistence on the natural liberty of individuals had led him to declare that all existing governments were illegitimate except insofar as they protected and furthered it. Since it was impossible, Tucker said, for a government to do nothing but advance natural liberty, all governments must fail this test, and Price was therefore an enemy to all governments existing or possible. Tucker's argument is visibly like Burke's; but there are some important differences.

In the first place, Burke's case for the legitimacy of existing governments makes much of their resting upon ancient and venerable traditions, habits established so deeply in the past of mankind as to make them part of human nature itself. Tucker, an English clergyman who corresponded with David Hume, Adam Smith, and other Scottish proponents of the new science of political economy, emphasises rather the contribution of civil government to the progress of wealth and commerce. It is important to keep in mind that Whig social theory held commercial progress to be part of the science of human nature and perfectly compatible with hereditary monarchy and landed aristocracy; we shall have to return to this point, since it is true of Burke as well as Tucker. What Tucker was saying, a decade before Burke said it, was that Price's radical insistence on the primacy of natural rights would destroy the commercial as well as the moral ties that bound human society together; but unlike Burke, he blamed Locke for this as well as Price. Far from seeing Locke as the philosophical progenitor of political economy and capitalist values, he thought him an archaic and reactionary ideologue; the acquisition of property and rights by men in a state of nature could lead only to the wandering life of food-gathering savages, followed by the power of masters over slaves in an ancient Mediterranean (or modern American) economy, or that of lords over serfs in a feudal system. To portray John Locke an apologist for feudalism may have been unfair; the remarkable thing is that it could be done at all.

(v)

Tucker's critique of Locke raises the question of the relation of Whig aristocracy to modern commerce; but as a clergyman of the Church of England, he found a further reason to argue that both the American colonists and their English sympathisers were acting as Locke's disciples. He knew—as did Burke in 1775[30]—that New England Congregationalism was producing in some cases an undogmatic religion of free enquiry, increasingly anti-Trinitarian in tone; and he knew that Richard Price was a leader, along with Joseph Priestley and others, of a campaign to free English Dissenters of the civil disabilities imposed on them in the late seventeenth century. This campaign arose less from the older nonconformist churches—Presbyterians, Congregationalists, and Baptists—than from a new militant Unitarianism, and its demands went beyond toleration to the separation of church and state. Tucker came to believe that there was a transatlantic alliance sharing this aim, with a strategy of keeping the colonies within the empire until disestablishment could be achieved in both Britain and America. He wanted to see the colonies driven out before this could happen, and bitterly attacked Burke[31] for seeking to maintain imperial unity by his Speech on Conciliation with America. To us this may seem comically extravagant, but it still may have been ringing in Burke's ears in 1790, when he attacked Price for seeking the disestablishment of the Church of England by praising the Revolutionary reconstitution of the Church in France.

Tucker's polemic (which Burke does not mention) was not altogether extravagant. The Glorious Revolution had indeed won the support of English Dissenters, who might otherwise have preferred James II's Declaration of Indulgence, by passing a Toleration Act which guaranteed most of them the liberty of worshipping undisturbed, and Locke's *Letters on Toleration* could be read as endorsing that policy. But at the same time, the Revolution had lessened the opposition of the Church of England by retaining the Test and Corporation Acts passed under Charles II, which ensured that Dissenters could not hold office under the Crown, sit in Parliament, or attend the ancient universities. There was more at stake here than the persecuting zeal of Anglican divines; the compromise retained the position that membership in the Church of England was identical with full membership in the English civil order, and that there were limits to the latter's will to legislate the conditions of the former's existence. At stake too was a question posed to the Church by the Revolution, when it saw the King who was its supreme head and governor replaced against its will by secular political action. Was the Church in England a mere extension of the ruling order, as some of Henry VIII's legislation might seem to suggest; or was it also an apostolic communion, part of Christ's mystical body enduring upon earth, as doctrines which Henry VIII had been determined to retain also suggested? The Whig regime of the eighteenth century was based, at the least, on keeping this question open, which meant that both answers remained possible.[32]

This is one reason why anti-Trinitarians as well as Catholics were specifically excluded from the benefits of the Toleration Act.[33] To those for whom all intolerance is ridiculous and unnecessary, it is hard to imagine a world in which differences in religious belief had serious political consequences; but if Jesus Christ were less than an equal person of the holy and undivided Trinity, still more if he were a divinely appointed human being and not himself divine, there could be no thought that the Church—any Church—was part of his continuing divine presence on earth, or in any corporate sense part of the presence of God among men. Religion could only be a community of belief or opinion among those who voluntarily held beliefs or opinions in common; it could not be the institutional form of a communion between God and men. So far from any ministers of the Church holding authority which was theirs from God's presence therein, the Church could be nothing but a voluntary association among individuals holding the same opinions, and the only authority it could recognise must be that of the civil magistrate. Whether the magistrate gained power when God was no longer his rival, or lost it when he ceased to be part of God's fellowship, was a question hotly debated.

These were not ridiculous positions; men of the highest intelligence debated them very seriously, and even those who thought they were ridiculous hated them very much. In viewing the exclusion of anti-Trinitarians from the Act of Toleration, we must understand that there were those who refused to assert, denied, or sought to diminish the full divinity of Jesus for the precise reason that they knew its assertion must place the Church alongside the civil order, rather than in it, and loathed beyond anything else the thought that priests might exercise authority in the civil order which they did not derive from it. John Locke was probably such an anti-Trinitarian; so certainly was John Milton; and Richard Price, in the Revolution sermon to which Burke objected, praised Milton and Locke as true lovers of their country, along with Benjamin Hoadly who, though a bishop of the Church of England, had been prepared to pronounce it no more than a voluntary association. Joseph Priestley, who thought Jesus a man sent from God, held that his return had been indefinitely delayed by the false churches proclaiming his false divinity, and expected the fall of the civil power to be brought about by God before the false alliance of church and state could be disestablished. Both the pious Burke and the sceptic Gibbon pointed to this passage from Priestley's writings[34] as evidence that the wild fanaticism (or "enthusiasm") of the seventeenth-century sectarians was not extinct. Nor was it. There were reasons why Unitarians might be revolutionaries, as some were in America, or fellow travellers with revolution, as some were in England; and when they pursued the radical implications of Locke's thought on civil government, it was sometimes in the knowledge that he was no less radical on the relations of church and state. This had been evident to Tucker; was it the vehemence of Tucker's criticism of Burke that prevented the latter from acknowledging it?

(vi)

The Whig aristocratic order that Burke defended against its radical critics, and against the French revolutionaries whom the latter admired, was a political system, and a political economy, with some very definite characteristics. To begin with, it was Whig, and we should never be lured into calling Burke a Tory, merely because he was a monarchist, a traditionalist, and a churchman. He mentions Tories only once in the *Reflections,* and then in order to distance himself from them. To him, as to everyone he knew, it was self-evident that any administration formed by the King must be a Whig administration, since only Whigs could be relied on as friends of the monarchy and the principles on which it was founded. When with Rockingham or Fox, Burke expressed fears that George III was working against the formation of Whig administrations,[35] these (quite unjustified) fears accused the monarchy itself of becoming Tory and undermining its own foundations. "Tories" could be variously defined.[36] They might be Jacobites (extinct at the death of the last exiled Stuart), or Anglican ultras who still silently held that the monarchy of 1689 or 1714 enjoyed only a provisional authority. They might be partisans of exploded ideas of patriarchal monarchy and divine right, or more radical "country" figures who denounced the Whig regime as oligarchical and corrupt, and—following Bolingbroke, the last notable Tory theorist[37]—urged the King or Prince of Wales to set himself up against the Whig aristocracy. Burke speaks slightingly of Bolingbroke[38] but was allied with those who feared that George III had succumbed to his ideas. It was after Burke's time that "Tories" came to mean the last-ditch defenders of the eighteenth-century Whig regime, which "Whigs" themselves were by then prepared to modify.

When Tories embraced a "country" language and depicted the regime as an oligarchy of selfish aristocrats, they became hard to distinguish from the doctrinaire Old Whigs or Commonwealthmen,[39] who held that true Whig principles had been deserted at the Revolution. Theirs was a criticism of the ways in which Whig aristocracy was perceived as working, and in particular of the ways in which the great aristocrats were supposed to join their "influence" or "interest" with that of the crown, in order to ensure that all Britain was ruled by an oligarchy of the managers of patronage. Whatever the facts about the role of patronage in eighteenth-century government, there can be no doubt that the Whig regime was aristocratic to the bone, or that the aristocrat was expected to dispense favour, interest and influence in return for the deference of his inferiors. There was very little that was feudal about this; the great political aristocrats were certainly great landowners and builders of great country houses, but the patronage they dispensed was that of a state structure which had been growing since the later middle ages, and had been burgeoning since the growth of trade and commerce had begun enabling the state to diversify its activities. Whig Britain was consciously postfeudal; its cardinal belief was in the natural harmony between landed and commercial wealth; and we shall never understand the *ancien regime,* whether in France or in England, if we do not realise that it believed itself to be modern, and even progressive.

There were criticisms of the regime in which landed aristocrats managed a commercial society. Country ideology, whether Tory or Old Whig, expressed the fear that the control of patronage had made the executive too powerful with respect to the other branches of government; and there were persistent worries about the moral health of a society in which comfortable civilians paid the government to defend them by means of a professional army, maintained out of the public revenue. Behind this lay a philosophical question, which found expression in what we now know as the "republican" thesis of government.[40] According to the humanist values of an age which assiduously studied the classics, the moral health of a political society depended upon "virtue", the quality which made men engage in war or politics to serve the public good; no moral equivalent or alternative was certainly known to exist. To display virtue, men must possess enough property to make them masters and not servants, and to give them the leisure to enter the public service; there was room for both an aristocracy and a democracy within this broad definition. They must not be so poor that their lives were taken up in labour, or so rich that they were distracted or corrupted from serving the public good. Such had been the ideal, variously expressed, of the ancient Greeks and Romans. But was there any room for virtue in a commercial society, where property became a medium of exchange, and the exchange of goods for services took the place of service to the public good? In such a society, men might find themselves driven to specialise, paying others to perform for them actions, such as war and government, in which alone virtue could be found; yet how could a society be healthy or free where no man was virtuous in himself?

The problem for eighteenth-century theorists was not that government was held to exist for the defence of property, so much as how property in land, existing to maintain the personality's independence and virtue, should be related to property in goods or capital, existing to satisfy its appetites and diversify its capacities. Nobody thought this problem could be dealt with by means of a simple choice between land and commerce; but for this very reason it became a central and complex problem in eighteenth-century ethical, political, and historical theory. To deal with it was the enterprise of David Hume, Adam Smith and the great thinkers of the Scottish Enlightenment,[41] as of Montesquieu and some of his successors in France.

They argued that the virtuous man of antiquity was obliged by the lack of a free market to live off the labour of the slaves who worked his land and gave him the leisure to serve the republic. His "virtue" made him harsh and barbaric; even his moral personality was impoverished by his inability to exchange goods with his fellows. As in the course of history the market developed, he became capable of interacting with them in many more ways, and there took shape elaborate codes of manners and morals in which they articulated a common culture in the end far richer than that of antiquity. The rigid and fragile virtue of antique man was replaced by the greater flexibility of "manners"; yet these were seen as resting upon a complex historical process, leading men from savagery to civilisation, and there was no guarantee that this could not be corrupted or destroyed. The luxury and effeminacy of the rich, the barbarity and desperation of the underclass, were threats to the progress of civilisation; and as students of religion added their quota to the science of society, superstition, monasticism, and enthusiasm appeared as phenomena of the mind which might endanger it in other ways.

One further fear proved particularly hard to exorcise. The economies of eighteenth-century states were economies of public credit; the state borrowed from the economy and anticipated its revenues in the future.[42] Every state was in debt to itself, and there grew up a class of public creditors who traded in the promises to repay which the state had issued to gain itself loans, as if these were in themselves a species of wealth. Since the rate at which these changed hands came to determine the rate at which money could be borrowed, there was perceived to be a danger that paper credit would determine the value of money, and the activities of the public creditors exercise a kind of tyranny over property itself. In an age where social personality seemed to depend upon property, that was a frightening prospect; a threat to the coherence of the mind itself, and the universe which it perceived. The Scottish philosopher, historian, and political economist David Hume was tough and placid of mind, but his essay "Of Public Credit" presents a nightmare vision of the dissolution of society itself, as the proliferation of paper renders all value meaningless. In *Thoughts Concerning Civil Liberty,* published in 1776, the year of Hume's death, Richard Price cited him at length in arguing that the attempt to tax America had been brought on by the burden of the British national debt; and Adam Smith's *Inquiry Concerning the Nature and Causes of the Wealth of Nations,* published in the same year, has a concluding section[43] which shows that the father of modern economics was none too sure that the British economy could bear the burden of debt it had imposed on itself.

Burke, a friend though perhaps a critic of Smith and the Scottish economists, was less perturbed.[44] It was one of his strengths as a parliamentarian that he diligently studied governmental data on the finances and really knew what was going on there; and we find him making the claim that public virtue is nowhere better displayed than in the management of the public revenue.[45] In parliamentary practice Burke affirmed what Hume, Smith, and Tucker declared in theory: that there was no reason why a modern commercial economy should not be stabilised and rendered more dynamic through control by a landed aristocracy who knew their business. This was his profession of modernity, very typical of his age, and it renders doubtful the claim that aristocracy and "bourgeoisie" were at war in his mind or his world. When his eyes turned to the French Revolution, however, he saw a monstrous paper-money despotism being installed on the ruins of the Church. This is the key to all his analyses of the Revolution, and it is bound to remind us of earlier Tories who, in the reign of Queen Anne, had attacked the Whig "monied interest" and declared that "the Church was in danger".

(vii)

What then was the impact of the revolution in France during 1789 on English affairs and on Burke's perceptions as shaped by them?[46] To frame this question is not to say that he saw the French Revolution in exclusively English terms. On the contrary, he recognised it immediately—as did every observer of any intelligence—as an event of European and possibly global significance; but it was with his perception of its meaning for England that his perception of its wider meanings began. But Burke's was a powerful, highly emotional, and deeply egocentric mind; and we must begin a study of his response to happenings in France with a study of his personal situation in 1789. This was, very largely, the situation of a politician who had lost his way and despaired of finding it again.

Burke's friends had been in political opposition since 1783, when a coalition between Fox and Lord North had been broken up by the actions of George III and William Pitt.[47] The coalition had brought in a bill for reconstructing the relations between the Crown and the East India Company in the government of British India, and the King had engineered its defeat by letting it be known in the House of

Lords that he would consider no man who voted for it his friend. He had subsequently upheld William Pitt's ministry in the face of repeated defeats in Parliament. Fox, and with him Burke, considered this a breach of constitutional convention; the King should accept as his ministers only those who could command the votes of the Houses. As a matter of fact, this was not yet the established convention which it became in the nineteenth century, but Fox and Burke saw in the King's conduct evidence that he was still under the control of hidden (indeed, nonexistent) Tory advisors who were working against the Whigs and the constitution. Their resentment increased beyond bounds when the parliamentary elections of 1784 gave Pitt and the King a secure control of both Houses of Parliament.

During 1789, Burke was involved in two parliamentary strategies resulting directly from the isolation of his friends in politics. George III fell ill and was, for a time, mentally disturbed by the disease which was to incapacitate him twenty years later. A Regency became probable, and the Foxites embarked on what was then known as the "reversionary" strategy of seeking to come to power through the heir to the throne. This had once been a Tory strategy, and Burke and Fox did themselves no good by the extravagance with which they pushed for an immediate and unqualified Regency in the hands of the Prince of Wales. The King's sudden recovery left them looking foolish and desperate.[48] During the same year, Burke embarked upon the impeachment of Warren Hastings, Governor-General of India. Obviously, he was attempting to injure Pitt and the King by means of the Indian issue which had helped bring Pitt to power; but he had a case, and threw himself into it, for years to come, with the same moral passion as he was to display in his crusade against the French Revolution. It is at times hard to tell which he thought the more important cause. Out of office, Burke was becoming a man of great moral issues; yet his political resentments fuelled his emotional convictions.

The Foxite Whigs—who were only one Whig group among several, though they claimed to speak for all—were tempted, while in opposition, to take up the issue of reform of the Whig structure of government itself.[49] The electoral influence of the Crown was a conspicuous feature of this structure; another was the electoral influence of the powerful Whig families; and when—as Whigs in opposition saw it— George III was successfully using the influence of the Crown against the influence of the Whig aristocracy, the latter might be tempted to endeavour a reduction of influence all around, hoping to do better in changed circumstances. One much-discussed way of reducing influence was to enlarge the electorate, thus rendering it harder to manipulate; and one great nobleman, the Duke of Richmond,[50] had in 1780 called for extending the right to vote to all adult males, though clearly he had no desire to see England a democracy and merely thought the natural leadership of the aristocracy would triumph over the Crown under those conditions. Fox had not adopted such ideas, and Burke had, since at latest 1782, been their outspoken opponent. He thought them too dangerous, since there were some radical democrats at large who attacked the influence of the aristocracy as vehemently as they attacked that of the Crown; and he saw Richmond, and other noblemen who played with such policies, in the classical role of aristocrats who betrayed their class and—like Catiline in ancient Rome—led the people from behind, as demagogues, instead of from above, as their natural superiors. Some of the most quoted utterances of Burke's conservative philosophy date from his oratory on this question.[51]

The role of Catiline had been played in 1780 by the mad Lord George Gordon, who had helped bring about a terrifying series of anti-Catholic riots in London,[52] and had later converted to Judaism. Whig Britain had its own fears of revolution, rooted in the memory of the religious radicalism of the previous century; this figures in the text of the *Reflections,* and so does Gordon.[53] But Catiline could also be played by aristocratic politicians, who took up radical causes to outflank the Foxites in the pursuit of office. One such was the Earl of Shelburne, a slightly mysterious figure in the history of the time, since it is hard to discover exactly why his contemporaries (including Burke) hated him as much as they did. He was a patron of radical intellectuals, such as Richard Price and Joseph Priestley; and they put him in association with a further strategy of reform, which we must see as providing one of the most powerful motives behind Burke's writing of the *Reflections.* This was the relief of Protestant Dissenters from their disabilities under the Test and Corporation Acts, and its logical implication was the separation of church and state.

A campaign against these Acts had been pressed intermittently since 1772,[54] and we should remind ourselves that its movers came less from the mainly Trinitarian "old Dissent" which profited by the Toleration Act than from Unitarian circles whose liberties were formally, if not in practice, excluded from it; they arose in some cases from Presbyterian origins, but also from liberal Anglicans discontented with the Thirty-Nine Articles to which the Church required subscription. In addition to Shelburne, the Duke of Grafton and other noblemen lent their support to this demand and this is why the *Reflections* pillory Richard Price as an agent of heretical aristocrats as well as an heir of the seventeenth-century fanatics.[55] Probably he was neither, but we are beginning to see why it was that his sermon to the Revolution Society on November 4, 1789, occupies so central a position in Burke's polemic against the revolution in France.

(viii)

When we think of the French Revolution, we visualize the fall of the Bastille, the abolition of feudalism, the Reign of Terror and the execution of Louis XVI, and finally the great wars in which the armies of the Republic overthrew the *ancien regime* in Europe. It has to be remembered that, at the time when Burke was writing the *Reflections,* only the first two of these had occurred, and they do not figure very prominently in his pages; the others lay in a future of which Burke lived to see only the opening stages. "The revolution in France" meant, primarily, Louis XVI's summoning of the States General, over which he swiftly lost control, and its conversion by the Third Estate into a single National Assembly. This alone was enough to constitute a revolution in English eyes, for France had long been recognised as the greatest of the absolute monarchies with which Britain was regularly compared; and the fall of such a power was an event of the greatest significance, the weakening of an old enemy and its possible transformation into a constitutional monarchy on English lines. The greatest event that had ever happened in the world, said Fox, exaggerating the case somewhat, and by far the best. Burke was more cautious and said he would wait to see what would happen; he had known for some time that some drastic solution must be found for the huge problem of the French government's debts.[56] Price in 1776 had represented British finances as in nearly as bad a state, but the growing health of the British economy was held to secure the National Debt.

By the time the young Frenchman Charles-François Depont[57] wrote to ask his opinion of events in France, Burke's doubts were greater, but there are three events which stand out as dominating the pages of the *Reflections* as he wrote it in subsequent months. These are: beginning with the great abolition of feudal rights in August 1789, the expropriation of the lands of the French Church and their use to guarantee the floating of a new loan by the National Assembly; the march of the Parisians to Versailles on October 5–6, and the forcible bringing of the royal family to Paris; and Price's sermon to the Revolution Society in London on November 4. We have to bring these together and understand their significance in Burke's mind; and we should start by linking the first and third. Burke's emotions, and his rhetoric, were most deeply stirred by the events of October 6; but it is the Revolution's attack on the Church, and the praise of the Revolution by an anti-Trinitarian preacher in London, which provide the *Reflections* with much of its structure.

Richard Price desired more than toleration for Protestant Dissenters; he desired a full equality of civil rights, irrespective of denominational membership or doctrinal subscription. To us the case for such equality seems among those truths which are self-evident, and it was becoming enacted law in both Virginia and the Constitution of the United States. But we have to be clear in our minds what it meant. It meant the separation of church and state, and this was a revolutionary proposal; Priestley in 1782 had said it might not be achieved without the fall of the civil powers, and only revolutionary Americans (and not yet all of them) had made it their goal. The separation of church and state would mean that the sacred character of the latter had no ecclesiastical or institutional expression, and could be affirmed only by such undenominational religion as men were able to agree on, irrespective of church membership or doctrinal belief; in the words sometimes ascribed to President Eisenhower, society would be based on a fundamental religious faith, but it wouldn't matter what it was.[58] The existence of civil society would have either no religious justification, or one so unspecific that it could be organised into no institutional communion or church; and for those who thought that a church was more than a voluntary association of persons with the same religious opinions, but rather a communion with Christ himself, there was no real difference between these alternatives. Unitarians like Priestley and deists like Jefferson did not think of Christ as a divine being who was with them always, even to the end of the world, but as a supremely significant being, concerning whom a diversity of opinions might be held; and since a church was no more than an association of persons sharing one or more of these opinions, they did not want to see civil society—the state—commit itself to any single ecclesiastical structure. The issue to their conservative opponents was not whether one opinion was better than another; it was whether Christ's presence and redemptive action in the world could be anything more than an opinion. Burke himself was unsure;

there is a sentence in the *Reflections* where he declares the case for religious toleration to be, not that all opinions are of equal value, but that justice can be done as between them.[59]

We may now understand why the political theory of Price and other Dissenters was strongly Lockean. If civil society could not be justified by one set of religious beliefs better than by another, it could have no ecclesiastical justification; and those who wanted it to have no ecclesiastical structure were interested in justifying it by a theory of natural rights which made no appeal to a theology of redemption. If civil rights were the same for all men irrespective of religious affiliation, they were the same for all irrespective of other distinctions or criteria; men who were radically equal irrespective of church might be radically equal irrespective of class, and Price was a strong advocate of some kind of parliamentary reform. A theory of civil society based on a radical equality of rights must offer a radical explanation of the Revolution of 1688–89; and Price, no less than Burke, saw the events in France a hundred years later as an occasion for talking about what had happened in England then. But we should not think of the issue of church and state merely as leading to a debate between the conservative and radical interpretations of the English Revolution as an event in secular politics. The converse is just as likely to be true. The debate about the Revolution had always been a debate about the place of the Church relative to the English civil order, and one hundred years later, Price and Burke were continuing the debate, in circumstances transformed by two major developments. In England, there was now a militant (and anti-Trinitarian) movement with goals extending as far as a separation of church and state; in France, there was a revolutionary movement, attacking monarchy and aristocracy, aiming at the reduction of the Church to a branch of the national government, and employing the rhetoric of an anti-Christian philosophical deism. This was why Price's sermon in praise of the French triggered Burke's *Reflections* as a vindication of the Church of England's role as more than a branch of the English government, and of that government as recognising the Church in that role.[60]

What the French revolutionaries had done was to declare the lands of the Church repossessed by the nation, arguing that the clergy could never possess lands by any right valid against the claims of the nation,[61] and to move towards what became the Civil Constitution of the Clergy, guaranteeing them a financial endowment which was less like the property owned by an order or estate of the realm than like the income enjoyed by the salaried functionaries of the state. Burke was horrified by this development and set out to defend the right of the Church of England to own property in its capacity as an estate; as a Whig he believed that every element of ruling society should possess property in its own right, and as an Anglican he believed that the Church should be an element of the ruling order and not a branch of the salaried civil service. Price and those like him had no intention of duplicating the French achievement; like Jefferson and the Virginia House of Assembly, they believed that subscription to a religious association, whether doctrinal or financial, should be purely voluntary. The Civil Constitution in France probably did not go far enough for them in the direction of disestablishment; nevertheless Price applauded what was going on in France, and Burke thought he was applauding (perhaps on millenarian grounds) that "fall of the civil powers" which Priestley had said might be the necessary prelude to disestablishment.

(ix)

Burke had no doctrinaire desire to impose the landowning Church of England on other societies. His Speech on Conciliation shows him accepting American religious fragmentation as a fact of political life, and his Irish speeches and writings show that he saw no reason why the Protestant Church of Ireland should dominate a society in which most worshippers were Catholics. But where a landed clergy was established as part of the civil order of any nation, any attempt to disestablish or expropriate it was, in his eyes, an attack on both religion and property.

The French National Assembly had taken control of the lands of the Church in order to use them as security in issuing a great national loan, designed to remedy the desperate state of French national finances by encouraging the public to invest in them. The Glorious Revolution in England had been followed by the establishment of the Bank of England, with the same end in view; and the system of public credit had been successful enough to encourage the practice of borrowing on the security of anticipated public revenues, known as the National Debt. Bank of England notes were promises to pay gold or silver on demand; they had been supported by the authority of Parliament, reinforced by the great reform of the coinage in which John

xxviii

Locke had taken a hand, and were ultimately guaranteed by the increase of British trade, commerce, national income, and public revenue. What disturbed such political economists as Price, Hume, and Adam Smith was the practice of speculating in government stock, which affected the rates of interest as the National Debt rose. In France during 1789 and after, the *assignats,* or paper guarantees issued to investors in the Revolutionary loan, were supported by the authority of the National Assembly, but had no security to back them other than the Church lands; there was as yet little sign of political stability or commercial prosperity. Both the English and the French Revolutions had issued loans which were invitations to invest in the future of the revolutionary regime, but in Burke's eyes the *assignats* had nothing behind them but an act of confiscation, itself designed to destroy established religion.

During the War of the Spanish Succession in the reign of Queen Anne, English Tories—among them Jonathan Swift—had developed a press campaign against the "monied interest" of speculators in the public funds, by whose aid the Whig regime was supposedly support-ing the war and its own continuance in power. This was not necessar-ily identical with the "trading interest", since it invested capital in the power and stability of the state, rather than in commerce and enter-prise; but it was regularly opposed to the "landed interest" or country gentry, who were said to pay the taxes on which it flourished to their ruin. The campaign against it was coupled with the cry that "the church was in danger", since the Whigs and their Dissenting allies were supposed to be undermining the Test and Corporation Acts and the Anglican supremacy; however, nothing was going on comparable to the Unitarian agitation in the times of Price and Burke. What has to be examined now is the way in which the Whig Burke took up the originally Tory notion of the "monied interest", and used it in his explanation of the Revolutionary seizure of the lands of the French Church. "By the vast debts of France," he tells us, an extensive monied interest had arisen,[62] which grasped the opportunity of Louis XVI's capitulation to the National Assembly to take control of the finances of France. The aim of this "monied interest" was not to secure repayment of their loans, but to extend their power and that of the state; Burke saw them as active, inflationary, and insatiable, and it was this which had moved them to something never attempted in England—to increase the power of public credit through confiscation of the property of one of the great estates of the realm. The only parallel in English history had been the seizure and sale of the lands of the monasteries by Henry VIII, and this had not been an operation of public-credit finance.

In this act of spoliation, the revolutionary creditors of the state had been aided by a second class, "the political men of letters".[63] The French literati, Burke tells us, had been organised into public bodies, the various *académies,* by Louis XIV, but that monarch's successors had not maintained his patronage and control over them. They had, therefore, become an organised and independently acting political force, increasingly led by *philosophes* who aimed at nothing less than the elimination of the Christian religion from politics. Two bodies of dynamic activists, overdominant in the States General[64] and the National Assembly, had combined to force through the expropriation of the Church and the issue of the *assignats,* the two political acts which Burke saw as constituting the Revolution as he understood it in 1789–90. He says surprisingly little about the abolition of feudal and seigneurial rights; it is the assault on the Church which is at the center of his vision; but he is clear that the monied interest was striking through the Church at the nobility and monarchy.[65] We need to ask, however, whether this combination of public creditors and men of letters constitutes a "bourgeoisie" as we are accustomed to use the word; and the answer must depend in part on how we are using it. In its older sense, it means the freemen of incorporated towns, or "third estate"; in its modern sense, it means those dependent on the investment of private capital in commercial and industrial enterprises. Burke says that the outcome of the Revolution will be the political dominance of the towns and the "burghers" who live there;[66] it is a puzzle why he uses this anglicized Dutch word, instead of the French *bourgeois* which must have been known to him. By "burghers", however, he does not mean primarily those who invest their capital in commerce and industry, and the evidence runs contrary to the view that he thought a trading "bourgeoisie" was assuming control of the French state. The revolutionary "burghers" as he describes them consist not of merchants and businessmen, so much as the inhabitants of Paris supported by provincial lawyers and petty officials, and others whose professions fit them for speculation in the public funds; and their alliance with the "men of letters", literati or intelligentsia, has directed their revolutionary activity against the Church, as the road towards the seizure of the state. This combination of forces, Burke thought, was becoming a threat to the stability of Europe; everywhere states were running deeper in debt, and becoming vulnerable to antireligious conspiracies like that of the Bavarian Illuminati.[67] He was not far from that identification of Freemasons and Jews as the revolutionary underground which was to haunt the imagination of the Catholic Right for at least a century and a half, but he did not articulate it;[68] and how far he saw the anti-Trinitarian Dissenters as the English expression of a universal malignancy is left for us to guess.

This was not the conspiracy of commerce against land, or in that sense of a bourgeois against a feudal order. Burke was a typical thinker of his age in his firm belief in the natural harmony of land and money, which he thought had been institutionalised in the relations between aristocracy and commerce prevailing in England.[69] Faced with the Revolution in France, he said, gold and silver "had disappeared and hid themselves in the earth from whence they came";[70] but what had driven them there was the subversion of property, and this in turn was the work of a revolutionary alliance aiming at a despotism of paper securities, the common enemy of land and money, erected upon the destruction of religion. Church, aristocracy, and commerce would all be destroyed by this systematic subversion; but to see how the three were related in Burke's mind we must turn to his attack on the third great crime of the Revolution as he saw it, that perpetrated on October 6, 1789.

(x)

On that day a large crowd of Parisian men and women had marched to Versailles, where the royal family resided and the National Assembly was meeting. There had been a bread shortage, and there were rumours of counterrevolution. Fighting broke out between the crowds and the royal bodyguards, and people were killed on both sides. There was an attack on the queen's apartments and two of her guards perished, though not the sentry whose death Burke inaccurately recounts;[71] their heads were brought back to Paris, in the kind of ritual decapitation of which there had been several instances since July 14. The crowd, and the national guardsmen with them, obliged the royal family to accompany them to Paris, and the Assembly, which had refused to offer the king any support, followed some days later. It was a dramatically effective humiliation of a monarchy increasingly impotent, the end of the Revolution of 1789 and the beginning of further stages of revolution as yet unplanned and unknown.[72] It also brought about the flight to England of several of Burke's French informants.

These events shocked Burke deeply, and he gives a highly coloured account of them which concludes with a kind of apotheosis of Marie Antoinette, as he had once seen her at Versailles. This leads him to lament the end of an age of chivalry in which no nobility would have suffered a woman of rank to be so treated.[73] Burke's emotions rise to a height that struck many of his contemporary readers as extraordinary and unacceptable; it was of the Marie Antoinette passage that Thomas Paine wrote "he pities the plumage, but forgets the dying bird",[74] whatever that means exactly. Many modern interpreters have dwelt upon this section of the *Reflections* in an attempt to penetrate Burke's inner feelings, his psychological condition, or the structure of his rhetoric. If we want to penetrate his historical understanding of the phenomena of revolution, however, we may do best to focus our attention on what he has to say about chivalry.

"Chivalry" was not a mere emotive term, but the name of a complex historical phenomenon. The great historians of the Enlightenment had seen a dark age of barbarism as putting an end to the virtue and philosophy of Greek and Roman antiquity, and had sought a way of explaining the transition from barbarism to the commerce, intellect, and civilised manners of modern times; this was particularly important if (like Burke) one regarded the superiority of "manners" over primitive "virtue" as explaining the superiority of European over Greco-Roman civilisation.[75] The Scottish historian William Robertson had selected the rise of a chivalric ethos as marking an important moment in this transition;[76] it showed the knightly class moving out of brutal warrior courage, acquiring a code of manners, and systematising a sense of responsibility towards others, notably women. It was in the encounter between the genders that the development of "manners"—courtesy, morality, a language of interpersonal behaviour—largely occurred. Ancient man, Adam Ferguson thought, had depended on nothing but his own character; modern man was civilised by a higher level of interaction with his fellow social beings.[77]

Commerce, arising within feudal society and showing it the way out of barbarism, was a further motor in the growth of manners, and there was an association in Robertson's mind between chivalry, courtly love, and the opening up of commerce in Europe after the Crusades. It could also be said that chivalry had been a civilising movement among the nobility, just as scholastic and juristic learning had indicated the revival of literacy among the medieval priests and monks; commerce and letters were media of communication and encouraged the growth of manners, but the remarkable thing about chivalry was that it showed the warrior nobility moving towards the generation of manners on their own. To emphasise medieval chivalry had therefore the ideological effect of explaining how noblemen and gentlemen could play their part in the polite modern Europe of the *ancien regime*. A chivalrous nobility and a learned and charitable clergy belonged to the same historical process as the enlightened townsmen of the age of commerce. It was the decline of all three that Burke was lamenting when he described chivalry crumbling under the impact of revolution. This part of the *Reflections* is both emotionally extravagant and historically sophisticated; Burke was turning the historical theses of Robertson and Ferguson into an indictment of the Revolution in France.

Increasingly—both in the *Reflections* and in later writings—he took the view that the Revolution was a destructive movement of the human intellect, aimed at the utter subversion of the codes of manners and social behaviour which had grown up in the centuries of European history. The two groups aiming at this subversion—paper-money speculators and irresponsible intellectuals—had struck first at the Church by destroying its property, then at the nobility and monarchy by the destruction of chivalry; and there was no doubt in Burke's mind, as many passages show,[78] that they would proceed to the subversion of commerce, the third historical foundation of manners. He stressed, however, that it was only the third; there is a passage in which he differs from "our economical politicians"—a phrase which, since "politician" still meant "political theorist", seems to point at the political economists of Scotland—in holding that commerce is not the sole force generating manners in history.[79] On the contrary, a foundation in manners must be laid before commerce is possible, and the feudal and clerical cultural codes generated in the middle ages are part of what Robertson had called "the progress of society in Europe"; to destroy them is to undermine what has been built upon them. The Revolutionary conspiracy against manners is therefore a conspiracy against history. The strange vehemence with which Burke portrayed both Marie Antoinette—who may not have deserved it—and the violence committed against her—which may have been less terrible than he suggested—is the occasion of a complex piece of conservative thinking, in which tradition and progress find themselves reconciled.

Of the two groups identified as revolutionary in Burke's mind, the speculators in paper money and public debt were perhaps the less durable image. This may be the moment at which to point out that this Introduction makes no attempt to tell the true story of the French Revolution, or to offer criticism of Burke's account of it; we are concerned solely with the processes by which this account took shape in his mind. But fear of a "monied interest" in this sense had usually been expressed by Tories and Commonwealthmen, and directed against the Whig order to which Burke had joined himself; it is a little odd to find him elaborating such an invective, and he is obliged to spend time[80] explaining why English public finances are not vulnerable to debt in the way Price (and later Paine) thought they were. Perhaps this is why we hear less about the paper-money men in Burke's later anti-Revolutionary writings. But the specter of the atheist *philosophes* grows stronger and more terrible, and their conspiracy against "manners" and morals (it is nearly the same word[81]) will lead to their being regularly compared to cannibals when Burke is writing after the Reign of Terror. In the *Reflections,* what is noteworthy is the emphasis laid on their organised and collective activity, unlike that of the earlier English deists, who "never acted in corps, never were known as a faction in the state".[82] Burke seems to envisage the organised *académies* created by Louis XIV—and abolished during the Revolution—giving place, long before it, to spontaneously organised enterprises such as the *Encyclopèdie* and then to the Revolution itself. Leaving aside the question how far the latter was the work of *philosophes* acting together, what needs attention here is Burke's perception of the techniques of control which a regime may exert over its intellectuals and literary men. Louis XIV brigaded them into academies; his successors failed to control them; Napoleon, after Burke's time, was to signal his agreement with this thesis by re-creating the academies. But exactly what were the means of control which the *ancien regime* failed to exercise?

Burke seems to have had two in mind, both typical of the England in which he lived: namely, land and patronage. With regard to the former, we should remember that the "men of letters" were the social group which might be coming to replace the clergy as educators and disciplinarians of the people; the original meaning of "clergy" was not "priesthood" or "ministry" but "literati", the "clerks" or "lettered men" of medieval society. In England, the "men of letters" were not organised into academies in the French sense, but into the "universities" dominated by the Anglican clergy and their competitors, the "dissenting academies", where ministers such as Price and Priestley taught; or if not aiming at ecclesiastical careers, they made for London where they were not organised or incorporated, but lived under the patronage of great men or by the sale of their works on a publishers' market. It followed that one of the principal means of securing literary and intellectual talent to the English social order was the landowning Church of England; and in his lengthy passages in praise of this establishment,[83] Burke is saying that England both commits itself to the sacred order of nature by investing the Church with property, and by the same means harnesses the restless energy of the human intellect to a social order which is sacred, natural, and the product of history. The clergy nourish manners, let us remember, and manners nourish commerce.

This is probably what accounts for one of the apparently "Tory" passages in the *Reflections:* the lengthy quotations from Sir John Denham's *Cooper's Hill,*[84] a poem of the Civil War period in the previous century, which denounce Henry VIII for his seizure of the lands of the monasteries a hundred years earlier still. There need be no nostalgia for the monastic life here; Denham and Burke were carrying on a line of thought continuous in the Church of England, which had long lamented that these lands had not been used to endow learning and an even more secure clergy, instead of passing into the hands of greedy and improvident laymen. The argument looked towards the greater independence of the Church, and therefore seems Tory, if we do not agree with Burke that an established and landed clergy formed an integral part of the Whig order. The only reason why we should not think so is that many landed Whig families owed their beginnings and much of their wealth to lands which had once been monastic, and that they knew it. It was not always clear that the Whig aristocracy were the mainstay of the Church party.

A disestablishment of the Church might threaten its place in the social order as well as the state. As late as 1830, the University of Durham was founded by a bishop and cathedral chapter who feared that their lands would be taken from them by godless reformers and, therefore, used them to endow clerical learning. This fear is somewhere in Burke's mind when he attacks Price's apparent sympathy with the National Assembly's proceedings against the French Church, and it is part of his portrait of the reforming dissenters as types of the rootless intellectual who can think only against the social order and never with it. The social order in his mind was natural; it was an alliance between heaven and earth; and property (as the republican James Harrington had also seen[85]) was the means by which the human actor assumed a place in this natural, but also dynamic and historical, order. A landed clergy was therefore one way of enlisting and controlling the intellectual energy of the "men of letters" or "clerisy". Milton had thought this a perversion of religion and had wanted[86] to see the clergy paid by their congregations, but Burke was a product of the Anglican Restoration. In France, he was beginning to see what intellectual energy might do when it ran outside the channels of established society, and while the reforming dissenters of London might be very unlike the anti-Christian *philosophes* of Paris, he thought them headed in the same direction. If they were not revolutionaries, they were misguided fellow-travellers.

The patronage of great men, landed aristocrats who were pillars of the social order, was the second means by which men of letters and talent found admission to the regime and learned to accept its discipline. We must never forget that Burke himself was a literary adventurer of talent; and he was, like many talented dependents on great men, inclined both to idealise the patron-client relationship and to denounce it. He admired the Whig aristocracy for their leisured magnanimity and railed against them for their complacent irresponsibility, and when he found any of them, like Shelburne, seeming to betray their order, "the rage of Edmund Burke"[87] knew no bounds. A few years after the *Reflections,* Burke was granted a pension by the Crown, and when the immensely rich Duke of Bedford—a Whig of the left—jeered at this, Burke wrote him *A Letter to a Noble Lord,* reminding him in no uncertain terms that his family's wealth originated in a grant of monastic lands by Henry VIII. The *Letter* almost reads as an attack on the whole aristocracy, but Burke was raging against Bedford for deserting his proper role, which included courtesy and protection towards such as Burke himself.

(xii)

His last work on the Revolution in France is the *Letters on a Regicide Peace,* published in 1796–97. By that time Louis XVI and his queen had been guillotined, the Terror had come and gone, the armies of the Revolution were overrunning Western Europe, and the British government was contemplating a treaty with France; and Burke—bereaved of his son, dying of cancer, and utterly isolated in politics—was wilder in his language than ever. The *Letters on a Regicide Peace* are well worth reading but do not contain the makings of a classic. They are mentioned here because they display the culmination of the thinking which underlies the *Reflections*. The earlier work proclaims and explores France's descent into chaos; not long after, Burke was declaring that "France" no longer existed; but by the end he came to hold, prophetically and obsessively, that Britain was not at war with a nation, but with a revolutionary conspiracy, which he termed an "armed doctrine"[88] and a "dreadful energy". We can say that he was wrong; it was still France that had been transformed by revolution; but his diagnosis, while poor political practice, was great political prophecy, in the sense that it enabled him to isolate and describe something recognisable in the holocausts and purges of our own times. Burke seems to have known more about what revolution could become than about what it was yet like.

The "dreadful energy" is that of human intellect set free from all social restraints, so that it is free to be constructive or destructive as it chooses, and it frequently chooses the latter in sheer assertion of its own power. A revolutionary intelligentsia is still the main vehicle of this energy, but its allies are less the "monied interest" of the *Reflections*—and still less the "burghers", about whom nothing is said—than the bureaucrats and technocrats of national power,[89] replacing the provincial attorneys and speculators of Burke's earlier analysis; and instead of the *académiciens* and *encyclopèdistes* of 1790, the intelligentsia is now described as the underground hack-writers recently studied by Robert Darnton,[90] risen—says Burke—to the government of an empire from "the miserable servitude of the desk".[91] This confederate *trahison des clercs* has erected a state which has no purpose but the assertion of its own power and will readily lay waste the very provinces it is supposed to govern.[92] We may protest that France in 1797 was in full retreat from Jacobinism; but the emergence of the Nazis, the Red Guards, and the Khmer Rouge in our time suggests that Burke's last work was the *1984* of its generation. He had discovered the theory of totalitarianism and was enlarging it into prophecy.

One thread in Burke's account of how all this came about is the decay of aristocratic patronage. When lesser men (including men of letters) followed great patrons, society was vertically divided into cliques of clientage, and the political intelligence of the follower was focused—as Burke's had once been—on the person of his leader, who was no charismatic demagogue but a natural leader in a society constructed on the model of nature. But with the concentration of more and more wealth in the hands of the "middle classes"—Burke says this, and we must follow his meaning closely—patronage decayed, society ceased to be divided into the great and the less, and there came into existence, not a capitalist bourgeoisie, but an ideologised mass, in whom political opinions were instantaneously communicated by the electric fluid of the print medium, and the reflective caution of a managerial aristocracy could no longer delay the generation of new kinds of fanaticism.[93] In the early twentieth century, the sociological historian Augustin Cochin[94] diagnosed the Revolution as the rise of what he called *sociétés de pensée,* which sound very like this; though clearly, Cochin was not using an eighteenth-century Whig sociology to account for the phenomena.

The patronage and influence of an aristocracy were in Burke's mind part of the natural order of things, as were the distribution and exchange of property throughout the social structure. What began with the decay of aristocratic patronage over men of letters ended with "the dreadful energy of a state in which property has nothing to do with the government . . . and where nothing rules but the mind of desperate men".[95] The concentration of wealth in the middle classes did not produce a society governed by capitalist relations following known laws, but an anarchy in which men of talent, energy, and intellect thought themselves free to remodel society, but could only destroy it because nothing was left by which their energy could be guided. *La carrière ouverte aux talents* was a Revolutionary slogan, but Burke asked what would happen if literally everything was *ouverte aux talents;* would they not destroy themselves along with everything? He posed this problem by means of the phrase "Jacobinism is the revolt of the enterprising talents of a country against its property";[96] and by "property" he meant neither simple aristocratic nor simple capitalist ownership, but everything which could involve individuals in the material and moral structure of society (including its "manners"). He had no faith in the fraternity of activism, in which revolutionaries deeply believe.

(xiii)

The analysis of Burke's thinking has been carried past the *Reflections* to the *Letters on a Regicide Peace,* in order to indicate one of the directions in which it could develop. He was defending a complex governing order—monarchic, clerical, aristocratic, commercial—

against the inroads of the revolutionary intellect, and the social class or group which he most feared was neither a bourgeoisie nor a proletariat, but what in such nineteenth-century language would best be termed an intelligentsia. In comparing the French *ancien regime* with the English, he was concerned to show that landed and commercial wealth were more harmoniously related in the latter, so that it was not vulnerable to the alliance of financial and intellectual speculators which was overthrowing the former. The second half of the *Reflections* is devoted to showing why the Revolutionary experiments in public finance, state-building and military power cannot possibly construct a governing order as stable as the English—it is here that we find Burke's most detailed criticisms of French practice—and similarly, the *Third Letter on a Regicide Peace* concludes with a demonstration[97] why English public finance must outlast the French even under wartime conditions (as for the next twenty years, it arguably did). Burke had few fears for the economic stability of the Whig regime and little sense that the aristocratic and commercial components of English society were at odds; that awareness was not general until the enactment of the Corn Laws. He did not fear the capitalist classes (Marxists are compelled to dither between denouncing him as a reactionary and denouncing him as a bourgeois)[98] and there is little to be found in the *Reflections* about the radical English artisans who read Paine and loudly supported the French a few years later.[99] Burke was afraid of the power of the human intelligence when divorced from all social restraints; he offered a sociological explanation of how this divorce might come about, but at its heart is always the vision of an intellectual and professional class which is not a bourgeoisie—though it may invest its earnings—but, equally, is no longer a clergy or content to be the clients of liberal aristocratic patrons. Here we may indeed find sources for Burke's thought in the ambivalence of his personal position. He was no longer a follower of great men, but he had not succeeded in becoming one himself. Men of intellect could rise to the peerage and found titled families, but he had not done so. The death of his idolised son, which crushed him in his last years, must have been part of this vision of personal failure.

The role in society of men of letters and talents offers one key to the understanding of how the *Reflections* was received by contemporaries and became part of the history of British political discourse. About this reception we do not know as much as we may be tempted to take for granted. The first printed responses we have were all the works of adversaries: sympathisers with the French Revolution, whether Whig, Unitarian or belonging to the new strains of political radicalism being developed by Thomas Paine, Mary Wollstonecraft or William Godwin.[100] A laudable desire for political fairness causes most studies of the *Reflections* to conclude with an examination of these replies, and it is curious to see modern paperback editions of Burke whose cover designs, in fact, glorify revolution,[101] planting the Tree of Liberty where he praised the British Oak. But this introduction is concerned with the *Reflections* as a conservative classic, and the story of how it became one is not yet well understood, in part because British politics and society changed so much over the next half-century that conservatism, liberalism, and radicalism—if not appearing for the first time—took on many new meanings.

Since the *Reflections* appeared in a context formed by the disintegration of the Whig party, and indeed contributed to the schism between the followers of Fox and other Whig groups, it had a mixed reception, and we cannot say that it immediately became the bible of counterrevolutionary thought. There is a story that George III thanked Burke for pleading the cause "of all the gentlemen", but this rests on Jane Burke's account of what her husband had told her the King had said to him[102] and is not much evidence of the dissemination of Burke's ideas. Certainly, the French Revolution marked the beginning of a long period of aristocratic rigour in British politics, and there was popular conservatism as well as democratic and radical insurgency; but the process by which the text of the *Reflections* entered the vocabulary of conservatism needs much further study. The counterrevolutionary associations which were formed in and after 1793 seem to have relied less on Burke for their polemics than on William Paley, Hannah More, and other authoritarian elements lying deep in Whig and Tory tradition.[103] Burke himself remained a lonely and distrusted figure. The Foxites hated him as an apostate, the other Whig groups had never liked him, and the Church looked askance at his views on Ireland; while the strange vehemence of his style, apparent in the *Reflections* and growing stronger afterwards, repelled readers then as it often disturbs them today. Emotional misery rendered him wild and extravagant, and his last years were unhappy.

Burke was a European as well as an English figure, though as we have seen, the *Reflections* is a very English book which might not be expected to travel well. Abroad, however, there was keen interest in the Revolution and what others thought of it, and Burke was taken up by an international booksellers' market. A French translation—

evidently the manifesto of a faction of political moderates—was in circulation between 1790 and 1791, until intimidation closed the bookseller down; there were German and Italian translations between 1791 and 1793, American editions in 1791 and 1792.[104] But for Burke's thought to sink deep into the conservative intelligence of any nation but his own, readers and writers of that nation would have to translate Burke's understanding of both nature and history into that possible for its culture; and Burke's role in the making of European philosophies of history—of which many were generated by the Revolution and the reactions to it—is a complex and various subject. It has been argued that Burke can have had very little influence on counterrevolutionary thought in Europe because, though he was widely read and studied, nobody really understood him, and he therefore transmitted no messages. This leaves out of account the question of what those who misunderstood him thought he was saying and what their misunderstandings helped them to say themselves.

So far as we know, he was most attentively read and studied in Germany, where his chief disciple was Friedrich Gentz,[105] but the understanding of human nature and history taking shape there was very different from that in England or Scotland. We think of political ideas in the era following the French Revolution as "romantic",[106] built around the importance of popular and individual experience, shaping an inheritance from the ancestral past and set in opposition to the "rationalism" attributed to both the state and the revolutionary (or reactionary) program for reconstructing it. "Romantic" thinking could play either a revolutionary or a counterrevolutionary role, depending on whether the *ancien regime* or the revolution were targetted as the "rationalism" to be replaced; and there are cases of both German and English romantics who passed from one position to the other. It is easy to see how Burke's dramatic appeal to history against revolutionary "metaphysics" could help frame such a discourse,[107] but there is the difficulty that his vision of history is in no way romantic or populist, but Whig, aristocratic and clerical. Perhaps the greatest of British romantic conservatives is Sir Walter Scott, an admirer of Burke who was never a Jacobin; but the English Lake Poets completed the transition from Jacobinism (in an English sense) to legitimism, and there is a sonnet of Wordsworth's addressed to the "Genius of Burke" which helps us see what part he played in it.[108]

The best evidence we have of Burke's role in shaping British conservatism seems to come from those of whom, directly or indirectly, he made converts. The Scot Sir James Mackintosh wrote *Vindiciae*

Gallicae as one of the *Reflection*'s critics but later dramatically re-canted and took part in the conservative reshaping of Scottish scientific Whiggism.[109] The Holland House Whigs—in blood and ideas the heirs of Charles James Fox—helped in a laborious reshaping of Whig reformist thinking, which by 1832 enabled orators such as Macaulay to present parliamentary reform as necessary to the preservation of English historical continuity;[110] and Macaulay's *History of England*, which began to appear in 1848, gave an essentially Burkean account of the Revolution of 1688–89. It was because England had passed through a "preserving revolution" in the seventeenth century, said Macaulay, that there had been no "destroying revolution" 100 or 160 years later.[111]

Burke might have agreed, however, with a recent historian[112] that Catholic Emancipation in 1829, and the repeal of the Test and Corporation Acts which followed it, marked the true end of the *ancien regime* in England; though his feelings about the former would presumably have differed from those about the latter. These measures marked deep changes in the relations between the state and its established church; and if the Anglican clergy were no longer to be the profession solely charged with maintaining the sacred values of the legally established order, the question arose how they were to be maintained in the future. This lay very near the roots of Burke's fear of revolution as the release of intellectual energy from sacred or social control; and here Samuel Taylor Coleridge—a great poet and a second-rate but interesting philosopher—perhaps saw deepest into what Burke had been contending for. Coleridge's last major work, *On the Constitution of the Church and State According to the Idea of Each* (1830) is a complex synthesis of Burke, Kant, and Plato. It imagines society as an alliance between conservative landowners, progressive merchants and industrialists, and a "clerisy" or "national church" consisting of men of letters whose end is the maintenance of culture rather than creed, and for whose support a proportion of the nation's land should be set aside. Coleridge had clearly perceived that Burke's central concern was for the integration of the intellectual and lettered class with national tradition, and that his formula for doing so was ultimately an Anglican one. The *Constitution of Church and State* is a piece of utopian conservatism, but it points accurately, in its own way, towards the association of the literary and professional classes with the gentility rather than the bourgeoisie, which is one of the keys to British history in the nineteenth and twentieth centuries. A great deal of Victorian political and social thought is now perceived as thinking about the proper social role of the "clerisy", and of this Burke may properly be regarded as the herald and prophet.[113]

(xiv)

All his antirevolutionary writings are aimed against a secular intelligence and intelligentsia which have become separated from the social—and also from the sacred—order. The decay of the patronal relationships characteristic of an aristocratic society are important to him, but not more so than the decay of established churches which link intellect to the sacred and the social. In England—whatever he knew of post-Independence America—he feared the Unitarian dissenters who would separate church from state and reduce all religion to free enquiry; in France, and far more vividly and terribly, he feared the associations of intellectuals against Christianity itself. We have seen how he synthesized the clerical, aristocratic, and commercial components of Whig society and sought to defend them against its enemies. But what makes the *Reflections* a classic of conservative thought is that it states the case against intelligence which seeks to unmake the social order, in terms which can be translated out of the specifically Whig language in which Burke stated it. To understand just what Burke was saying, we have to reconstitute his language as that of an eighteenth-century Whig, founded on certain assumptions, making certain allusions, and carrying certain implications. But to understand how he has been read by publics who did not necessarily belong to that English political culture, we have to generalise and abstract his language where it examines the relations of intelligence to the social order; and because Burke was a man of intellectual and literary genius, we shall find that he has done much of that work for us.

The passages from the *Reflections on the Revolution in France* that have been most read by subsequent publics and most studied by subsequent scholars are those directed against Price's equation of the English and French Revolutions, against French doctrines of the Rights of Man, and against the reconstruction of the French state by the National Assembly. They have not been those directed against Revolutionary paper-money finance or the spoliation of the Church, and even the lament for the age of chivalry, while recognised from the start as crucial, has not always been read in the appropriate context. But in the passages that have been read so as to make the *Reflections* a classic, interpreters have correctly understood that a case is being made against political action taken on grounds which liberate the intellect and permit it to engage in a total criticism and a total reconstruction of the social order. Burke does not cite the words of the Abbé Sieyès: "What is the Third Estate? Everything. What has it been permitted to be? Nothing. What does it desire to be? Something";[114] but they form an excellent statement of what he was against. He would have said that Sieyès could not possibly be right; the Third Estate must hitherto have been something, and for this reason it could not have absolute power to determine what it was to be henceforth. There was already a moderating commitment to history, and this is what revolutionaries deny. Did Paine and Jefferson (he might have asked) really mean that the earth belonged to the living, and that they might do what they liked with it?

Burke's central doctrine is that the social order antedates the human intellect and sets the moral and practical conditions under which both theory and practice must be carried on. We cannot be fully human unless we already inhabit a society and a culture, which furnishes us with the context in and on which we must act, and with the moral and practical reasons for acting in and on it. It follows that we cannot possibly destroy and replace the whole fabric of culture without destroying our own intelligences and our capacity to replace it, since we shall be destroying the only reasons for acting, and even living, which we can possibly have. The victims of Auschwitz and Kampuchea were having this done to them, but their killers were also doing it to themselves. If we accept this premise—that human culture precedes human reason—there remain only two questions. In what terms shall we describe human culture and state its primacy? What moral and practical limitations will we find ourselves setting to human action? Applied to Burke, the first question becomes a historical one: in what terms did he affirm the primacy of the social order? The second question is more likely to be a critical one: if we employ and follow Burke's language, what limits to action are we likely to set? The first question is about Burke's intentions, the second about our interpretations; but there are connections between the two.

Burke defined the social order in the terms accessible to an eighteenth-century Whig who inhabited a high culture making use of a wide range of complex idioms of thought. For this reason he defined it, and asserted its primacy, from a variety of points of view, which he thought entirely harmonious with one another. It is possible for scholars to examine what these were and ask whether they were as harmonious as he thought. Furthermore, there is a practice among students of Burke that complicates the problem further: that of examining all his writings during an active life extending over forty years and seeking to extract from them a common philosophy or ideology which remained with Burke all his days. That practice has not been followed here. Taking the *Reflections on the Revolution in France* as a single text, we can see that the social system is being vindicated, in the first place, as sacred: as part of a chain of eternal order linking man to God, which is why it must include the organisation of a Church; in the second place, as natural: as part of the eternal law implanted by God in the constitution of things and the constitution of the human mind, which is why the mind cannot destroy and reconstitute the social order without trying to destroy and reconstitute itself; in the third place, as historical: as the product of the progress of society from barbarism to manners and commerce, which is why the ancient orders cannot be undermined without undermining the modern as well; last—though least has been said of this here—as traditional: as founded in the English practice of relying on the custom, precedent, inheritance, and gradual adaptation of the common law and the ancient constitution, which are seen as reinforcing the order of history and nature in their own way.

Debate among Burke scholars has often been aimed at deciding whether any one of these ways of vindicating the social order enjoyed primacy over the others, in the sense that it was the most deeply ingrained in Burke's mind and was a matrix out of which the others developed; or at analysing the implications of each in turn, and asking whether they were at harmony or in tension; or at considering the synthesis of them all as itself a historical artefact, produced by the conditions of a given time and place and beginning to undergo change into something else. All of these can be historical enquiries, more or less well conceived and conducted. But if we take Burke as a possible guide in our own perplexities in our own times, we are likely to find that we do not think as English Whigs thought in the late eighteenth century and must translate Burke, to some extent, into our own ways of thinking. We shall then ask whether we agree that there is a previously existing social or historical order which sets the conditions for our moral and practical thinking and, therefore, sets moral and practical limitations to our criticism of, or action upon it. If we do agree, we must next ask in what terms we define that order and the limitations it imposes on us, and whether these terms are at all like Burke's. Finally, we ought to enquire what the revolutionaries have had to say for themselves since the Declaration of the Rights of Man (they have of course had a great deal to say); whether they have come up with any theories of revolution more sophisticated than those Burke found in Paris or London, or have been capable of offering better accounts of how we are shaped by history and how we may act in and on it. The twentieth century has been an age of revolutions, and the debate between revolutionary and conservative positions has been fundamentally a debate about the relations between political man and his history.

(xv)

This being so, any thinker desiring to make use of a Burkean strategy must ask her or himself in what society the strategy is to be carried out; what has been the "past" of that society, meaning the processes of both change and preservation by which the society has come to be what it is; what, if any, commitment the society has to its past, meaning by "commitment" the acknowledgment that there are conditions which cannot be changed if the society is to remain recognisable to itself; and—should there be revolutionaries at large whose aim avowedly is to change society so utterly that its former self becomes unrecognisable—on what grounds the pursuit of such an aim can be evaluated. It is probably the nature of "past" and "commitment" which will differentiate the conservatism of one society from that of another; and the situation is greatly complicated by the fact that the "past" of many societies now includes the experience of revolutionary change, as was not the case when Burke wrote in 1790. Pasts are now dynamic as often as they are traditional, and we very much doubt whether the history of any society can be called "a link in the great chain of eternal order". History and nature are farther apart for us than they were for Burke.

Nevertheless, his writings have brought to the conservative canon an abhorrence of systematic rational reform, of the mind that sets itself against history, which can be brought into play whenever reformers come forward with systematic plans for doing anything. His writings usefully ask the questions how the reformer proposes to act upon others, and for what actions by other persons or agencies he proposes to substitute action directly by himself. But there has arisen a Burkean cant, used to suggest that the wisdom of others is always and necessarily greater than that of the critic or reformer. Jeremy Bentham called this "the wisdom-of-our-ancestors fallacy",[115] and it was much employed in the late nineteenth and twentieth centuries, as liberal reform was succeeded by socialist planning.

Burke was an enemy of rational reform only insofar as it threatened to substitute the active intellect for the social order of which it was part. In defence of that order he mobilised all the resources of nature, history, and tradition. Whenever his rhetorical strategy was repeated, it became a question what resources there were in the tradition which were to be defended; and it is interesting to see how often, in the debate between governmental action and the free market, the role of Burkean tradition has been played by the market and its "invisible hand." The play of invisible forces is held to produce a spontaneous and unplanned order, and the presumptuous intellect that seeks to substitute itself is accused of starting human society down "the road to serfdom".[116] Burke might not have disagreed; he was a friend of Adam Smith and certainly held that the order of commerce was part of the order of nature;[117] but, again as a friend of Smith and the other Scottish historians, he knew that commerce had emerged from a long and complex human history and still had need of its historical preconditions. It is, therefore, the intensity and complexity of previous history at which we are left looking when we attempt to decide how appropriately Burke's rhetoric may be employed in any given society; and this is important to the question of the applicability of Burke's thought in American political culture.

The difficulty here lies in the presumed nature of the American political tradition. It is held by some that there could never have been an American Burke—though the title has been claimed for the Loyalist Thomas Hutchinson[118]—because American history contains no traditions other than those of Lockean politics and the free market,[119] and the Atlantic Ocean lies between the United States and Burke's appeal to the clerical and chivalric underpinnings of the commercial prosperity of Europe; to what John Adams, in his own way a conservative, had already dismissed as "the canon and the feudal law". American historical conservatism has usually been expressed by lawyers, aware that American law has its roots in English common law and that in turn has deep roots in the Middle Ages; but the great jurists have been a venerated minority in American society. Since pre-Revolutionary times the belief has persisted that America has little history of its own and even less that it shares with Europe, and attempts to provide it with a pre-Revolutionary history have often found themselves far from welcome. No doubt this is why the most energetic school of American Burkeans known to have existed presented the master as a philosopher of nature rather than history (he was, of course, both). Led by Russell Kirk and Peter Stanlis,[120] this school flourished about thirty years ago and saw its discovery that Burke was a theorist of natural law as part of the vindication of universal human society against the barbarities of Hitler and Stalin. It is now out of vogue and condemned by association with the Cold War, but a more substantive criticism might be to ask whether American civilisation can be vindicated by a philosophy that relies so much on nature and so little on history. The conservatives of the 1950s found in the author of the *Reflections on the Revolution in France* a defender of liberal society against revolutionary totalitarianism. It might be argued that Burke, crying aloud his discovery of the latter, was at the same time asking how the former had emerged from history and was to persist in it. He certainly thought it needed the support of the aristocracy and clergy who had never struck roots in America. What American thinkers are to make of Burke must depend, in the last analysis, on what they think of America's pre-Revolutionary history, or rather on whether they think America has any early history except the preparations for a Revolution profoundly unlike the French.

Editor's Notes to the Introduction

1. This is perhaps why a general history of "conservative" doctrine cannot be written; too many minds have been trying to "conserve" too many things for too many reasons.

2. For a study of how works become classics, see Conal J. Condren, *The Status and Appraisal of Classical Texts* (Princeton University Press, 1985).

3. The phrase is that of Quentin Skinner, *The Foundations of Modern Political Thought* (Cambridge University Press, 1978), Vol. I, p. xi.

4. The best current biographies are Sir Philip Magnus, *Edmund Burke: A Life* (London, J. Murray 1939) and Carl B. Cone, *Burke and the Nature of Politics:* Vol. I, *The Age of the American Revolution* (Lexington: University of Kentucky Press, 1957); Vol. II, *The Age of the French Revolution (ibidem,* 1964). Since changes are constantly occurring in historical perspective, a new biography would be convenient. Burke's letters have been published by Thomas W. Copeland (general editor), *The Correspondence of Edmund Burke* (Cambridge University Press and University of Chicago Press, 10 vols., 1958–78) and his writings are in process of being published by Paul Langford (general editor), *Writings and Speeches of Edmund Burke* (Oxford, 1981–   ; to be completed in 12 volumes).

5. The most suggestive study of Burke as an Irishman is that of Conor Cruise O'Brien, in his Penguin Classics edition of the *Reflections on the Revolution in France* (Harmondsworth, 1968). See also T. H. D. Mahoney, *Edmund Burke and Ireland* (London, 1960).

6. Ross J. S. Hoffman, *The Marquis: A Study of Lord Rockingham, 1730–1782* (New York, 1973).

[7.] Ian Christie, *Wars and Revolutions: Britain, 1760–1815* (Cambridge, MA, 1982); John W. Derry, *Charles James Fox* (New York, St. Martin's Press, 1972).

[8.] John Ehrman, *The Younger Pitt: The Years of Acclaim* (London, 1969); *The Younger Pitt: The Reluctant Minister* (London, 1983).

[9.] *A Letter to a Noble Lord*, in *The Works of the Right Honourable Edmund Burke* (London: C. and J. Rivington, 1826), Vol. VIII, pp. 1–76, hereafter cited as *Works*. The "Rivington" edition is the standard version of Burke's writings, now in process of supersession (see note 4 above).

[10.] Isaac F. Kramnick, *The Rage of Edmund Burke: The Conscience of an Ambivalent Conservative* (New York, Basic Books 1979).

[11.] For the first phase of this debate, see J. P. Kenyon, *Revolution Principles: the Politics of Party, 1688–1720* (Cambridge University Press, 1977).

[12.] The most recent attempt to weigh "Whig" against "revisionist" readings is Derek Hirst, *Authority and Conflict: England, 1603–58* (London and Cambridge, Mass., 1986).

[13.] See below, p. 42.

[14.] See below, pp. 10, 57–58. Burke calls him "Peters", but "Peter" appears to be the better spelling. See also n. iii to p. 10.

[15.] For the political thought of the Interregnum, see Perez Zagorin, *A History of Political Thought in the English Revolution* (London, 1954); John M. Wallace, *Destiny His Choice: the Loyalism of Andrew Marvell* (Cambridge University Press, 1968); J. G. A. Pocock, ed., *The Political Works of James Harrington* (Cambridge University Press, 1977), introduction, pp. 15–42; Margaret A. Judson, *From Tradition to Political Reality: a Study of the Ideas Set Forth in Support of Commonwealth Government in England* (Hamden, Conn., 1980).

[16.] C. B. Macpherson, ed., *Second Treatise of Government* (Hackett, 1980) Peter Laslett, ed., *Two Treatises of Government by John Locke* (Cambridge University Press, 1960); John Dunn, *The Political Thought of John Locke* (Cambridge University Press, 1969); Julian H. Franklin, *John Locke and the Theory of Sovereignty* (Cambridge University Press, 1978); Richard Ashcraft, *Revolutionary Politics and John Locke's Treatise of Government* (Princeton University Press, 1986).

[17.] There was a brief civil war in Scotland, and a major one—completing the process of English conquest—in Ireland.

[18.] Howard A. Nenner, *By Color of Law: Legal Culture and Constitutional Politics in England, 1660–1689* (University of Chicago Press, 1977); J. G. A. Pocock, *The Ancient Constitution and the Feudal Law* (Cambridge University Press, 1957; second rev. ed., 1987); *Virtue, Commerce and History* (Cambridge University Press, 1985), pp. 223–30.

[19.] Keith Feiling, *A History of the Tory Party, 1640–1714* (Oxford, 1924), p. 285.

1

20. Richard Ashcraft and Maurice M. Goldsmith, "Locke, Revolution Principles, and the Formation of Whig Ideology", *Historical Journal,* XXVI, 4 (1983), pp. 773–800.

21. David Hume, *Essays Moral, Political and Literary,* ed. Eugene F. Miller, (Indianapolis, 1985), pp. 472–3, 486–7.

22. Sir William Blackstone, *Commentaries on the Laws of England* (Oxford, 1775), I, pp. 161–2.

23. Lord Macaulay, *A History of England from the Accession of James II* (first published 1848), in particular chapter XI. Ashcraft (n. 16, pp. 370–2) argues that there has been a wish to maintain a "myth of Locke's political innocence".

24. For alternative readings, see Bernard Bailyn, *The Ideological Origins of the American Revolution* (Belknap Press of Harvard University Press, 1967); J. G. A. Pocock, *The Machiavellian Moment* (Princeton University Press, 1975), ch. 15; Garry Wills, *Inventing America: Jefferson's Declaration of Independence* (Garden City, Doubleday, 1978). The best short statement of Locke's actual role is Ronald Hamowy, "Declaration of Independence", in Jack P. Greene, ed., *Encyclopedia of American Political History* (New York, 1984), Vol. 1, pp. 455–65.

25. For this see generally Cone, *Burke and the Nature of Politics* (note 4 above).

26. Friedrich Gentz, *The French and American Revolutions Compared,* translated by John Quincy Adams, ed., with an introduction by Russell Kirk (Chicago, 1955).

27. Richard Price (1723–91); see Carl B. Cone, *Torchbearer of Freedom: the Influence of Richard Price on Eighteenth-Century Thought* (Lexington: University of Kentucky Press, 1952) and D. O. Thomas, *The Honest Mind: The Thought and Work of Richard Price* (Oxford: Clarendon Press, 1977).

28. Josiah Tucker (1711–99); see George Shelton, *Dean Tucker and Eighteenth-Century Economic and Political Thought* (New York, 1981) and Pocock, "Josiah Tucker on Burke, Locke and Price: a study in the varieties of eighteenth-century conservatism", in *Virtue, Commerce and History* (note 18 above).

29. It was Price's gift to provoke conservative responses. The French statesman Turgot's letter to him on American government moved John Adams to compose *A Defence of the Constitutions of the United States* (1787).

30. See his *Speech on Conciliation with America (Works,* Vol. III); Pocock, *op. cit.,* pp. 164–7.

31. Especially in *A Letter to Edmund Burke, Esq. . . .* (Gloucester, 1775); Pocock, pp. 162–6.

32. The most recent study of this issue is J. C. D. Clark, *English Society, 1660–1832* (Cambridge University Press, 1985), an important study of

eighteenth-century orthodox churchmanship and its opponents.

[33.] E. N. Williams, *The Eighteenth-Century Constitution* (Cambridge University Press, 1960), pp. 42–6.

[34.] Joseph Priestley, *A History of the Corruptions of Christianity* (Birmingham, 1782), Vol. II, p. 484; Burke, p. 50 below; Gibbon, *History of the Decline and Fall of the Roman Empire* (concluding footnote to chapter 54 in any complete edition).

[35.] He had first done so in *Thoughts on the Cause of the Present Discontents* (1770).

[36.] Clark, *English Society;* Pocock, *op. cit.;* Linda Colley, *In Defiance of Oligarchy: the Tory Party, 1714–60* (Cambridge University Press, 1982).

[37.] Isaac F. Kramnick, *Bolingbroke and His Circle: the Politics of Nostalgia in the Age of Walpole* (Harvard University Press, 1968); H. T. Dickinson, *Bolingbroke* (London, 1970).

[38.] Below, pp. 78, 110.

[39.] Caroline Robbins, *The Eighteenth-Century Commonwealthman* (Harvard University Press, 1959).

[40.] J. G. A. Pocock, *The Machiavellian Moment: Florentine Political Thought and the Atlantic Republican Tradition* (Princeton University Press, 1975).

[41.] Istvan Hont and Michael Ignatieff, eds., *Wealth and Virtue: the Shaping of Political Economy in the Scottish Enlightenment* (Cambridge University Press, 1983).

[42.] P. G. M. Dickson, *The Financial Revolution in England: a Study in the Development of Public Credit* (London, 1967).

[43.] Book V, chapter iii.

[44.] See, e.g., p. 204, below.

[45.] Below, pp. 199–200.

[46.] The best recent study of the making of the *Reflections* is F. P. Lock, *Burke's Reflections on the Revolution in France* (London, 1985).

[47.] John Cannon, *The Fox-North Coalition: Crisis of the Constitution, 1782–4* (Cambridge University Press, 1969).

[48.] J. W. Derry, *The Regency Crisis and the Whigs, 1788–9* (Cambridge University Press, 1963).

[49.] See Christie, note 7 above.

[50.] Alison G. Olson, *The Radical Duke* (London, 1965).

[51.] Pocock, "Burke and the Ancient Constitution: a Problem in the History of Ideas", in *Politics, Language and Time* (New York, Atheneum, 1971).

[52.] Christopher Hibbert, *King Mob: the Story of Lord George Gordon and the Riots of 1780* (London, 1958).

[53.] Below, pp. 73–74.

[54.] Clark, *English Society,* pp. 307–24.

[55.] Below, pp. 6, 10-13, 41-42, 63-64.

[56.] O'Brien, Penguin Classics edition of *Reflections,* p. 13.

[57.] For him see Robert Forster, *Merchants, Landlords, Magistrates: the Depont Family in Eighteenth-Century France* (Baltimore: John Hopkins University Press, 1980).

[58.] Usually quoted as "Our society makes no sense unless it's founded on a fundamental religious faith, and I don't care what it is".

[59.] Below, p. 132.

[60.] For this reading of Burke, see Clark, *English Society,* pp. 247–58; cf. O'Brien, note 5 above, pp. 27–30, and Frederick Dreyer, "Burke's Religion", *Studies in Burke and His Time,* XVII, 3 (1976), pp. 199–212. Burke once declared that his Christian feelings arose "much from conviction, more from affection" *(Correspondence,* Vol. VI, p. 215).

[61.] Georges Lefebvre, *The Coming of the French Revolution,* trans. R. R. Palmer (Princeton University Press, 1967), pp. 166–7.

[62.] Below, p. 45–46.

[63.] Below, p. 96–97.

[64.] Below, pp. 35–38.

[65.] Below, p. 96.

[66.] Below, pp. 170–172.

[67.] Below, p. 137 and Burke's n. 43.

[68.] His references to Jews are usually contemptuous but not obsessive; he does not seem to mention Freemasons at all.

[69.] See the contrast between France and England on pp. 124–5 below.

[70.] Below, p. 34.

[71.] Below, p. 62. Richard Burke met him at Coblentz among the emigrés in 1791 and wrote in some amusement to his father *(Correspondence,* Vol. VI, p. 372). For a short statement of what happened, see Lefebvre, *The Coming of the French Revolution,* pp. 198–205.

[72.] Lefebvre, p. 205.

[73.] Below, pp. 66–67.

[74.] Thomas Paine, *The Age of Reason* (Penguin ed., Harmondsworth, 1984), p. 51.

75. Below, pp. 67, 69–70.

76. William Robertson, *A View of the Progress of Society in Europe from the Subversion of the Roman Empire to the Beginning of the Sixteenth Century*. This essay forms the introduction to Robertson's *History of the Reign of the Emperor Charles V* (1769).

77. Adam Ferguson, *History of the Progress and Termination of the Roman Republic* (Edinburgh, 1799), Vol. V, p. 418 and n. Ferguson may be alluding to Burke's text at this point.

78. Below, pp. 34, 69–70, 115–118, 134, 164–70, 204–05.

79. Below, pp. 69–70.

80. Below, pp. 168, 204.

81. "Manners" in French might be *moeurs,* derived from the Latin *mores,* from which we derive "morals". However, they might also be *manières,* which need not be moral at all.

82. Below, p. 78.

83. Below, pp. 79–90.

84. Below, pp. 102–03.

85. J. G. A. Pocock, ed., *The Political Works of James Harrington* (Cambridge University Press, 1977).

86. Milton, *Considerations Touching the Likeliest Means to Remove Hirelings Out of the Church* (1659; in Robert W. Ayers, ed., *The Complete Prose Works of John Milton,* Vol. VII (New Haven, 1980), pp. 274–321.

87. Kramnick's phrase; note 10 above.

88. *Works,* VIII, p. 98.

89. *Works,* VIII, p. 172–3.

90. R. Darnton, *The Literary Underground of the Old Regime* (Cambridge, Mass., 1982).

91. *Works,* VIII, p. 256.

92. *Works,* VIII, p. 253.

93. *Works,* VIII, pp. 259–60.

94. Francois Furet, *Rethinking the French Revolution,* trans. Elborg Forster (Cambridge University Press, 1981), ch. 3.

95. *Works,* VIII, p. 256.

96. *Works,* VIII, p. 170.

97. *Works,* VIII, pp. 362–430.

[98.] Marx called him "an out-and-out vulgar bourgeois"; Marx was sometimes vulgar himself. The best Marxist account of Burke is that of C. B. Macpherson, *Edmund Burke* (Oxford, 1981).

[99.] Albert Goodwin, *The Friends of Liberty: the English Democratic Movement in the Age of the French Revolution* (Cambridge, Mass., 1979).

[100.] Marilyn Butler, ed., *Burke, Paine, Godwin. The French Revolution Controversy* (Cambridge 1984).

[101.] See the editions by William B. Todd (Rinehart Editions, New York, 1959), showing the Goddess Liberty summoning citizens to battle, and Conor Cruise O'Brien (Pelican Classics, Harmondsworth, 1968), showing the planting of the Tree of Liberty. What would be a good pictorial representation of the view of politics expressed in the *Reflections?*

[102.] *Correspondence*, Vol. VI, p. 239.

[103.] Clark, *English Society,* pp. 258–65; Robert L. Dozier, *For King, Constitution and Country: the English Loyalists and the French Revolution* (Lexington, Ky., 1983); J. A. W. Gunn, *Beyond Liberty and Property: the Process of Self-Recognition in Eighteenth-Century Political Thought* (Kingston and Montreal, 1983).

[104.] See Appendix I. Mr. Velema acted as research assistant while this introduction was being prepared.

[105.] Golo Mann, *Secretary of Europe: the life of Friedrich Gentz, enemy of Napoleon* (New Haven, 1946).

[106.] H. G. Schenck, *The Mind of the European Romantics: an Essay in Cultural History* (London, 1966); H. S. Reiss, *The Political Thought of the German Romantics* (Oxford, 1955); Crane Brinton, *The Political Ideas of the English Romantics* (London, 1926).

[107.] Alfred Cobban, *Edmund Burke and the Revolt Against the Eighteenth Century* (London, 1962).

[108.] James D. Chandler, *Wordsworth's Second Nature: A Study of the Poetry and Politics* (Chicago, 1984).

[109.] Stefan Collini, Donald Winch and John Burrow, *That Noble Science of Politics: A Study in Nineteenth-Century Intellectual History* (Cambridge, 1983), pp. 45–6.

[110.] These speeches are to be found in Volume VIII of Lady Trevelyan, ed., *The Works of Lord Macaulay* (New York, 1897). For Macaulay's relation to Burke see John Burrow, *A Liberal Descent: Victorian Historians and the English Past* (Cambridge, 1981).

[111.] *Works,* Vol. II, p. 398; close of ch. X of the *History.*

[112.] Clark, *English Society.*

[113.] Harold Perkin, *Origins of Modern English Society* (London, 1969), part

VII, c. 4; Ben Knights, *The Idea of the Clerisy in the Nineteenth Century* (Cambridge, 1978).

[114.] Emmanuel Joseph Sieyès, *What is the Third Estate?* trans. M. Blondel (London, 1963).

[115.] Jeremy Bentham, *The Handbook of Political Fallacies* (Baltimore, 1952; New York, 1962).

[116.] F. A. von Hayek, *The Road to Serfdom* (Chicago, 1944).

[117.] See his *Thoughts and Details on Scarcity* (London, 1800); Gertrude Himmelfarb, *The Idea of Poverty: England in the Early Industrial Age* (New York, 1984), pp. 66–72; Macpherson, *Edmund Burke.*

[118.] William J. Pencak, *America's Burke: the Mind of Thomas Hutchinson* (Washington, 1982).

[119.] Clinton Rossiter, *Conservatism in America: the Thankless Persuasion* (New York, 1955); Louis Hartz, *The Liberal Tradition in America* (New York, 1955).

[120.] Compare the critical analyses of this school by O'Brien, (note 5 above, pp. 56–67) and Lock, *Burke's Reflections,* pp. 192–4), the former ideological and the latter methodological. A journal, *The Burke Newsletter,* later *Burke and His Times,* has now lost its predominantly Burkean character as *The Eighteenth Century: Theory and Interpretation* (Texas Tech University).

Note on the Text

This edition is based on that published by the Library of Liberal Arts in 1955 and edited by Oskar Piest. Burke did not divide the text of the *Reflections* into chapters, and in the introductory note acknowledges that it would have been easier for the reader had he done so; the work as we have it is too long for a pamphlet, and too unsystematic for a book. Piest therefore inserted chapter headings, subheadings, and even subsubheadings in the text where he thought they would best guide the reader. These have been removed in the present edition, since the editor believes it better to let the reader wrestle with the text in his/her own way than to impose his own organisation on what Burke wrote. Rhetoric and style are all-important in the reading of the *Reflections,* and the unity of Burke's language should not be chopped up and interrupted by the words of an editor.

The definitive text of the *Reflections* has since been established by William B. Todd (Rinehart Books, 1959) and will be employed in the Oxford edition of Burke's *Writings and Speeches.* This edition has been checked against Todd's but Piest's punctuation has often been allowed to stand. Footnotes by Burke dated 1803 were added by him to later printings of the *Reflections* and published posthumously in that year.

Reflections on the
Revolution in France
and on the Proceedings in Certain Societies
in London Relative to That Event in a Letter
Intended to Have Been Sent
to a Gentleman in Paris, 1790

IT MAY NOT BE UNNECESSARY to inform the reader that the following Reflections had their origin in a correspondence between the Author and a very young gentleman at Paris, who did him the honor of desiring his opinion upon the important transactions which then, and ever since, have so much occupied the attention of all men. An answer was written some time in the month of October 1789, but it was kept back upon prudential considerations. That letter is alluded to in the beginning of the following sheets. It has been since forwarded to the person to whom it was addressed. The reasons for the delay in sending it were assigned in a short letter to the same gentleman. This produced on his part a new and pressing application for the Author's sentiments.

The Author began a second and more full discussion on the subject. This he had some thoughts of publishing early in the last spring; but, the matter gaining upon him, he found that what he had undertaken not only far exceeded the measure of a letter, but that its importance required rather a more detailed consideration than at that time he had any leisure to bestow upon it. However, having thrown down his first thoughts in the form of a letter, and, indeed, when he sat down to write, having intended it for a private letter, he found it difficult to change the form of address when his sentiments had grown into a greater extent and had received another direction. A different plan, he is sensible, might be more favorable to a commodious division and distribution of his matter.

3

DEAR SIR,

You are pleased to call again, and with some earnestness, for my thoughts on the late proceedings in France. I will not give you reason to imagine that I think my sentiments of such value as to wish myself to be solicited about them. They are of too little consequence to be very anxiously either communicated or withheld. It was from attention to you, and to you only, that I hesitated at the time when you first desired to receive them. In the first letter I had the honor to write to you, and which at length I send, I wrote neither for, nor from, any description of men, nor shall I in this. My errors, if any, are my own. My reputation alone is to answer for them.

You see, Sir, by the long letter I have transmitted to you, that though I do most heartily wish that France may be animated by a spirit of rational liberty, and that I think you bound, in all honest policy, to provide a permanent body in which that spirit may reside, and an effectual organ by which it may act, it is my misfortune to entertain great doubts concerning several material points in your late transactions.

YOU IMAGINED, WHEN YOU WROTE LAST, that I might possibly be reckoned among the approvers of certain proceedings in France, from the solemn public seal of sanction they have received from two clubs of gentlemen in London, called the Constitutional Society and the Revolution Society.

I certainly have the honor to belong to more clubs than one, in which the constitution of this kingdom and the principles of the glorious Revolution are held in high reverence, and I reckon myself among the most forward in my zeal for maintaining that constitution and those principles in their utmost purity and vigor. It is because I do so, that I think it necessary for me that there should be no mistake. Those who cultivate the memory of our Revolution and those who are attached to the constitution of this kingdom will take good care how they are involved with persons who, under the pretext of zeal toward the Revolution and constitution, too frequently wander from their true principles and are ready on every occasion to depart from the firm but cautious and deliberate spirit which produced the one, and which presides in the other. Before I proceed to answer the more material particulars in your letter, I shall beg leave to give you such information as I have been able to obtain of the two clubs which have thought proper, as bodies, to interfere in the concerns of France, first assuring you that I am not, and that I have never been, a member of either of those societies.

The first, calling itself the Constitutional Society, or Society for Constitutional Information, or by some such title, is, I believe, of seven or eight years standing. The institution of this society appears to be of a charitable and so far of a laudable nature; it was intended for the circulation, at the expense of the members, of many books which few others would be at the expense of buying, and which might lie on the hands of the booksellers, to the great loss of an useful body of men. Whether the books, so charitably circulated, were ever as charitably read is more than I know. Possibly several of them have been exported to France and, like goods not in request here, may with you have found a market. I have heard much talk of the lights to be drawn from books that are sent from hence. What improvements they have had in their passage (as it is said some liquors are meliorated by crossing the sea) I cannot tell; but I never heard a man of common judgment or the least degree of information speak a word in praise of the greater part of the publications circulated by that society, nor have their proceedings been accounted, except by some of themselves, as of any serious consequence.

Your National Assembly seems to entertain much the same opinion that I do of this poor charitable club. As a nation, you reserved the whole stock of your eloquent acknowledgments for the Revolution Society, when their fellows in the Constitutional were, in equity, entitled to some share. Since you have selected the Revolution Society as the great object of your national thanks and praises, you will think me excusable in making its late conduct the subject of my observations. The National Assembly of France has given importance to these gentlemen by adopting them; and they return the favor by acting as a committee in England for extending the principles of the National Assembly. Henceforward we must consider them as a kind of privileged persons, as no inconsiderable members in the diplomatic body. This is one among the revolutions which have given splendor to obscurity, and distinction to undiscerned merit. Until very lately I do not recollect to have heard of this club. I am quite sure that it never occupied a moment of my thoughts, nor, I believe, those of any person out of their own set. I find, upon inquiry, that on the anniversary of the Revolution in 1688, a club of dissenters, but of what denomination I know not, have long had the custom of hearing a sermon in one of their churches; and that afterwards they spent the day cheerfully, as other clubs do, at the tavern. But I never heard that any public measure or political system, much less that the merits of the constitution of any foreign nation, had been the subject of a formal proceeding at their festivals, until, to my inexpressible surprise, I found them in a sort of public capacity, by a congratulatory address, giving an authoritative sanction to the proceedings of the National Assembly in France.

In the ancient principles and conduct of the club, so far at least as they were declared, I see nothing to which I could take exception. I think it very probable that for some purpose new members may have entered among them, and that some truly Christian politicians, who love to dispense benefits but are careful to conceal the hand which distributes the dole, may have made them the instruments of their pious designs. Whatever I may have reason to suspect concerning private management, I shall speak of nothing as of a certainty but what is public.

For one, I should be sorry to be thought, directly or indirectly, concerned in their proceedings. I certainly take my full share, along with the rest of the world, in my individual and private capacity, in speculating on what has been done or is doing on the public stage in any place ancient or modern; in the republic of Rome or the republic of Paris; but having no general apostolical mission, being a citizen of a particular state and being bound up, in a considerable degree, by its public will, I should think it at least improper and irregular for me to open a formal public correspondence with the actual government of a foreign nation, without the express authority of the government under which I live.

I should be still more unwilling to enter into that correspondence under anything like an equivocal description, which to many, unacquainted with our usages, might make the address, in which I joined, appear as the act of persons in some sort of corporate capacity acknowledged by the laws of this kingdom and authorized to speak the sense of some part of it. On account of the ambiguity and uncertainty of unauthorized general descriptions, and of the deceit which may be practiced under them, and not from mere formality, the House of Commons would reject the most sneaking petition for the most trifling object, under that mode of signature to which you have thrown open the folding doors of your presence chamber, and have ushered into your National Assembly with as much ceremony and parade, and with as great a bustle of applause, as if you have been

6

visited by the whole representative majesty of the whole English nation. If what this society has thought proper to send forth had been a piece of argument, it would have signified little whose argument it was. It would be neither the more nor the less convincing on account of the party it came from. But this is only a vote and resolution. It stands solely on authority; and in this case it is the mere authority of individuals, few of whom appear. Their signatures ought, in my opinion, to have been annexed to their instrument. The world would then have the means of knowing how many they are; who they are; and of what value their opinions may be, from their personal abilities, from their knowledge, their experience, or their lead and authority in this state. To me, who am but a plain man, the proceeding looks a little too refined and too ingenious; it has too much the air of a political strategem adopted for the sake of giving, under a high-sounding name, an importance to the public declarations of this club which, when the matter came to be closely inspected, they did not altogether so well deserve. It is a policy that has very much the complexion of a fraud.

I flatter myself that I love a manly, moral, regulated liberty as well as any gentleman of that society, be he who he will; and perhaps I have given as good proofs of my attachment to that cause in the whole course of my public conduct. I think I envy liberty as little as they do to any other nation. But I cannot stand forward and give praise or blame to anything which relates to human actions, and human concerns, on a simple view of the object, as it stands stripped of every relation, in all the nakedness and solitude of metaphysical abstraction. Circumstances (which with some gentlemen pass for nothing) give in reality to every political principle its distinguishing color and discriminating effect. The circumstances are what render every civil and political scheme beneficial or noxious to mankind. Abstractedly speaking, government, as well as liberty, is good; yet could I, in common sense, ten years ago, have felicitated France on her enjoyment of a government (for she then had a government) without inquiry what the nature of that government was, or how it was administered? Can I now congratulate the same nation upon its freedom? Is it because liberty in the abstract may be classed amongst the blessings of mankind, that I am seriously to felicitate a madman, who has escaped from the protecting restraint and wholesome darkness of his cell, on his restoration to the enjoyment of light and liberty? Am I to congratulate a highwayman and murderer who has broke prison upon the recovery of his natural rights? This would be

7

to act over again the scene of the criminals condemned to the galleys, and their heroic deliverer, the metaphysic Knight of the Sorrowful Countenance.[i]

When I see the spirit of liberty in action, I see a strong principle at work; and this, for a while, is all I can possibly know of it. The wild *gas*, the fixed air, is plainly broke loose; but we ought to suspend our judgment until the first effervescence is a little subsided, till the liquor is cleared, and until we see something deeper than the agitation of a troubled and frothy surface. I must be tolerably sure, before I venture publicly to congratulate men upon a blessing, that they have really received one. Flattery corrupts both the receiver and the giver, and adulation is not of more service to the people than to kings. I should, therefore, suspend my congratulations on the new liberty of France until I was informed how it had been combined with government, with public force, with the discipline and obedience of armies, with the collection of an effective and well-distributed revenue, with morality and religion, with the solidity of property, with peace and order, with civil and social manners. All these (in their way) are good things, too, and without them liberty is not a benefit whilst it lasts, and is not likely to continue long. The effect of liberty to individuals is that they may do what they please; we ought to see what it will please them to do, before we risk congratulations which may be soon turned into complaints. Prudence would dictate this in the case of separate, insulated, private men, but liberty, when men act in bodies, is *power*. Considerate people, before they declare themselves, will observe the use which is made of *power*, and particularly of so trying a thing as *new* power in *new* persons of whose principles, tempers, and dispositions they have little or no experience, and in situations where those who appear the most stirring in the scene may possibly not be the real movers.

ALL these considerations, however, were below the transcendental dignity of the Revolution Society. Whilst I continued in the country, from whence I had the honor of writing to you, I had but an imperfect idea of their transactions. On my coming to town, I sent for an account of their proceedings, which had been published by their authority, containing a sermon of Dr. Price, with the Duke de Rochefoucault's and the Archbishop of Aix's letter, and several other documents annexed. The whole of that publication, with the manifest design of connecting the affairs of France with those of England by drawing us into an imitation of the conduct of the National Assembly, gave me a considerable degree of uneasiness. The effect of that conduct upon the power, credit, prosperity, and tranquility of France became every day more evident. The form of constitution to be settled for its future polity became more clear. We are now in a condition to discern, with tolerable exactness, the true nature of the object held up to our imitation. If the prudence of reserve and decorum dictates silence in some circumstances, in others prudence of a higher order may justify us in speaking our thoughts. The beginnings of confusion with us in England are at present feeble enough, but, with you, we have seen an infancy still more feeble growing by moments into a strength to heap mountains upon mountains and to wage war with heaven itself. Whenever our neighbor's house is on fire, it cannot be amiss for the engines to play a little on our own. Better to be despised for too anxious apprehensions than ruined by too confident a security.

Solicitous chiefly for the peace of my own country, but by no means unconcerned for yours, I wish to communicate more largely what was at first intended only for your private satisfaction. I shall still keep your affairs in my eye and continue to address myself to you. Indulging myself in the freedom of epistolary intercourse, I beg leave to throw out my thoughts and express my feelings just as they arise in my mind, with very little attention to formal method. I set out with the proceedings of the Revolution Society, but I shall not confine myself to them. Is it possible I should? It appears to me as if I were in a great crisis, not of the affairs of France alone, but of all Europe, perhaps of more than Europe. All circumstances taken together, the French revolution is the most astonishing that has hitherto happened in the world. The most wonderful things are brought about, in many instances by means the most absurd and ridiculous, in the most ridiculous modes, and apparently by the most contemptible instruments. Everything seems out of nature in this strange chaos of levity and ferocity, and of all sorts of crimes jumbled together with all sorts of follies. In viewing this monstrous tragicomic scene, the most opposite passions necessarily succeed and sometimes mix with each other in the mind: alternate contempt and indignation, alternate laughter and tears, alternate scorn and horror.

It cannot, however, be denied that to some this strange scene appeared in quite another point of view. Into them it inspired no other sentiments than those of exultation and rapture. They saw nothing in what has been done in France but a firm and temperate exertion of freedom, so consistent, on the whole, with morals and with piety as to make it deserving not only of the secular applause of dashing Machiavellian politicians, but to render it a fit theme for all the devout effusions of sacred eloquence.

On the forenoon of the fourth of November last, Doctor Richard Price, a non-conforming minister of eminence, preached, at the dissenting meeting house of the Old Jewry, to his club or society, a very extraordinary miscellaneous sermon, in which there are some good moral and religious sentiments, and not ill expressed, mixed up in a sort of porridge of various political opinions and reflections; but the Revolution in France is the grand ingredient in the cauldron.[ii] I consider the address transmitted by the Revolution Society to the National Assembly, through Earl Stanhope, as originating in the principles of the sermon and as a corollary from them. It was moved by the preacher of that discourse. It was passed by those who came reeking from the effect of the sermon without any censure or qualification, expressed or implied. If, however, any of the gentlemen concerned shall wish to separate the sermon from the resolution, they know how to acknowledge the one and to disavow the other. They may do it: I cannot.

For my part, I looked on that sermon as the public declaration of a man much connected with literary caballers and intriguing philosophers, with political theologians and theological politicians both at home and abroad. I know they set him up as a sort of oracle, because, with the best intentions in the world, he naturally *philippizes* and chants his prophetic song in exact unison with their designs.

That sermon is in a strain which I believe has not been heard in this kingdom, in any of the pulpits which are tolerated or encouraged in it, since the year 1648, when a predecessor of Dr. Price, the Rev. Hugh Peters, made the vault of the king's own chapel at St. James's ring with the honor and privilege of the saints, who, with the "high praises of God in their mouths, and a *two*-edged sword in their hands, were to execute judgment on the heathen, and punishments upon the *people;* to bind their *kings* with chains, and their *nobles* with fetters of iron".[1] Few harangues from the pulpit, except in the days of your league in France or in the days of our Solemn League and Covenant in England,[iii] have ever breathed less of the spirit of moderation than this lecture in the Old Jewry. Supposing, however, that something like moderation were visible in this political sermon, yet politics and the pulpit are terms that have little agreement. No sound ought to be

---

[1] Psalm CXLIX.

heard in the church but the healing voice of Christian charity. The cause of civil liberty and civil government gains as little as that of religion by this confusion of duties. Those who quit their proper character to assume what does not belong to them are, for the greater part, ignorant both of the character they leave and of the character they assume. Wholly unacquainted with the world in which they are so fond of meddling, and inexperienced in all its affairs on which they pronounce with so much confidence, they have nothing of politics but the passions they excite. Surely the church is a place where one day's truce ought to be allowed to the dissensions and animosities of mankind.

This pulpit style, revived after so long a discontinuance, had to me the air of novelty, and of a novelty not wholly without danger. I do not charge this danger equally to every part of the discourse. The hint given to a noble and reverend lay divine, who is supposed high in office in one of our universities,[2] and other lay divines "of *rank* and literature" may be proper and seasonable, though somewhat new. If the noble *Seekers*[iv] should find nothing to satisfy their pious fancies in the old staple of the national church, or in all the rich variety to be found in the well-assorted warehouses of the dissenting congregations, Dr. Price advises them to improve upon non-conformity and to set up, each of them, a separate meeting house upon his own particular principles.[3] It is somewhat remarkable that this reverend divine should be so earnest for setting up new churches and so perfectly indifferent concerning the doctrine which may be taught in them. His zeal is of a curious character. It is not for the propagation of his own opinions, but of any opinions. It is not for the diffusion of truth, but for the spreading of contradiction. Let the noble teachers but dissent, it is no matter from whom or from what. This great point once secured, it is taken for granted their religion will be rational and manly. I doubt whether religion would reap all the benefits which the calculating divine computes from this "great company of great preachers". It would certainly be a valuable addition of nondescripts

[J.S. Mill On Liberty]

---

[2] *Discourse on the Love of our Country,* Nov. 4, 1789, by Dr. Richard Price, 3d ed., pp. 17, 18.

[3] "Those who dislike that mode of worship which is prescribed by public authority, ought, if they can find *no* worship *out* of the church which they approve, *to set up a separate worship for themselves;* and by doing this, and giving an example of a rational and manly worship, men of *weight* from their *rank* and literature may do the greatest service to society and the world".—P. 18, Dr. Price's Sermon. (Burke's italics.)

to the ample collection of known classes, genera and species, which at present beautify the *hortus siccus*[v] of dissent. A sermon from a noble duke, or a noble marquis, or a noble earl, or baron bold would certainly increase and diversify the amusements of this town, which begins to grow satiated with the uniform round of its vapid dissipations. I should only stipulate that these new *Mess-Johns*[vi] in robes and coronets should keep some sort of bounds in the democratic and leveling principles which are expected from their titled pulpits. The new evangelists will, I dare say, disappoint the hopes that are conceived of them. They will not become, literally as well as figuratively, polemic divines, nor be disposed so to drill their congregations that they may, as in former blessed times, preach their doctrines to regiments of dragoons and corps of infantry and artillery. Such arrangements, however favorable to the cause of compulsory freedom, civil and religious, may not be equally conducive to the national tranquility. These few restrictions I hope are no great stretches of intolerance, no very violent exertions of despotism.

BUT I may say of our preacher *"utinam nugis tota illa dedisset tempora saevitiae"*.[vii]—All things in this his fulminating bull are not of so innoxious a tendency. His doctrines affect our constitution in its vital parts. He tells the Revolution Society in this political sermon that his Majesty "is almost the *only* lawful king in the world because the *only* one who owes his crown to the *choice of his people*". As to the kings of *the world,* all of whom (except one) this archpontiff of the *rights of men,* with all the plenitude and with more than the boldness of the papal deposing power in its meridian fervor of the twelfth century,[viii] puts into one sweeping clause of ban and anathema and proclaims usurpers by circles of longitude and latitude, over the whole globe, it behooves them to consider how they admit into their territories these apostolic missionaries who are to tell their subjects they are not lawful kings. That is their concern. It is ours, as a domestic interest of some moment, seriously to consider the solidity of the *only* principle upon which these gentlemen acknowledge a king of Great Britain to be entitled to their allegiance.

This doctrine, as applied to the prince now on the British throne, either is nonsense and therefore neither true nor false, or it affirms a most unfounded, dangerous, illegal, and unconstitutional position. According to this spiritual doctor of politics, if his Majesty does not owe his crown to the choice of his people, he is no *lawful king.* Now nothing can be more untrue than that the crown of this kingdom is so held by his Majesty. Therefore, if you follow their rule, the king of Great Britain, who most certainly does not owe his high office to any form of popular election, is in no respect better than the rest of the gang of usurpers who reign, or rather rob, all over the face of this our miserable world without any sort of right or title to the allegiance of their people. The policy of this general doctrine, so qualified, is evident enough. The propagators of this political gospel are in hopes that their abstract principle (their principle that a popular choice is necessary to the legal existence of the sovereign magistracy) would be overlooked, whilst the king of Great Britain was not affected by it. In the meantime the ears of their congregations would be gradually habituated to it, as if it were a first principle admitted without dispute. For the present it would only operate as a theory, pickled in the preserving juices of pulpit eloquence, and laid by for future use. *Condo et compono quae mox depromere possim.*[ix] By this policy, whilst our government is soothed with a reservation in its favor, to which it has no claim, the security which it has in common with all governments, so far as opinion is security, is taken away.

Thus these politicians proceed whilst little notice is taken of their doctrines; but when they come to be examined upon the plain meaning of their words and the direct tendency of their doctrines, then equivocations and slippery constructions come into play. When they say the king owes his crown to the choice of his people and is therefore the only lawful sovereign in the world, they will perhaps tell us they mean to say no more than that some of the king's predecessors have been called to the throne by some sort of choice, and therefore he owes his crown to the choice of his people. Thus, by a miserable subterfuge, they hope to render their proposition safe by rendering it nugatory. They are welcome to the asylum they seek for their offense, since they take refuge in their folly. For if you admit this interpretation, how does their idea of election differ from our idea of inheritance?

And how does the settlement of the crown in the Brunswick line derived from James the First come to legalize our monarchy rather than that of any of the neighboring countries? At some time or other, to be sure, all the beginners of dynasties were chosen by those who called them to govern. There is ground enough for the opinion that all the kingdoms of Europe were, at a remote period, elective, with more or fewer limitations in the objects of choice. But whatever kings might have been here or elsewhere a thousand years ago, or in whatever manner the ruling dynasties of England or France may have begun, the king of Great Britain is, at this day, king by a fixed rule of succession according to the laws of his country; and whilst the legal conditions of the compact of sovereignty are performed by him (as they are performed), he holds his crown in contempt of the choice of the Revolution Society, who have not a single vote for a king amongst them, either individually or collectively, though I make no doubt they would soon erect themselves into an electoral college if things were ripe to give effect to their claim. His Majesty's heirs and successors, each in his time and order, will come to the crown with the same contempt of their choice with which his Majesty has succeeded to that he wears.

Whatever may be the success of evasion in explaining away the gross error of *fact,* which supposes that his Majesty (though he holds it in concurrence with the wishes) owes his crown to the choice of his people, yet nothing can evade their full explicit declaration concerning the principle of a right in the people to choose; which right is directly maintained and tenaciously adhered to. All the oblique insinuations concerning election bottom in this proposition and are referable to it. Lest the foundation of the king's exclusive legal title should pass for a mere rant of adulatory freedom, the political divine proceeds dogmatically to assert[4] that, by the principles of the Revolution, the people of England have acquired three fundamental rights, all which, with him, compose one system and lie together in one short sentence, namely, that we have acquired a right:

(1) to choose our own governors.
(2) to cashier them for misconduct.
(3) to frame a government for ourselves.

This new and hitherto unheard-of bill of rights, though made in the name of the whole people, belongs to those gentlemen and their faction only. The body of the people of England have no share in it. They utterly disclaim it. They will resist the practical assertion of it with their lives and fortunes. They are bound to do so by the laws of their country made at the time of that very Revolution which is appealed to in favor of the fictitious rights claimed by the Society which abuses its name.

---

[4] *Discourse on the Love of our Country,* by Dr. Price, p. 34.

14

THESE GENTLEMEN OF THE OLD JEWRY, in all their reasonings on the Revolution of 1688, have a revolution which happened in England about forty years before and the late French revolution, so much before their eyes and in their hearts that they are constantly confounding all the three together. It is necessary that we should separate what they confound. We must recall their erring fancies to the *acts* of the Revolution which we revere, for the discovery of its true *principles*. If the *principles* of the Revolution of 1688 are anywhere to be found, it is in the statute called the *Declaration of Right*.* In that most wise, sober, and considerate declaration, drawn up by great lawyers and great statesmen, and not by warm and inexperienced enthusiasts, not one word is said, nor one suggestion made, of a general right "to choose our own *governors,* to cashier them for misconduct, and to *form* a government for *ourselves".*

This Declaration of Right (the act of the 1st of William and Mary, sess. 2, ch. 2) is the cornerstone of our constitution as reinforced, explained, improved, and in its fundamental principles for ever settled. It is called, "An Act for declaring the rights and liberties of the subject, and for *settling* the *succession* of the crown". You will observe that these rights and this succession are declared in one body and bound indissolubly together.

A few years after this period, a second opportunity offered for asserting a right of election to the crown. On the prospect of a total failure of issue from King William, and from the Princess, afterwards Queen Anne, the consideration of the settlement of the crown and of a further security for the liberties of the people again came before the legislature. Did they this second time make any provision for legalizing the crown on the spurious revolution principles of the Old Jewry? No. They followed the principles which prevailed in the Declaration of Right, indicating with more precision the persons who were to inherit in the Protestant line. This act also incorporated, by the same policy, our liberties and an hereditary succession in the same act. Instead of a right to choose our own governors, they declared that the *succession* in that line (the Protestant line drawn from James the First), was absolutely necessary "for the peace, quiet, and security of the realm", and that it was equally urgent on them "to maintain a *certainty in the succession* thereof, to which the subjects may safely have recourse for their protection". Both these acts, in which are heard the unerring, unambiguous oracles of revolution policy, instead of countenancing the delusive, gipsy predictions of a "right to choose our governors", prove to a demonstration how totally adverse the wisdom of the nation was from turning a case of necessity into a rule of law.

Unquestionably, there was at the Revolution, in the person of King William, a small and a temporary deviation from the strict order of a regular hereditary succession; but it is against all genuine principles of jurisprudence to draw a principle from a law made in a special case and regarding an individual person. *Privilegium non transit in exemplum.*[xi] If ever there was a time favorable for establishing the principle that a king of popular choice was the only legal king, without all doubt it was at the Revolution. Its not being done at that time is a proof that the nation was of opinion it ought not to be done at any time. There is no person so completely ignorant of our history as not to know that the majority in parliament of both parties were so little disposed to anything resembling that principle that at first they were determined to place the vacant crown, not on the head of the Prince of Orange, but on that of his wife Mary, daughter of King James, the eldest born of the issue of that king, which they acknowledged as undoubtedly his. It would be to repeat a very trite story, to recall to your memory all those circumstances which demonstrated that their accepting King William was not properly a *choice;* but to all those who did not wish, in effect, to recall King James or to deluge their country in blood and again to bring their religion, laws, and liberties into the peril they had just escaped, it was an act of *necessity,* in the strictest moral sense in which necessity can be taken.

In the very act in which for a time, and in a single case, parliament departed from the strict order of inheritance in favor of a prince who, though not next, was, however, very near in the line of succession, it is curious to observe how Lord Somers, who drew the bill called the Declaration of Right, has comported himself on that delicate occasion. It is curious to observe with what address this temporary solution of continuity is kept from the eye, whilst all that could be found in this act of necessity to countenance the idea of an hereditary succession is brought forward, and fostered, and made the most of, by this great man and by the legislature who followed him. Quitting the dry, imperative style of an act of parliament, he makes the Lords and Commons fall to a pious, legislative ejaculation and declare that they consider it "as a marvellous providence and merciful goodness of God to this nation to preserve their said Majesties' *royal* persons most happily to reign over us *on the throne of their ancestors,* for which, from the bottom of their hearts, they return their humblest thanks and praises".—The legislature plainly had in view the act of recognition of the first of Queen Elizabeth, chap. 3rd, and of that of James the First, chap. 1st, both acts strongly declaratory of the inheritable nature of the crown; and in many parts they follow, with a nearly literal precision, the words and even the form of thanksgiving which is found in these old declaratory statutes.

The two Houses, in the act of King William, did not thank God that they had found a fair opportunity to assert a right to choose their own governors, much less to make an election the *only lawful* title to the crown. Their having been in a condition to avoid the very appearance of it, as much as possible, was by them considered as a providential escape. They threw a politic, well-wrought veil over every circumstance tending to weaken the rights which in the meliorated order of succession they meant to perpetuate, or which might furnish a precedent for any future departure from what they had then settled forever. Accordingly, that they might not relax the nerves of their monarchy, and that they might preserve a close conformity to the practice of their ancestors, as it appeared in the declaratory statutes of Queen Mary[5] and Queen Elizabeth, in the next clause they vest, by recognition, in their Majesties *all* the legal prerogatives of the crown, declaring "that in them they are most *fully*, rightfully, and *entirely* invested, incorporated, united, and annexed". In the clause which follows, for preventing questions by reason of any pretended titles to the crown, they declare (observing also in this the traditionary language, along with the traditionary policy of the nation, and repeating as from a rubric the language of the preceding acts of Elizabeth and James,) that on the preserving "a *certainty* in the SUCCESSION thereof, the unity, peace, and tranquillity of this nation doth, under God, wholly depend".

They knew that a doubtful title of succession would but too much resemble an election, and that an election would be utterly destructive of the "unity, peace, and tranquillity of this nation", which they thought to be considerations of some moment. To provide for these objects and, therefore, to exclude for ever the Old Jewry doctrine of "a right to choose our own governors", they follow with a clause containing a most solemn pledge, taken from the preceding act of Queen Elizabeth, as solemn a pledge as ever was or can be given in favor of an hereditary succession, and as solemn a renunciation as could be made of the principles by this Society imputed to them: The Lords spiritual and temporal, and Commons, do, in the name of all

[5] 1st Mary, sess. 3, ch. 1.

the people aforesaid, most humbly and faithfully submit *themselves, their heirs and posterities for ever;* and do faithfully promise that they will stand to maintain, and defend their said Majesties, and also the *limitation of the crown,* herein specified and contained, to the utmost of their powers, etc. etc.

So far is it from being true that we acquired a right by the Revolution to elect our kings that, if we had possessed it before, the English nation did at that time most solemnly renounce and abdicate it, for themselves and for all their posterity forever. These gentlemen may value themselves as much as they please on their whig principles, but I never desire to be thought a better whig than Lord Somers, or to understand the principles of the Revolution better than those by whom it was brought about, or to read in the Declaration of Right any mysteries unknown to those whose penetrating style has engraved in our ordinances, and in our hearts, the words and spirit of that immortal law.

It is true that, aided with the powers derived from force and opportunity, the nation was at that time, in some sense, free to take what course it pleased for filling the throne, but only free to do so upon the same grounds on which they might have wholly abolished their monarchy and every other part of their constitution. However, they did not think such bold changes within their commission. It is indeed difficult, perhaps impossible, to give limits to the mere *abstract* competence of the supreme power, such as was exercised by parliament at that time, but the limits of a *moral* competence subjecting, even in powers more indisputably sovereign, occasional will to permanent reason and to the steady maxims of faith, justice, and fixed fundamental policy, are perfectly intelligible and perfectly binding upon those who exercise any authority, under any name or under any title, in the state. The House of Lords, for instance, is not morally competent to dissolve the House of Commons, no, nor even to dissolve itself, nor to abdicate, if it would, its portion in the legislature of the kingdom. Though a king may abdicate for his own person, he cannot abdicate for the monarchy. By as strong, or by a stronger reason, the House of Commons cannot renounce its share of authority. The engagement and pact of society, which generally goes by the name of the constitution, forbids such invasion and such surrender. The constituent parts of a state are obliged to hold their public faith with each other and with all those who derive any serious interest under their engagements, as much as the whole state is bound to keep its faith with separate communities. Otherwise competence and power would soon be confounded and no law be left but the will of a prevailing force. On this principle the succession of the crown has always been what it now is, an hereditary succession by law; in the old line it was a succession by the common law; in the new, by the statute law operating on the principles of the common law, not changing the substance, but regulating the mode and describing the persons.[xii] Both these descriptions of law are of the same force and are derived from an equal authority emanating from the common agreement and original compact of the state, *communi sponsione reipublicae*,[xiii] and as such are equally binding on king and people, too, as long as the terms are observed and they continue the same body politic.

It is far from impossible to reconcile, if we do not suffer ourselves to be entangled in the mazes of metaphysic sophistry, the use both of a fixed rule and an occasional deviation: the sacredness of an hereditary principle of succession in our government with a power of change in its application in cases of extreme emergency. Even in that extremity (if we take the measure of our rights by our exercise of them at the Revolution), the change is to be confined to the peccant part only, to the part which produced the necessary deviation; and even then it is to be effected without a decomposition of the whole civil and political mass for the purpose of originating a new civil order out of the first elements of society.[xiv]

A state without the means of some change is without the means of its conservation. Without such means it might even risk the loss of that part of the constitution which it wished the most religiously to preserve. The two principles of conservation and correction operated strongly at the two critical periods of the Restoration and Revolution, when England found itself without a king. At both those periods the nation had lost the bond of union in their ancient edifice; they did not, however, dissolve the whole fabric. On the contrary, in both cases they regenerated the deficient part of the old constitution through the parts which were not impaired. They kept these old parts exactly as they were, that the part recovered might be suited to them. They acted by the ancient organized states in the shape of their old organization, and not by the organic *moleculae* of a disbanded people. At no time, perhaps, did the sovereign legislature manifest a more tender regard to that fundamental principle of British constitutional policy than at the time of the Revolution, when it deviated from the direct line of hereditary succession. The crown was carried somewhat out of the line in which it had before moved, but the new line was derived from the same stock. It was still a line of hereditary descent, still an hereditary descent in the same blood, though an hereditary descent qualified with Protestantism. When the legislature altered the direction, but kept the principle, they showed that they held it inviolable.

On this principle, the law of inheritance had admitted some amendment in the old time, and long before the era of the Revolution. Some time after the Conquest, great questions arose upon the legal principles of hereditary descent. It became a matter of doubt whether the heir *per capita* or the heir *per stirpes*xv was to succeed; but whether the heir *per capita* gave way when the heirdom *per stirpes* took place, or the Catholic heir when the Protestant was preferred, the inheritable principle survived with a sort of immortality through all transmigrations—*multosque per annos stat fortuna domus, et avi numerantur avorum.*xvi This is the spirit of our constitution, not only in its settled course, but in all its revolutions. Whoever came in, or however he came in, whether he obtained the crown by law or by force, the hereditary succession was either continued or adopted.

The gentlemen of the Society for Revolution see nothing in that of 1688 but the deviation from the constitution; and they take the deviation from the principle for the principle. They have little regard to the obvious consequences of their doctrine, though they must see that it leaves positive authority in very few of the positive institutions of this country. When such an unwarrantable maxim is once established, that no throne is lawful but the elective, no one act of the princes who preceded this era of fictitious election can be valid. Do these theorists mean to imitate some of their predecessors who dragged the bodies of our ancient sovereigns out of the quiet of their tombs? Do they mean to attaint and disable backward all the kings that have reigned before the Revolution, and consequently to stain the throne of England with the blot of a continual usurpation? Do they mean to invalidate, annul, or to call into question, together with the titles of the whole line of our kings, that great body of our statute law which passed under those whom they treat as usurpers, to annul laws of inestimable value to our liberties—of as great value at least as any which have passed at or since the period of the Revolution? If kings who did not owe their crown to the choice of their people had no title to make laws, what will become of the statute *de tallagio non concedendo?*—of the *petition of right?*—of the act of *habeas corpus?*xvii Do these new doctors of the rights of men presume to assert that King James the Second, who came to the crown as next of blood, according to the rules of a then unqualified succession, was not to all intents and purposes a lawful king of England before he had done any of those acts which were justly construed into an abdication of his crown? If he was not, much trouble in parliament might have been saved at the period these gentlemen commemorate. But King James was a bad king with a good title, and not an usurper. The princes who succeeded, according to the act of parliament which settled the crown on the Electress Sophia and on her descendants, being Protestants, came in as much by a title of inheritance as King James did. He came in according to the law as it stood at his accession to the crown; and the princes of the House of Brunswick came to the inheritance of the crown, not by election, but by the law as it stood at their several accessions of Protestant descent and inheritance, as I hope I have shown sufficiently.

The law by which this royal family is specifically destined to the succession is the act of the 12th and 13th of King William.[xviii] The terms of this act bind "us and our *heirs,* and our *posterity,* to them, their *heirs,* and their *posterity*", being Protestants, to the end of time, in the same words as the Declaration of Right had bound us to the heirs of King William and Queen Mary. It therefore secures both an hereditary crown and an hereditary allegiance. On what ground, except the constitutional policy of forming an establishment to secure that kind of succession which is to preclude a choice of the people forever, could the legislature have fastidiously rejected the fair and abundant choice which our country presented to them and searched in strange lands for a foreign princess from whose womb the line of our future rulers were to derive their title to govern millions of men through a series of ages?

The Princess Sophia was named in the act of settlement of the 12th and 13th of King William for a *stock* and root of *inheritance* to our kings, and not for her merits as a temporary administratrix of a power which she might not, and in fact did not, herself ever exercise. She was adopted for one reason, and for one only, because, says the act, "the most excellent Princess Sophia, Electress and Duchess Dowager of Hanover, is *daughter* of the most excellent Princess Elizabeth, late Queen of Bohemia, *daughter* of our late *sovereign lord* King James the First, of happy memory, and is hereby declared to be the next in *succession* in the Protestant line etc., etc., and the crown shall continue to the *heirs* of her body, being Protestants." This limitation was made by parliament, that through the Princess Sophia an inheritable line not only was to be continued in future, but (what they thought very material) that through her it was to be connected with the old stock of inheritance in King James the First, in order that the monarchy might preserve an unbroken unity through all ages and might be preserved (with safety to our religion) in the old approved mode by descent, in which, if our liberties had been once endangered, they had often, through all storms and struggles of prerogative and privilege, been preserved. They did well. No experience has taught us that in any other course or method than that of an *hereditary crown* our liberties can be regularly perpetuated and preserved sacred as our *hereditary right*. An irregular, convulsive movement may be necessary to throw off an irregular, convulsive disease. But the course of succession is the healthy habit of the British constitution. Was it that the legislature wanted, at the act for the limitation of the crown in the Hanoverian line, drawn through the female descendants of James the First, a due sense of the inconveniences of having two or three, or possibly more, foreigners in succession to the British throne? No!—they had a due sense of the evils which might happen from such foreign rule, and more than a due sense of them. But a more decisive proof cannot be given of the full conviction of the British nation that the principles of the Revolution did not authorize them to elect kings at their pleasure, and without any attention to the ancient fundamental principles of our government, than their continuing to adopt a plan of hereditary Protestant succession in the old line, with all the dangers and all the inconveniences of its being a foreign line full before their eyes and operating with the utmost force upon their minds.

A few years ago I should be ashamed to overload a matter so capable of supporting itself by the then unnecessary support of any argument; but this seditious, unconstitutional doctrine is now publicly taught, avowed, and printed. The dislike I feel to revolutions, the signals for which have so often been given from pulpits; the spirit of change that is gone abroad; the total contempt which prevails with you, and may come to prevail with us, of all ancient institutions when set in opposition to a present sense of convenience or to the bent of a present inclination: all these considerations make it not unadvisable, in my opinion, to call back our attention to the true principles of our own domestic laws; that you, my French friend, should begin to know, and that we should continue to cherish them. We ought not, on either side of the water, to suffer ourselves to be imposed upon by the counterfeit wares which some persons, by a double fraud, export to you in illicit bottoms as raw commodities of British growth, though wholly alien to our soil, in order afterwards to smuggle them back again into this country, manufactured after the newest Paris fashion of an improved liberty.

The people of England will not ape the fashions they have never tried, nor go back to those which they have found mischievous on trial. They look upon the legal hereditary succession of their crown as among their rights, not as among their wrongs; as a benefit, not as a grievance; as a security for their liberty, not as a badge of servitude. They look on the frame of their commonwealth, *such as it stands,* to be of inestimable value, and they conceive the undisturbed succession of the crown to be a pledge of the stability and perpetuity of all the other members of our constitution.

I shall beg leave, before I go any further, to take notice of some paltry artifices which the abettors of election, as the only lawful title to the crown, are ready to employ in order to render the support of the just principles of our constitution a task somewhat invidious. These sophisters substitute a fictitious cause and feigned personages, in whose favor they suppose you engaged whenever you defend the inheritable nature of the crown. It is common with them to dispute as if they were in a conflict with some of those exploded fanatics of slavery, who formerly maintained what I believe no creature now maintains, "that the crown is held by divine hereditary and indefeasible right".—These old fanatics of single arbitrary power dogmatized as if hereditary royalty was the only lawful government in the world, just as our new fanatics of popular arbitrary power maintain that a popular election is the sole lawful source of authority. The old prerogative enthusiasts, it is true, did speculate foolishly, and perhaps impiously too, as if monarchy had more of a divine sanction than any other mode of government; and as if a right to govern by inheritance were in strictness *indefeasible* in every person who should be found in the succession to a throne, and under every circumstance, which no civil or political right can be. But an absurd opinion concerning the king's hereditary right to the crown does not prejudice one that is rational and bottomed upon solid principles of law and policy. If all the absurd theories of lawyers and divines were to vitiate the objects in which they are conversant, we should have no law and no religion left in the world. But an absurd theory on one side of a question forms no justification for alleging a false fact or promulgating mischievous maxims on the other.

23

THE second claim of the Revolution Society is "a right of cashiering their governors for *misconduct*". Perhaps the apprehensions our ancestors entertained of forming such a precedent as that "of cashiering for misconduct" was the cause that the declaration of the act, which implied the abdication of King James, was, if it had any fault, rather too guarded and too circumstantial.[6] But all this guard and all this accumulation of circumstances serves to show the spirit of caution which predominated in the national councils in a situation in which men irritated by oppression, and elevated by a triumph over it, are apt to abandon themselves to violent and extreme courses; it shows the anxiety of the great men who influenced the conduct of affairs at that great event to make the Revolution a parent of settlement, and not a nursery of future revolutions.

No government could stand a moment if it could be blown down with anything so loose and indefinite as an opinion of "misconduct". They who led at the Revolution grounded the virtual abdication of King James upon no such light and uncertain principle. They charged him with nothing less than a design, confirmed by a multitude of illegal overt acts, to *subvert the Protestant church and state,* and their *fundamental,* unquestionable laws and liberties; they charged him with having broken the *original* contract between king and people. This was more than *misconduct*. A grave and overruling necessity obliged them to take the step they took, and took with infinite reluctance, as under that most rigorous of all laws. Their trust for the future preservation of the constitution was not in future revolutions. The grand policy of all their regulations was to render it almost impracticable for any future sovereign to compel the states of the kingdom to have again recourse to those violent remedies. They left the crown what, in the eye and estimation of law, it had ever been—perfectly irresponsible. In order to lighten the crown still further, they aggravated responsibility on ministers of state. By the statute of the 1st of King William, sess. 2nd, called "the act for declaring the rights and liberties of the subject, and for settling the succession of the crown", they enacted that the ministers should serve the crown on the terms of that declaration. They secured soon after the *frequent*

---

[6] "That King James the Second, having endeavored to *subvert the constitution* of the kingdom by breaking the *original contract* between king and people, and, by the advice of Jesuits and other wicked persons, having violated the *fundamental* laws, and *having withdrawn himself out of the kingdom,* hath *abdicated* the Government, and the throne is thereby *vacant*".

24

meetings of parliament, by which the whole government would be under the constant inspection and active control of the popular representative and of the magnates of the kingdom. In the next great constitutional act, that of the 12th and 13th of King William, for the further limitation of the crown and *better* securing the rights and liberties of the subject, they provided "that no pardon under the great seal of England should be pleadable to an impeachment by the Commons in parliament". The rule laid down for government in the Declaration of Right, the constant inspection of parliament, the practical claim of impeachment, they thought infinitely a better security, not only for their constitutional liberty, but against the vices of administration, than the reservation of a right so difficult in the practice, so uncertain in the issue, and often so mischievous in the consequences, as that of "cashiering their governors".

Dr. Price, in this sermon,[7] condemns very properly the practice of gross, adulatory addresses to kings. Instead of this fulsome style, he proposes that his Majesty should be told, on occasions of congratulation, that "he is to consider himself as more properly the servant than the sovereign of his people". For a compliment, this new form of address does not seem to be very soothing. Those who are servants in name, as well as in effect, do not like to be told of their situation, their duty, and their obligations. The slave, in the old play, tells his master, *"Haec commemoratio est quasi exprobatio"*.[xix] It is not pleasant as compliment; it is not wholesome as instruction. After all, if the king were to bring himself to echo this new kind of address, to adopt it in terms, and even to take the appellation of Servant of the People as his royal style, how either he or we should be much mended by it I cannot imagine. I have seen very assuming letters, signed "Your most obedient, humble servant". The proudest denomination that ever was endured on earth took a title of still greater humility than that which is ncw proposed for sovereigns by the Apostle of Liberty. Kings and nations were trampled upon by the foot of one calling himself "the Servant of Servants"; and mandates for deposing sovereigns were sealed with the signet of "the Fisherman".

I should have considered all this as no more than a sort of flippant, vain discourse, in which, as in an unsavory fume, several persons suffer the spirit of liberty to evaporate, if it were not plainly in support of the idea and a part of the scheme of "cashiering kings for

[7] Pp. 22-24.

25

misconduct". In that light it is worth some observation.

Kings, in one sense, are undoubtedly the servants of the people because their power has no other rational end than that of the general advantage; but it is not true that they are, in the ordinary sense (by our constitution, at least), anything like servants; the essence of whose situation is to obey the commands of some other and to be removable at pleasure. But the king of Great Britain obeys no other person; all other persons are individually, and collectively too, under him and owe to him a legal obedience. The law, which knows neither to flatter nor to insult, calls this high magistrate not our servant, as this humble divine calls him, but *"our sovereign Lord the king";* and we, on our parts, have learned to speak only the primitive language of the law, and not the confused jargon of their Babylonian pulpits.[xx]

As he is not to obey us, but as we are to obey the law in him, our constitution has made no sort of provision toward rendering him, as a servant, in any degree responsible. Our constitution knows nothing of a magistrate like the *Justicia* of Aragon, nor of any court legally appointed, nor of any process legally settled, for submitting the king to the responsibility belonging to all servants. In this he is not distinguished from the Commons and the Lords, who, in their several public capacities, can never be called to an account for their conduct, although the Revolution Society chooses to assert, in direct opposition to one of the wisest and most beautiful parts of our constitution, that "a king is no more than the first servant of the public, created by it, *and responsible to it".*

Ill would our ancestors at the Revolution have deserved their fame for wisdom if they had found no security for their freedom but in rendering their government feeble in its operations, and precarious in its tenure; if they had been able to contrive no better remedy against arbitrary power than civil confusion. Let these gentlemen state who that *representative* public is to whom they will affirm the king, as a servant, to be responsible. It will then be time enough for me to produce to them the positive statute law which affirms that he is not.

The ceremony of cashiering kings, of which these gentlemen talk so much at their ease, can rarely, if ever, be performed without force. It then becomes a case of war, and not of constitution. Laws are commanded to hold their tongues amongst arms, and tribunals fall to the ground with the peace they are no longer able to uphold. The Revolution of 1688 was obtained by a just war, in the only case in which any war, and much more a civil war, can be just. *Justa bella quibus necessaria.*[xxi] The question of dethroning or, if these gentlemen like the phrase better, "cashiering kings" will always be, as it has always been, an extraordinary question of state, and wholly out of the law— a question (like all other questions of state) of dispositions and of means and of probable consequences rather than of positive rights. As it was not made for common abuses, so it is not to be agitated by common minds. The speculative line of demarcation where obedience ought to end and resistance must begin is faint, obscure, and not easily definable. It is not a single act, or a single event, which determines it. Governments must be abused and deranged, indeed, before it can be thought of; and the prospect of the future must be as bad as the experience of the past. When things are in that lamentable condition, the nature of the disease is to indicate the remedy to those whom nature has qualified to administer in extremities this critical, ambiguous, bitter potion to a distempered state. Times and occasions and provocations will teach their own lessons. The wise will determine from the gravity of the case; the irritable, from sensibility to oppression; the high-minded, from disdain and indignation at abusive power in unworthy hands; the brave and bold, from the love of honorable danger in a generous cause; but, with or without right, a revolution will be the very last resource of the thinking and the good.

THE third head of right, asserted by the pulpit of the Old Jewry, namely, the "right to form a government for ourselves", has, at least, as little countenance from anything done at the Revolution, either in precedent or principle, as the two first of their claims. The Revolution was made to preserve our *ancient,* indisputable laws and liberties and that *ancient* constitution of government which is our only security for law and liberty. If you are desirous of knowing the spirit of our constitution and the policy which predominated in that great period which has secured it to this hour, pray look for both in our histories, in our records, in our acts of parliament, and journals of parliament, and not in the sermons of the Old Jewry and the after-dinner toasts of the Revolution Society. In the former you will find other ideas and another language. Such a claim is as ill-suited to our temper and wishes as it is unsupported by any appearance of authority. The very idea of the fabrication of a new government is enough to fill us with disgust and horror. We wished at the period of the Revolution, and do now wish, to derive all we possess as *an inheritance from our fore-*

fathers. Upon that body and stock of inheritance we have taken care not to inoculate any cyon alien to the nature of the original plant. All the reformations we have hitherto made have proceeded upon the principle of reverence to antiquity; and I hope, nay, I am persuaded, that all those which possibly may be made hereafter will be carefully formed upon analogical precedent, authority, and example.

Our oldest reformation is that of Magna Charta. You will see that Sir Edward Coke, that great oracle of our law, and indeed all the great men who follow him, to Blackstone,[8] are industrious to prove the pedigree of our liberties. They endeavor to prove that the ancient charter, the Magna Charta of King John, was connected with another positive charter from Henry I, and that both the one and the other were nothing more than a reaffirmance of the still more ancient standing law of the kingdom. In the matter of fact, for the greater part these authors appear to be in the right; perhaps not always; but if the lawyers mistake in some particulars, it proves my position still the more strongly, because it demonstrates the powerful prepossession toward antiquity, with which the minds of all our lawyers and legislators, and of all the people whom they wish to influence, have been always filled, and the stationary policy of this kingdom in considering their most sacred rights and franchises as an *inheritance.*

In the famous law of the 3rd of Charles I, called the Petition of Right, the parliament says to the king, "Your subjects have *inherited* this freedom", claiming their franchises not on abstract principles "as the rights of men", but as the rights of Englishmen, and as a patrimony derived from their forefathers. Selden and the other profoundly learned men who drew this Petition of Right were as well acquainted, at least, with all the general theories concerning the "rights of men" as any of the discoursers in our pulpits or on your tribune; full as well as Dr. Price or as the Abbé Sieyès. But, for reasons worthy of that practical wisdom which superseded their theoretic science, they preferred this positive, recorded, *hereditary* title to all which can be dear to the man and the citizen, to that vague speculative right which exposed their sure inheritance to be scrambled for and torn to pieces by every wild, litigious spirit.

The same policy pervades all the laws which have since been made for the preservation of our liberties. In the 1st of William and Mary, in the famous statute called the Declaration of Right, the two Houses

---

[8] See Blackstone's Magna Charta, printed at Oxford, 1759.

utter not a syllable of "a right to frame a government for themselves". You will see that their whole care was to secure the religion, laws, and liberties that had been long possessed, and had been lately endangered. "Taking[9] into their most serious consideration the *best* means for making such an establishment, that their religion, laws, and liberties might not be in danger of being again subverted", they auspicate[xxii] all their proceedings by stating as some of those *best* means, "in the *first place*" to do "as their *ancestors in like cases have usually* done for vindicating their *ancient* rights and liberties, to *declare*"— and then they pray the king and queen "that it may be *declared* and enacted that *all and singular* the rights and liberties *asserted and declared* are the true *ancient* and indubitable rights and liberties of the people of this kingdom".

You will observe that from Magna Charta to the Declaration of Right it has been the uniform policy of our constitution to claim and assert our liberties as an *entailed inheritance* derived to us from our forefathers, and to be transmitted to our posterity—as an estate specially belonging to the people of this kingdom, without any reference whatever to any other more general or prior right. By this means our constitution preserves a unity in so great a diversity of its parts. We have an inheritable crown, an inheritable peerage, and a House of Commons and a people inheriting privileges, franchises, and liberties from a long line of ancestors.

This policy appears to me to be the result of profound reflection, or rather the happy effect of following nature, which is wisdom without reflection, and above it. A spirit of innovation is generally the result of a selfish temper and confined views. People will not look forward to posterity, who never look backward to their ancestors. Besides, the people of England well know that the idea of inheritance furnishes a sure principle of conservation and a sure principle of transmission, without at all excluding a principle of improvement. It leaves acquisition free, but it secures what it acquires. Whatever advantages are obtained by a state proceeding on these maxims are locked fast as in a sort of family settlement, grasped as in a kind of mortmain[xxiii] forever. By a constitutional policy, working after the pattern of nature, we receive, we hold, we transmit our government and our privileges in the same manner in which we enjoy and transmit our

[9] W. and M.

property and our lives. The institutions of policy, the goods of fortune, the gifts of providence are handed down to us, and from us, in the same course and order. Our political system is placed in a just correspondence and symmetry with the order of the world and with the mode of existence decreed to a permanent body composed of transitory parts, wherein, by the disposition of a stupendous wisdom, molding together the great mysterious incorporation of the human race, the whole, at one time, is never old or middle-aged or young, but, in a condition of unchangeable constancy, moves on through the varied tenor of perpetual decay, fall, renovation, and progression. Thus, by preserving the method of nature in the conduct of the state, in what we improve we are never wholly new; in what we retain we are never wholly obsolete. By adhering in this manner and on those principles to our forefathers, we are guided not by the superstition of antiquarians, but by the spirit of philosophic analogy. In this choice of inheritance we have given to our frame of polity the image of a relation in blood, binding up the constitution of our country with our dearest domestic ties, adopting our fundamental laws into the bosom of our family affections, keeping inseparable and cherishing with the warmth of all their combined and mutually reflected charities our state, our hearths, our sepulchres, and our altars.

Through the same plan of a conformity to nature in our artificial institutions, and by calling in the aid of her unerring and powerful instincts to fortify the fallible and feeble contrivances of our reason, we have derived several other, and those no small, benefits from considering our liberties in the light of an inheritance. Always acting as if in the presence of canonized forefathers, the spirit of freedom, leading in itself to misrule and excess, is tempered with an awful gravity. This idea of a liberal descent inspires us with a sense of habitual native dignity which prevents that upstart insolence almost inevitably adhering to and disgracing those who are the first acquirers of any distinction. By this means our liberty becomes a noble freedom. It carries an imposing and majestic aspect. It has a pedigree and illustrating ancestors. It has its bearings and its ensigns armorial. It has its gallery of portraits, its monumental inscriptions, its records, evidences, and titles. We procure reverence to our civil institutions on the principle upon which nature teaches us to revere individual men: on account of their age and on account of those from whom they are descended. All your sophisters cannot produce anything better adapted to preserve a rational and manly freedom than the course that we have pursued, who have chosen our nature rather than our speculations, our breasts rather than our inventions, for the great conservatories and magazines of our rights and privileges.

YOU MIGHT, IF YOU PLEASED, have profited of our example and have given to your recovered freedom a correspondent dignity. Your privileges, though discontinued, were not lost to memory. Your constitution, it is true, whilst you were out of possession, suffered waste and dilapidation; but you possessed in some parts the walls and in all the foundations of a noble and venerable castle. You might have repaired those walls; you might have built on those old foundations. Your constitution was suspended before it was perfected, but you had the elements of a constitution very nearly as good as could be wished. In your old states[xxiv] you possessed that variety of parts corresponding with the various descriptions of which your community was happily composed; you had all that combination and all that opposition of interests; you had that action and counteraction which, in the natural and in the political world, from the reciprocal struggle of discordant powers, draws out the harmony of the universe. These opposed and conflicting interests which you considered as so great a blemish in your old and in our present constitution interpose a salutary check to all precipitate resolutions. They render deliberation a matter, not of choice, but of necessity; they make all change a subject of *compromise,* which naturally begets moderation; they produce *temperaments* preventing the sore evil of harsh, crude, unqualified reformations, and rendering all the headlong exertions of arbitrary power, in the few or in the many, for ever impracticable. Through that diversity of members and interests, general liberty had as many securities as there were separate views in the several orders, whilst, by pressing down the whole by the weight of a real monarchy, the separate parts would have been prevented from warping and starting from their allotted places.

You had all these advantages in your ancient states, but you chose to act as if you had never been molded into civil society and had everything to begin anew. You began ill, because you began by despising everything that belonged to you. You set up your trade without a capital. If the last generations of your country appeared without much luster in your eyes, you might have passed them by and derived your claims from a more early race of ancestors. Under a pious predilection for those ancestors, your imaginations would have realized in them a standard of virtue and wisdom beyond the vulgar practice of the hour; and you would have risen with the example to whose imitation you aspired. Respecting your forefathers, you would have been taught to respect yourselves. You would not have chosen to consider the French as a people of yesterday, as a nation of low-born servile wretches until the emancipating year of 1789. In order to furnish, at the expense of your honor, an excuse to your apologists here for several enormities of yours, you would not have been content to be represented as a gang of Maroon slaves[xxv] suddenly broke loose from the house of bondage, and therefore to be pardoned for your abuse of the liberty to which you were not accustomed and ill fitted. Would it not, my worthy friend, have been wiser to have you thought, what I, for one, always thought you, a generous and gallant nation, long misled to your disadvantage by your high and romantic sentiments of fidelity, honor, and loyalty; that events had been unfavorable to you, but that you were not enslaved through any illiberal or servile disposition; that in your most devoted submission you were actuated by a principle of public spirit, and that it was your country you worshiped in the person of your king? Had you made it to be understood that in the delusion of this amiable error you had gone further than your wise ancestors, that you were resolved to resume your ancient privileges, whilst you preserved the spirit of your ancient and your recent loyalty and honor; or if, diffident of yourselves and not clearly discerning the almost obliterated constitution of your ancestors, you had looked to your neighbors in this land who had kept alive the ancient principles and models of the old common law of Europe meliorated and adapted to its present state—by following wise examples you would have given new examples of wisdom to the world. You would have rendered the cause of liberty venerable in the eyes of every worthy mind in every nation. You would have shamed despotism from the earth by showing that freedom was not only reconcilable, but, as when well disciplined it is, auxiliary to law. You would have had an unoppressive but a productive revenue. You would have had a flourishing commerce to feed it. You would have had a free constitution, a potent monarchy, a disciplined army, a reformed and venerated clergy, a mitigated but spirited nobility to lead your virtue, not to overlay it; you would have had a liberal order of commons to emulate and to recruit that nobility; you would have had a protected, satisfied, laborious, and obedient people, taught to seek and to recognize the happiness that is to be found by virtue in all conditions; in which consists the true moral equality of mankind, and not in that monstrous fiction which, by inspiring false ideas and vain expectations into men destined to travel in the obscure walk of laborious life, serves only to aggravate and embitter that real inequality which it never can remove, and which the order of civil life establishes as much for the benefit of those whom it must leave in a humble state as those whom it is able to exalt to a condition more splendid, but not more happy. You had a smooth and easy career of felicity and glory laid open to you, beyond anything recorded in the history of the world, but you have shown that difficulty is good for man.

COMPUTE your gains: see what is got by those extravagant and presumptuous speculations which have taught your leaders to despise all their predecessors, and all their contemporaries, and even to despise themselves until the moment in which they become truly despicable. By following those false lights, France has bought undisguised calamities at a higher price than any nation has purchased the most unequivocal blessings! France has bought poverty by crime! France has not sacrificed her virtue to her interest, but she has abandoned her interest, that she might prostitute her virtue. All other nations have begun the fabric of a new government, or the reformation of an old, by establishing originally or by enforcing with greater exactness some rites or other of religion. All other people have laid the foundations of civil freedom in severer manners and a system of a more austere and masculine morality. France, when she let loose the reins of regal authority, doubled the license of a ferocious dissoluteness in manners and of an insolent irreligion in opinions and practice, and has extended through all ranks of life, as if she were communicating some privilege or laying open some secluded benefit, all the unhappy corruptions that usually were the disease of wealth and power. This is one of the new principles of equality in France.

France, by the perfidy of her leaders, has utterly disgraced the tone of lenient council in the cabinets of princes, and disarmed it of its most potent topics. She has sanctified the dark, suspicious maxims of tyrannous distrust, and taught kings to tremble at (what will hereafter be called) the delusive plausibilities of moral politicians. Sovereigns will consider those who advise them to place an unlimited confidence in their people as subverters of their thrones, as traitors who aim at their destruction by leading their easy good-nature, under specious pretenses, to admit combinations of bold and faithless men into a participation of their power. This alone (if there were nothing else) is an irreparable calamity to you and to mankind. Remember that your parliament of Paris told your king that, in calling the states together, he had nothing to fear but the prodigal excess of their zeal in providing for the support of the throne. It is right that these men should hide their heads. It is right that they should bear their part in the ruin which their counsel has brought on their sovereign and their country. Such sanguine declarations tend to lull authority asleep; to encourage it rashly to engage in perilous adventures of untried policy; to neglect those provisions, preparations, and precautions which distinguish benevolence from imbecility, and without which no man can answer for the salutary effect of any abstract plan of government or of freedom. For want of these, they have seen the medicine of the state corrupted into its poison. They have seen the French rebel against a mild and lawful monarch with more fury, outrage, and insult than ever any people has been known to rise against the most illegal usurper or the most sanguinary tyrant. Their resistance was made to concession, their revolt was from protection, their blow was aimed at a hand holding out graces, favors, and immunities.

This was unnatural. The rest is in order. They have found their punishment in their success: laws overturned; tribunals subverted; industry without vigor; commerce expiring; the revenue unpaid, yet the people impoverished; a church pillaged, and a state not relieved; civil and military anarchy made the constitution of the kingdom; everything human and divine sacrificed to the idol of public credit, and national bankruptcy the consequence; and, to crown all, the paper securities of new, precarious, tottering power, the discredited paper securities of impoverished fraud and beggared rapine, held out as a currency for the support of an empire in lieu of the two great recognized species[xxvi] that represent the lasting, conventional credit of mankind, which disappeared and hid themselves in the earth from whence they came, when the principle of property, whose creatures and representatives they are, was systematically subverted.

Were all these dreadful things necessary? Were they the inevitable results of the desperate struggle of determined patriots, compelled to wade through blood and tumult to the quiet shore of a tranquil and prosperous liberty? No! nothing like it. The fresh ruins of France, which shock our feelings wherever we can turn our eyes, are not the devastation of civil war; they are the sad but instructive monuments of rash and ignorant counsel in time of profound peace. They are the display of inconsiderate and presumptuous, because unresisted and irresistible, authority. The persons who have thus squandered away the precious treasure of their crimes, the persons who have made this prodigal and wild waste of public evils (the last stake reserved for the ultimate ransom of the state) have met in their progress with little or rather with no opposition at all. Their whole march was more like a triumphal procession than the progress of a war. Their pioneers have gone before them and demolished and laid everything level at their feet. Not one drop of *their* blood have they shed in the cause of the country they have ruined. They have made no sacrifices to their projects of greater consequence than their shoebuckles, whilst they were imprisoning their king, murdering their fellow citizens, and bathing in tears and plunging in poverty and distress thousands of worthy men and worthy families. Their cruelty has not even been the base result of fear. It has been the effect of their sense of perfect safety, in authorizing treasons, robberies, rapes, assassinations, slaughters, and burnings throughout their harassed land. But the cause of all was plain from the beginning.

THIS unforced choice, this fond election of evil, would appear perfectly unaccountable if we did not consider the composition of the National Assembly. I do not mean its formal constitution, which, as it now stands, is exceptionable enough, but the materials of which, in a great measure, it is composed, which is of ten thousand times greater consequence than all the formalities in the world. If we were to know nothing of this assembly but by its title and function, no colors could paint to the imagination anything more venerable. In that light the mind of an inquirer, subdued by such an awful image as that of the virtue and wisdom of a whole people collected into a focus, would pause and hesitate in condemning things even of the very worst aspect. Instead of blamable, they would appear only mysterious. But no name, no power, no function, no artificial institution whatsoever can make the men of whom any system of authority is composed any other than God, and nature, and education, and their habits of life have made them. Capacities beyond these the people have not to give. Virtue and wisdom may be the objects of their choice, but their choice confers neither the one nor the other on those upon whom they lay their ordaining hands. They have not the engagement of nature, they have not the promise of revelation, for any such powers.

After I had read over the list of the persons and descriptions elected into the *Tiers Etat,* nothing which they afterwards did could appear astonishing. Among them, indeed, I saw some of known rank, some of shining talents; but of any practical experience in the state, not one man was to be found. The best were only men of theory. But whatever the distinguished few may have been, it is the substance and mass of the body which constitutes its character and must finally determine its direction. In all bodies, those who will lead must also, in a considerable degree, follow. They must conform their propositions to the taste, talent, and disposition of those whom they wish to conduct; therefore, if an assembly is viciously or feebly composed in a very great part of it, nothing but such a supreme degree of virtue as very rarely appears in the world, and for that reason cannot enter into calculation, will prevent the men of talent disseminated through it from becoming only the expert instruments of absurd projects! If, what is the more likely event, instead of that unusual degree of virtue, they should be actuated by sinister ambition and a lust of meretricious glory, then the feeble part of the assembly, to whom at first they conform, becomes in its turn the dupe and instrument of their designs. In this political traffic, the leaders will be obliged to bow to the ignorance of their followers, and the followers to become subservient to the worst designs of their leaders.

To secure any degree of sobriety in the propositions made by the leaders in any public assembly, they ought to respect, in some degree perhaps to fear, those whom they conduct. To be led any otherwise than blindly, the followers must be qualified, if not for actors, at least for judges; they must also be judges of natural weight and authority. Nothing can secure a steady and moderate conduct in such assemblies but that the body of them should be respectably composed, in point of condition in life or permanent property, of education, and of such habits as enlarge and liberalize the understanding.

In the calling of the States-General of France, the first thing that struck me was a great departure from the ancient course. I found the representation for the Third Estate composed of six hundred persons. They were equal in number to the representatives of both the other orders. If the orders were to act separately, the number would not, beyond the consideration of the expense, be of much moment. But when it became apparent that the three orders were to be melted down into one, the policy and necessary effect of this numerous representation became obvious. A very small desertion from either of the other two orders must throw the power of both into the hands of the third. In fact, the whole power of the state was soon resolved into that body. Its due composition became therefore of infinitely the greater importance.

Judge, Sir, of my surprise when I found that a very great proportion of the assembly (a majority, I believe, of the members who attended) was composed of practitioners in the law. It was composed, not of distinguished magistrates, who had given pledges to their country of their science, prudence, and integrity; not of leading advocates, the glory of the bar; not of renowned professors in universities;—but for the far greater part, as it must in such a number, of the inferior, unlearned, mechanical, merely instrumental members of the profession. There were distinguished exceptions, but the general composition was of obscure provincial advocates, of stewards of petty local jurisdictions, country attornies, notaries, and the whole train of the ministers of municipal litigation, the fomenters and conductors of the petty war of village vexation. From the moment I read the list, I saw distinctly, and very nearly as it has happened, all that was to follow.

The degree of estimation in which any profession is held becomes the standard of the estimation in which the professors hold themselves. Whatever the personal merits of many individual lawyers might have been, and in many it was undoubtedly very considerable, in that military kingdom no part of the profession had been much regarded except the highest of all, who often united to their professional offices great family splendor, and were invested with great power and authority. These certainly were highly respected, and even with no small degree of awe. The next rank was not much esteemed; the mechanical part was in a very low degree of repute.

Whenever the supreme authority is vested in a body so composed, it must evidently produce the consequences of supreme authority placed in the hands of men not taught habitually to respect themselves, who had no previous fortune in character at stake, who could not be expected to bear with moderation, or to conduct with discretion, a power which they themselves, more than any others, must be surprised to find in their hands. Who could flatter himself that these men, suddenly and, as it were, by enchantment snatched from the humblest rank of subordination, would not be intoxicated with their unprepared greatness? Who could conceive that men who are habitually meddling, daring, subtle, active, of litigious dispositions and unquiet minds would easily fall back into their old condition of obscure contention and laborious, low, unprofitable chicane? Who could doubt but that, at any expense to the state, of which they understood nothing, they must pursue their private interests, which they understand but too well? It was not an event depending on chance or contingency. It was inevitable; it was necessary; it was planted in the nature of things. They must *join* (if their capacity did not permit them to *lead*) in any project which could procure to them a *litigious constitution;* which could lay open to them those innumerable lucrative jobs which follow in the train of all great convulsions and revolutions in the state, and particularly in all great and violent permutations of property. Was it to be expected that they would attend to the stability of property, whose existence had always depended upon whatever rendered property questionable, ambiguous, and insecure? Their objects would be enlarged with their elevation, but their disposition and habits, and mode of accomplishing their designs, must remain the same.

Well! but these men were to be tempered and restrained by other descriptions, of more sober and more enlarged understandings. Were they then to be awed by the supereminent authority and awful dignity of a handful of country clowns who have seats in that assembly, some of whom are said not to be able to read and write, and by not a greater number of traders who, though somewhat more instructed and more conspicuous in the order of society, had never known anything beyond their counting house? No! Both these descriptions were more formed to be overborne and swayed by the intrigues and artifices of lawyers than to become their counterpoise. With such a dangerous disproportion, the whole must needs be governed by them. To the faculty of law was joined a pretty considerable proportion of the faculty of medicine. This faculty had not, any more than that of the law, possessed in France its just estimation. Its professors, therefore, must have the qualities of men not habituated to sentiments of dignity. But supposing they had ranked as they ought to do, and as with us they do actually, the sides of sickbeds are not the academies for forming statesmen and legislators. Then came the dealers in stocks and funds, who must be eager, at any expense, to change their ideal paper wealth for the more solid substance of land. To these were joined men of other descriptions, from whom as little knowledge of, or attention to, the interests of a great state was to be expected, and as little regard to the stability of any institution; men formed to be instruments, not controls. Such in general was the composition of the *Tiers Etat* in the National Assembly, in which was scarcely to be perceived the slightest traces of what we call the natural landed interest of the country.

We know that the British House of Commons, without shutting its doors to any merit in any class, is, by the sure operation of adequate causes, filled with everything illustrious in rank, in descent, in hereditary and in acquired opulence, in cultivated talents, in military, civil, naval, and politic distinction that the country can afford. But supposing, what hardly can be supposed as a case, that the House of Commons should be composed in the same manner with the *Tiers Etat* in France, would this dominion of chicane be borne with patience or even conceived without horror? God forbid I should insinuate anything derogatory to that profession which is another priesthood, administering the rights of sacred justice. But whilst I revere men in the functions which belong to them, and would do as much as one man can do to prevent their exclusion from any, I cannot, to flatter them, give the lie to nature. They are good and useful in the composition; they must be mischievous if they preponderate so as virtually to become the whole. Their very excellence in their peculiar functions may be far from a qualification for others. It cannot escape observation that when men are too much confined to professional and faculty habits and, as it were, inveterate in the recurrent employment of that narrow circle, they are rather disabled than qualified for whatever depends on the knowlege of mankind, on experience in mixed affairs, on a comprehensive, connected view of the various, complicated, external and internal interests which go to the formation of that multifarious thing called a state.

After all, if the House of Commons were to have a wholly professional and faculty composition, what is the power of the House of Commons, circumscribed and shut in by the immovable barriers of laws, usages, positive rules of doctrine and practice, counterpoised by the House of Lords, and every moment of its existence at the discretion of the crown to continue, prorogue, or dissolve us? The power of the House of Commons, direct or indirect, is indeed great; and long may it be able to preserve its greatness and the spirit belonging to true greatness at the full; and it will do so as long as it can keep the breakers of law in India from becoming the makers of law for England.[xxvii] The power, however, of the House of Commons, when least diminished, is as a drop of water in the ocean, compared to that residing in a settled majority of your National Assembly. That assembly, since the destruction of the orders, has no fundamental law, no strict convention, no respected usage to restrain it. Instead of finding themselves obliged to conform to a fixed constitution, they have a power to make a constitution which shall conform to their designs. Nothing in heaven or upon earth can serve as a control on them. What ought to be the heads, the hearts, the dispositions that are qualified or that dare, not only to make laws under a fixed constitution, but at one heat to strike out a totally new constitution for a great kingdom, and in every part of it, from the monarch on the throne to the vestry of a parish? But—"fools rush in where angels fear to tread". In such a state of unbounded power for undefined and undefinable purposes, the evil of a moral and almost physical inaptitude of the man to the function must be the greatest we can conceive to happen in the management of human affairs.

Having considered the composition of the Third Estate as it stood in its original frame, I took a view of the representatives of the clergy. There, too, it appeared that full as little regard was had to the general security of property or to the aptitude of the deputies for the public purposes, in the principles of their election. That election was so contrived as to send a very large proportion of mere country curates to the great and arduous work of new-modeling a state: men who never had seen the state so much as in a picture—men who knew nothing of the world beyond the bounds of an obscure village; who, immersed in hopeless poverty, could regard all property, whether secular or ecclesiastical, with no other eye than that of envy; among whom must be many who, for the smallest hope of the meanest dividend in plunder, would readily join in any attempts upon a body of wealth in which they could hardly look to have any share except in a general scramble. Instead of balancing the power of the active chicaners in the other assembly, these curates must necessarily become the active coadjutors, or at best the passive instruments, of those by whom they had been habitually guided in their petty village concerns. They, too, could hardly be the most conscientious of their kind who, presuming upon their incompetent understanding, could intrigue for a trust which led them from their natural relation to their flocks and their natural spheres of action to undertake the regeneration of kingdoms. This preponderating weight, being added to the force of the body of chicane in the *Tiers Etat,* completed that momentum of ignorance, rashness, presumption, and lust of plunder, which nothing has been able to resist.

To observing men it must have appeared from the beginning that the majority of the Third Estate, in conjunction with such a deputation from the clergy as I have described, whilst it pursued the destruction of the nobility, would inevitably become subservient to the worst designs of individuals in that class. In the spoil and humiliation of their own order these individuals would possess a sure fund for the pay of their new followers. To squander away the objects which made the happiness of their fellows would be to them no sacrifice at all. Turbulent, discontented men of quality, in proportion as they are puffed up with personal pride and arrogance, generally despise their own order. One of the first symptoms they discover of a selfish and mischievous ambition is a profligate disregard of a dignity which they partake with others. To be attached to the subdivision, to love the little platoon we belong to in society, is the first principle (the germ as it were) of public affections. It is the first link in the series by which we proceed toward a love to our country and to mankind. The interest of that portion of social arrangement is a trust in the hands of all those who compose it; and as none but bad men would justify it in abuse, none but traitors would barter it away for their own personal advantage.

There were in the time of our civil troubles in England (I do not know whether you have any such in your assembly in France) several persons, like the then Earl of Holland,[xxviii] who by themselves or their families had brought an odium on the throne by the prodigal dispensation of its bounties toward them, who afterwards joined in the rebellions arising from the discontents of which they were themselves the cause; men who helped to subvert that throne to which they owed, some of them, their existence, others all that power which they employed to ruin their benefactor. If any bounds are set to the rapacious demands of that sort of people, or that others are permitted to partake in the objects they would engross, revenge and envy soon fill up the craving void that is left in their avarice. Confounded by the complication of distempered passions, their reason is disturbed; their views become vast and perplexed; to others inexplicable, to themselves uncertain. They find, on all sides, bounds to their unprincipled ambition in any fixed order of things. Both in the fog and haze of confusion all is enlarged and appears without any limit.

When men of rank sacrifice all ideas of dignity to an ambition without a distinct object and work with low instruments and for low ends, the whole composition becomes low and base. Does not something like this now appear in France? Does it not produce something ignoble and inglorious—a kind of meanness in all the prevalent policy, a tendency in all that is done to lower along with individuals all the dignity and importance of the state? Other revolutions have been conducted by persons who, whilst they attempted or affected changes in the commonwealth, sanctified their ambition by advancing the dignity of the people whose peace they troubled. They had

41

long views. They aimed at the rule, not at the destruction, of their country. They were men of great civil and great military talents, and if the terror, the ornament of their age. They were not like Jew brokers, contending with each other who could best remedy with fraudulent circulation and depreciated paper the wretchedness and ruin brought on their country by their degenerate councils. The compliment made to one of the great bad men of the old stamp (Cromwell) by his kinsman, a favorite poet of that time, shows what it was he proposed, and what indeed to a great degree he accomplished, in the success of his ambition:

> Still as *you* rise, the *state* exalted too,
> Finds no distemper whilst 'tis changed by *you;*
> Changed like the world's great scene, when without noise
> The rising sun night's *vulgar* lights destroys.[xxix]

These disturbers were not so much like men usurping power as asserting their natural place in society. Their rising was to illuminate and beautify the world. Their conquest over their competitors was by outshining them. The hand that, like a destroying angel, smote the country communicated to it the force and energy under which it suffered. I do not say (God forbid), I do not say that the virtues of such men were to be taken as a balance to their crimes; but they were some corrective to their effects. Such was, as I said, our Cromwell. Such were your whole race of Guises, Condés, and Colignis. Such the Richelieus, who in more quiet times acted in the spirit of a civil war. Such, as better men, and in a less dubious cause, were your Henry the Fourth and your Sully, though nursed in civil confusions and not wholly without some of their taint. It is a thing to be wondered at, to see how very soon France, when she had a moment to respire, recovered and emerged from the longest and most dreadful civil war that ever was known in any nation.[xxx] Why? Because among all their massacres they had not slain the *mind* in their country. A conscious dignity, a noble pride, a generous sense of glory and emulation was not extinguished. On the contrary, it was kindled and inflamed. The organs also of the state, however shattered, existed. All the prizes of honor and virtue, all the rewards, all the distinctions remained. But your present confusion, like a palsy, has attacked the fountain of life itself. Every person in your country, in a situation to be actuated by a principle of honor, is disgraced and degraded, and can entertain no sensation of life except in a mortified and humiliated indignation.

But this generation will quickly pass away. The next generation of the nobility will resemble the artificers and clowns, and money-jobbers usurers, and Jews, who will be always their fellows, sometimes their masters.

BELIEVE ME, SIR, those who attempt to level, never equalize. In all societies, consisting of various descriptions of citizens, some description must be uppermost. The levelers, therefore, only change and pervert the natural order of things; they load the edifice of society by setting up in the air what the solidity of the structure requires to be on the ground. The association of tailors and carpenters, of which the republic (of Paris, for instance) is composed, cannot be equal to the situation into which by the worst of usurpations—an usurpation on the prerogatives of nature—you attempt to force them.

The Chancellor of France, at the opening of the states, said, in a tone of oratorical flourish, that all occupations were honorable. If he meant only that no honest employment was disgraceful, he would not have gone beyond the truth. But in asserting that anything is honorable, we imply some distinction in its favor. The occupation of a hairdresser or of a working tallow-chandler cannot be a matter of honor to any person—to say nothing of a number of other more servile employments. Such descriptions of men ought not to suffer oppression from the state; but the state suffers oppression if such as they, either individually or collectively, are permitted to rule. In this you think you are combating prejudice, but you are at war with nature.[10]

---

[10] Ecclesiasticus, chap. xxxviii. verses 24, 25. "The wisdom of a learned man cometh by opportunity of leisure; and he that hath little business shall become wise".—"How can he get wisdom that holdeth the plough, and that glorieth in the goad; that driveth oxen; and is occupied in their labours; and whose talk is of bullocks"?

Ver. 27. "So every carpenter and work-master that laboureth night and day", etc.

Ver. 33. "They shall not be sought for in public counsel, nor sit high in the congregation: they shall not sit on the judge's seat, nor understand the sentence of judgment; they cannot declare justice and judgment, and they shall not be found where parables are spoken".

Ver. 34. "But they will maintain the state of the world".

I do not determine whether this book be canonical, as the Gallican church (till lately) has considered it, or apocryphal, as here it is taken. I am sure it contains a great deal of sense and truth.

43

I do not, my dear Sir, conceive you to be of that sophistical, captious spirit, or of that uncandid dulness, as to require, for every general observation or sentiment, an explicit detail of the correctives and exceptions which reason will presume to be included in all the general propositions which come from reasonable men. You do not imagine that I wish to confine power, authority, and distinction to blood and names and titles. No, Sir. There is no qualification for government but virtue and wisdom, actual or presumptive. Wherever they are actually found, they have, in whatever state, condition, profession, or trade, the passport of Heaven to human place and honor. Woe to the country which would madly and impiously reject the service of the talents and virtues, civil, military, or religious, that are given to grace and to serve it, and would condemn to obscurity everything formed to diffuse luster and glory around a state. Woe to that country, too, that, passing into the opposite extreme, considers a low education, a mean contracted view of things, a sordid, mercenary occupation as a preferable title to command. Everything ought to be open, but not indifferently, to every man. No rotation; no appointment by lot; no mode of election operating in the spirit of sortition[xxxi] or rotation can be generally good in a government conversant in extensive objects. Because they have no tendency, direct or indirect, to select the man with a view to the duty or to accommodate the one to the other. I do not hesitate to say that the road to eminence and power, from obscure condition, ought not to be made too easy, nor a thing too much of course. If rare merit be the rarest of all rare things, it ought to pass through some sort of probation. The temple of honor ought to be seated on an eminence. If it be opened through virtue, let it be remembered, too, that virtue is never tried but by some difficulty and some struggle.

Nothing is a due and adequate representation of a state that does not represent its ability as well as its property. But as ability is a vigorous and active principle, and as property is sluggish, inert, and timid, it never can be safe from the invasion of ability unless it be, out of all proportion, predominant in the representation. It must be represented, too, in great masses of accumulation, or it is not rightly protected. The characteristic essence of property, formed out of the combined principles of its acquisition and conservation, is to be *unequal.* The great masses, therefore, which excite envy and tempt rapacity must be put out of the possibility of danger. Then they form a natural rampart about the lesser properties in all their gradations. The same quantity of property, which is by the natural course of things divided among many, has not the same operation. Its defensive power is weakened as it is diffused. In this diffusion each man's portion is less than what, in the eagerness of his desires, he may flatter himself to obtain by dissipating the accumulations of others. The plunder of the few would indeed give but a share inconceivably small in the distribution to the many. But the many are not capable of making this calculation; and those who lead them to rapine never intend this distribution.

The power of perpetuating our property in our families is one of the most valuable and interesting circumstances belonging to it, and that which tends the most to the perpetuation of society itself. It makes our weakness subservient to our virtue, it grafts benevolence even upon avarice. The possessors of family wealth, and of the distinction which attends hereditary possession (as most concerned in it), are the natural *securities* for this transmission. With us the House of Peers is formed upon this principle. It is wholly composed of hereditary property and hereditary distinction, and made, therefore, the third of the legislature and, in the last event, the sole judge of all property in all its subdivisions. The House of Commons, too, though not necessarily, yet in fact, is always so composed, in the far greater part. Let those large proprietors be what they will—and they have their chance of being amongst the best—they are, at the very worst, the ballast in the vessel of the commonwealth. For though hereditary wealth and the rank which goes with it are too much idolized by creeping sycophants and the blind, abject admirers of power, they are too rashly slighted in shallow speculations of the petulant, assuming, short-sighted coxcombs of philosophy. Some decent, regulated preeminence, some preference (not exclusive appropriation) given to birth is neither unnatural, nor unjust, nor impolitic.

IT is said that twenty-four millions ought to prevail over two hundred thousand. True; if the constitution of a kingdom be a problem of arithmetic. This sort of discourse does well enough with the lamppost for its second;[xxxii] to men who *may* reason calmly, it is ridiculous. The will of the many and their interest must very often differ, and great will be the difference when they make an evil choice. A government of five hundred country attornies and obscure curates is not good for twenty-four millions of men, though it were chosen by eight and forty millions, nor is it the better for being guided by a dozen of persons of quality who have betrayed their trust in order to obtain

45

that power. At present, you seem in everything to have strayed out of the high road of nature. The property of France does not govern it. Of course, property is destroyed and rational liberty has no existence. All you have got for the present is a paper circulation and a stock-jobbing constitution; and as to the future, do you seriously think that the territory of France, upon the republican system of eighty-three independent municipalities (to say nothing of the parts that compose them), can ever be governed as one body or can ever be set in motion by the impulse of one mind? When the National Assembly has completed its work, it will have accomplished its ruin. These commonwealths will not long bear a state of subjection to the republic of Paris. They will not bear that this body should monopolize the captivity of the king and the dominion over the assembly calling itself national. Each will keep its own portion of the spoil of the church to itself; and it will not suffer either that spoil, or the more just fruits of their industry, or the natural produce of their soil to be sent to swell the insolence or pamper the luxury of the mechanics of Paris. In this they will see none of the equality, under the pretense of which they have been tempted to throw off their allegiance to their sovereign as well as the ancient constitution of their country. There can be no capital city in such a constitution as they have lately made. They have forgot that, when they framed democratic governments, they had virtually dismembered their country. The person whom they persevere in calling king has not power left to him by the hundredth part sufficient to hold together this collection of republics. The republic of Paris will endeavor, indeed, to complete the debauchery of the army, and illegally to perpetuate the assembly, without resort to its constituents, as the means of continuing its despotism. It will make efforts, by becoming the heart of a boundless paper circulation, to draw everything to itself; but in vain. All this policy in the end will appear as feeble as it is now violent.

IF this be your actual situation, compared to the situation to which you were called, as it were, by the voice of God and man, I cannot find it in my heart to congratulate you on the choice you have made or the success which has attended your endeavors. I can as little recommend to any other nation a conduct grounded on such principles, and productive of such effects. That I must leave to those who can see farther into your affairs than I am able to do, and who best know how far your actions are favorable to their designs. The gentlemen of the Revolution Society, who were so early in their congratulations, appear to be strongly of opinion that there is some scheme of politics relative to this country in which your proceedings may, in some way, be useful. For your Dr. Price, who seems to have speculated himself into no small degree of fervor upon this subject, addresses his auditory in the following very remarkable words: "I cannot conclude without recalling *particularly* to your recollection a consideration which I have *more than once alluded to,* and which probably your thoughts have *been all along anticipating;* a consideration with which my *mind is impressed more than I can express.* I mean the consideration of the *favourableness of the present times to all exertions in the cause of liberty.*"

It is plain that the mind of this *political* preacher was at the time big with some extraordinary design; and it is very probable that the thoughts of his audience, who understood him better than I do, did all along run before him in his reflection and in the whole train of consequences to which it led.

Before I read that sermon, I really thought I had lived in a free country; and it was an error I cherished, because it gave me a greater liking to the country I lived in. I was, indeed, aware that a jealous, ever-waking vigilance to guard the treasure of our liberty, not only from invasion, but from decay and corruption, was our best wisdom and our first duty. However, I considered that treasure rather as a possession to be secured than as a prize to be contended for. I did not discern how the present time came to be so very favorable to all *exertions* in the cause of freedom. The present time differs from any other only by the circumstance of what is doing in France.[xxxiii] If the example of that nation is to have an influence on this, I can easily conceive why some of their proceedings which have an unpleasant aspect and are not quite reconcilable to humanity, generosity, good faith, and justice are palliated with so much milky good-nature toward the actors, and borne with so much heroic fortitude toward the sufferers. It is certainly not prudent to discredit the authority of an example we mean to follow. But allowing this, we are led to a very natural question: What is that cause of liberty, and what are those exertions in its favor to which the example of France is so singularly auspicious? Is our monarchy to be annihilated, with all the laws, all the tribunals, and all the ancient corporations of the kingdom? Is every landmark of the country to be done away in favor of a geometrical and arithmetical constitution? Is the House of Lords to be voted useless? Is episcopacy to be abolished? Are the church lands to be sold to Jews and jobbers or given to bribe new-invented municipal

47

REFLECTIONS ON THE REVOLUTION IN FRANCE

republics into a participation in sacrilege? Are all the taxes to be voted grievances, and the revenue reduced to a patriotic contribution or patriotic presents? Are silver shoebuckles to be substituted in the place of the land tax and the malt tax for the support of the naval strength of this kingdom? Are all orders, ranks, and distinctions to be confounded, that out of universal anarchy, joined to national bankruptcy, three or four thousand democracies should be formed into eighty-three, and that they may all, by some sort of unknown attractive power, be organized into one? For this great end, is the army to be seduced from its discipline and its fidelity, first, by every kind of debauchery and, then, by the terrible precedent of a donative[xxxiv] in the increase of pay? Are the curates to be seduced from their bishops by holding out to them the delusive hope of a dole out of the spoils of their own order? Are the citizens of London to be drawn from their allegiance by feeding them at the expense of their fellow subjects? Is a compulsory paper currency to be substituted in the place of the legal coin of this kingdom? Is what remains of the plundered stock of public revenue to be employed in the wild project of maintaining two armies to watch over and to fight with each other? If these are the ends and means of the Revolution Society, I admit that they are well assorted; and France may furnish them for both with precedents in point.

I see that your example is held out to shame us. I know that we are supposed a dull, sluggish race, rendered passive by finding our situation tolerable, and prevented by a mediocrity of freedom from ever attaining to its full perfection. Your leaders in France began by affecting to admire, almost to adore, the British constitution; but as they advanced, they came to look upon it with a sovereign contempt. The friends of your National Assembly amongst us have full as mean an opinion of what was formerly thought the glory of their country. The Revolution Society has discovered that the English nation is not free. They are convinced that the inequality in our representation is a "defect in our constitution *so gross and palpable* as to make it excellent chiefly in *form* and *theory*".[11] That a representation in the legislature of a kingdom is not only the basis of all constitutional liberty in it, but of *"all legitimate government;* that without it a *government* is nothing but an *usurpation";*—that "when the representation is *partial,* the kingdom possesses liberty only *partially;* and if extremely partial, it gives only a *semblance;* and if not only extremely partial,

[11] *Discourse on the Love of our Country,* 3d ed., p. 39.

but corruptly chosen, it becomes a *nuisance*". Dr. Price considers this inadequacy of representation as our *fundamental grievance;* and though, as to the corruption of this semblance of representation, he hopes it is not yet arrived to its full perfection of depravity, he fears that "nothing will be done towards gaining for us this *essential blessing,* until some *great abuse of power* again provokes our resentment, or some *great calamity* again alarms our fears, or perhaps till the acquisition of a *pure and equal representation by other countries,* whilst we are *mocked* with the *shadow,* kindles our shame." To this he subjoins a note in these words. "A representation chosen chiefly by the treasury, and a *few* thousands of the *dregs* of the people, who are generally paid for their votes".

You will smile here at the consistency of those democratists who, when they are not on their guard, treat the humbler part of the community with the greatest contempt, whilst, at the same time, they pretend to make them the depositories of all power. It would require a long discourse to point out to you the many fallacies that lurk in the generality and equivocal nature of the terms "inadequate representation". I shall only say here, in justice to that old-fashioned constitution under which we have long prospered, that our representation has been found perfectly adequate to all the purposes for which a representation of the people can be desired or devised. I defy the enemies of our constitution to show the contrary. To detail the particulars in which it is found so well to promote its ends would demand a treatise on our practical constitution. I state here the doctrine of the Revolutionists only that you and others may see what an opinion these gentlemen entertain of the constitution of their country, and why they seem to think that some great abuse of power or some great calamity, as giving a chance for the blessing of a constitution according to their ideas, would be much palliated to their feelings; you see *why they* are so much enamored of your fair and equal representation, which being once obtained, the same effects might follow. You see they consider our House of Commons as only "a semblance", "a form", "a theory", "a shadow", "a mockery", perhaps "a nuisance".

These gentlemen value themselves on being systematic, and not without reason. They must therefore look on this gross and palpable defect of representation, this fundamental grievance (so they call it) as a thing not only vicious in itself, but as rendering our whole government absolutely *illegitimate,* and not at all better than a downright *usurpation.* Another revolution, to get rid of this illegitimate and usurped government, would of course be perfectly justifiable, if not absolutely necessary. Indeed, their principle, if you observe it with any attention, goes much further than to an alteration in the election of the House of Commons; for, if popular representation, or choice, is necessary to the *legitimacy* of all government, the House of Lords is, at one stroke, bastardized and corrupted in blood. That House is no representative of the people at all, even in "semblance or in form". The case of the crown is altogether as bad. In vain the crown may endeavor to screen itself against these gentlemen by the authority of the establishment made on the Revolution. The Revolution which is resorted to for a title, on their system, wants a title itself. The Revolution is built, according to their theory, upon a basis not more solid than our present formalities, as it was made by a House of Lords, not representing any one but themselves, and by a House of Commons exactly such as the present, that is, as they term it, by a mere "shadow and mockery" of representation.

Something they must destroy, or they seem to themselves to exist for no purpose. One set is for destroying the civil power through the ecclesiastical; another, for demolishing the ecclesiastic through the civil. They are aware that the worst consequences might happen to the public in accomplishing this double ruin of church and state, but they are so heated with their theories that they give more than hints that this ruin, with all the mischiefs that must lead to it and attend it, and which to themselves appear quite certain, would not be unacceptable to them or very remote from their wishes. A man amongst them of great authority and certainly of great talents, speaking of a supposed alliance between church and state, says, "perhaps *we must wait for the fall of the civil powers* before this most unnatural alliance be broken. Calamitous no doubt will that time be. But what convulsion in the political world ought to be a subject of lamentation if it be attended with so desirable an effect?"[xxxv] You see with what a steady eye these gentlemen are prepared to view the greatest calamities which can befall their country.

IT is no wonder, therefore, that with these ideas of everything in their constitution and government at home, either in church or state, as illegitimate and usurped, or at best as a vain mockery, they look abroad with an eager and passionate enthusiasm. Whilst they are possessed by these notions, it is vain to talk to them of the practice of their ancestors, the fundamental laws of their country, the fixed form of a constitution whose merits are confirmed by the solid test of long experience and an increasing public strength and national prosperity. They despise experience as the wisdom of unlettered men; and as for the rest, they have wrought underground a mine that will blow up, at one grand explosion, all examples of antiquity, all precedents, charters, and acts of parliament. They have "the rights of men". Against these there can be no prescription, against these no agreement is binding; these admit no temperament and no compromise; anything withheld from their full demand is so much of fraud and injustice. Against these their rights of men let no government look for security in the length of its continuance, or in the justice and lenity of its administration. The objections of these speculatists, if its forms do not quadrate with their theories, are as valid against such an old and beneficent government as against the most violent tyranny or the greenest usurpation. They are always at issue with governments, not on a question of abuse, but a question of competency and a question of title. I have nothing to say to the clumsy subtilty of their political metaphysics. Let them be their amusement in the schools.— *"Illa se jactet in aula Aeolus, et clauso ventorum carcere regnet".*[xxxvi]— But let them not break prison to burst like a *Levanter,* to sweep the earth with their hurricane and to break up the fountains of the great deep to overwhelm us.

Far am I from denying in theory, full as far is my heart from withholding in practice (if I were of power to give or to withhold) the *real* rights of men. In denying their false claims of right, I do not mean to injure those which are real, and are such as their pretended rights would totally destroy. If civil society be made for the advantage of man, all the advantages for which it is made become his right. It is an institution of beneficence; and law itself is only beneficence acting by a rule. Men have a right to live by that rule; they have a right to do justice, as between their fellows, whether their fellows are in public function or in ordinary occupation. They have a right to the fruits of their industry and to the means of making their industry fruitful. They have a right to the acquisitions of their parents, to the nourishment and improvement of their offspring, to instruction in life, and to consolation in death. Whatever each man can separately do, without trespassing upon others, he has a right to do for himself; and he has a right to a fair portion of all which society, with all its combinations of skill and force, can do in his favor. In this partnership all men have equal rights, but not to equal things. He that has but five shillings in the partnership has as good a right to it as he that has five hundred pounds has to his larger proportion. But he has not a right to an equal dividend in the product of the joint stock; and as to the share of power, authority, and direction which each individual ought to have in the management of the state, that I must deny to be amongst the direct original rights of man in civil society; for I have in my contemplation the civil social man, and no other. It is a thing to be settled by convention.

If civil society be the offspring of convention, that convention must be its law. That convention must limit and modify all the descriptions of constitution which are formed under it. Every sort of legislative, judicial, or executory power are its creatures. They can have no being in any other state of things; *and how can any man claim under the conventions of civil society rights which do not so much as suppose its existence—rights which are absolutely repugnant to it?* One of the first motives to civil society, and which becomes one of its fundamental rules, is *that no man should be judge in his own cause.* By this each person has at once divested himself of the first fundamental right of uncovenanted man, that is, to judge for himself and to assert his own cause. He abdicates all right to be his own governor. He inclusively, in a great measure, abandons the right of self-defense, the first law of nature. Men cannot enjoy the rights of an uncivil and of a civil state together. That he may obtain justice, he gives up his right of determining what it is in points the most essential to him. That he may secure some liberty, he makes a surrender in trust of the whole of it.[xxxvii]

Government is not made in virtue of natural rights, which may and do exist in total independence of it, and exist in much greater clearness and in a much greater degree of abstract perfection; but their abstract perfection is their practical defect. By having a right to everything they want everything. Government is a contrivance of human wisdom to provide for human *wants.* Men have a right that these wants should be provided for by this wisdom. Among these wants is to be reckoned the want, out of civil society, of a sufficient restraint upon their passions. Society requires not only that the passions of individuals should be subjected, but that even in the mass and body, as well as in the individuals, the inclinations of men should frequently be thwarted, their will controlled, and their passions brought into subjection. This can only be done *by a power out of*

52

themselves, and not, in the exercise of its function, subject to that will and to those passions which it is its office to bridle and subdue. In this sense the restraints on men, as well as their liberties, are to be reckoned among their rights. But as the liberties and the restrictions vary with times and circumstances and admit to infinite modifications, they cannot be settled upon any abstract rule; and nothing is so foolish as to discuss them upon that principle.

The moment you abate anything from the full rights of men, each to govern himself, and suffer any artificial, positive limitation upon those rights, from that moment the whole organization of government becomes a consideration of convenience. This it is which makes the constitution of a state and the due distribution of its powers a matter of the most delicate and complicated skill. It requires a deep knowledge of human nature and human necessities, and of the things which facilitate or obstruct the various ends which are to be pursued by the mechanism of civil institutions. The state is to have recruits to its strength, and remedies to its distempers. What is the use of discussing a man's abstract right to food or medicine? The question is upon the method of procuring and administering them. In that deliberation I shall always advise to call in the aid of the farmer and the physician rather than the professor of metaphysics.

The science of constructing a commonwealth, or renovating it, or reforming it, is, like every other experimental science, not to be taught *a priori.* Nor is it a short experience that can instruct us in that practical science, because the real effects of moral causes are not always immediate; but that which in the first instance is prejudicial may be excellent in its remoter operation, and its excellence may arise even from the ill effects it produces in the beginning. The reverse also happens: and very plausible schemes, with very pleasing commencements, have often shameful and lamentable conclusions. In states there are often some obscure and almost latent causes, things which appear at first view of little moment, on which a very great part of its prosperity or adversity may most essentially depend. The science of government being therefore so practical in itself and intended for such practical purposes—a matter which requires experience, and even more experience than any person can gain in his whole life, however sagacious and observing he may be—it is with infinite caution that any man ought to venture upon pulling down an edifice which has answered in any tolerable degree for ages the common purposes of society, or on building it up again without having models and patterns of approved utility before his eyes.

These metaphysic rights entering into common life, like rays of light which pierce into a dense medium, are by the laws of nature refracted from their straight line. Indeed, in the gross and complicated mass of human passions and concerns the primitive rights of men undergo such a variety of refractions and reflections that it becomes absurd to talk of them as if they continued in the simplicity of their original direction. The nature of man is intricate; the objects of society are of the greatest possible complexity; and, therefore, no simple disposition or direction of power can be suitable either to man's nature or to the quality of his affairs. When I hear the simplicity of contrivance aimed at and boasted of in any new political constitutions, I am at no loss to decide that the artificers are grossly ignorant of their trade or totally negligent of their duty. The simple governments are fundamentally defective, to say no worse of them. If you were to contemplate society in but one point of view, all these simple modes of polity are infinitely captivating. In effect each would answer its single end much more perfectly than the more complex is able to attain all its complex purposes. But it is better that the whole should be imperfectly and anomalously answered than that, while some parts are provided for with great exactness, others might be totally neglected or perhaps materially injured by the over-care of a favorite member.

The pretended rights of these theorists are all extremes; and in proportion as they are metaphysically true, they are morally and politically false. The rights of men are in a sort of *middle,* incapable of definition, but not impossible to be discerned. The rights of men in governments are their advantages; and these are often in balances between differences of good, in compromises sometimes between good and evil, and sometimes between evil and evil. Political reason is a computing principle: adding, subtracting, multiplying, and dividing, morally and not metaphysically or mathematically, true moral denominations.

By these theorists the right of the people is almost always sophistically confounded with their power. The body of the community, whenever it can come to act, can meet with no effectual resistance; but till power and right are the same, the whole body of them has no right inconsistent with virtue, and the first of all virtues, prudence. Men have no right to what is not reasonable and to what is not for their benefit; for though a pleasant writer said, *liceat perire poetis,* when one of them, in cold blood, is said to have leaped into the flames of a volcanic revolution, *ardentem frigidus Aetnam insiluit,*[xxxviii] I consider such a frolic rather as an unjustifiable poetic license than as one of the franchises of Parnassus; and whether he was a poet, or divine, or politician that chose to exercise this kind of right, I think that more wise, because more charitable, thoughts would urge me rather to save the man than to preserve his brazen slippers as the monuments of his folly.

The kind of anniversary sermons to which a great part of what I write refers, if men are not shamed out of their present course in commemorating the fact, will cheat many out of the principles, and deprive them of the benefits, of the revolution they commemorate. I confess to you, Sir, I never liked this continual talk of resistance and revolution, or the practice of making the extreme medicine of the constitution its daily bread. It renders the habit of society dangerously valetudinary; it is taking periodical doses of mercury sublimate and swallowing down repeated provocatives of cantharides to our love of liberty.

This distemper of remedy, grown habitual, relaxes and wears out, by a vulgar and prostituted use, the spring of that spirit which is to be exerted on great occasions. It was in the most patient period of Roman servitude that themes of tyrannicide made the ordinary exercise of boys at school—*cum perimit saevos classis numerosa tyrannos.*[xxxix] In the ordinary state of things, it produces in a country like ours the worst effects, even on the cause of that liberty which it abuses with the dissoluteness of an extravagant speculation. Almost all the high-bred republicans of my time have, after a short space, become the most decided, thorough-paced courtiers; they soon left the business of a tedious, moderate, but practical resistance to those of us whom, in the pride and intoxication of their theories, they have slighted as not much better than Tories.[xl] Hypocrisy, of course, delights in the most sublime speculations, for, never intending to go beyond speculation, it costs nothing to have it magnificent. But even in cases where rather levity than fraud was to be suspected in these ranting speculations, the issue has been much the same. These professors, finding their extreme principles not applicable to cases which call only for a qualified or, as I may say, civil and legal resistance, in such cases employ no resistance at all. It is with them a war or a revolution, or it is nothing. Finding their schemes of politics not adapted to the state of the world in which they live, they often come to think lightly of all public principle, and are ready, on their part, to abandon for a very trivial interest what they find of very trivial value. Some, indeed, are of more steady and persevering natures, but these are eager politicians out of parliament who have little to tempt them to abandon their favorite projects. They have some change in the church or state, or both, constantly in their view. When that is the case, they are always bad citizens and perfectly unsure connections.^{xli} For, considering their speculative designs as of infinite value, and the actual arrangement of the state as of no estimation, they are at best indifferent about it. They see no merit in the good, and no fault in the vicious, management of public affairs; they rather rejoice in the latter, as more propitious to revolution. They see no merit or demerit in any man, or any action, or any political principle any further than as they may forward or retard their design of change; they therefore take up, one day, the most violent and stretched prerogative, and another time the wildest democratic ideas of freedom, and pass from one to the other without any sort of regard to cause, to person, or to party.

IN FRANCE, you are now in the crisis of a revolution and in the transit from one form of government to another—you cannot see that character of men exactly in the same situation in which we see it in this country. With us it is militant; with you it is triumphant; and you know how it can act when its power is commensurate to its will. I would not be supposed to confine those observations to any description of men or to comprehend all men of any description within them—No! far from it. I am as incapable of that injustice as I am of keeping terms with those who profess principles of extremities and who, under the name of religion, teach little else than wild and dangerous politics. The worst of these politics of revolution is this: they temper and harden the breast in order to prepare it for the desperate strokes which are sometimes used in extreme occasions. But as these occasions may never arrive, the mind receives a gratuitous taint; and the moral sentiments suffer not a little when no political purpose is served by the depravation. This sort of people are so taken up with their theories about the rights of man that they have totally forgotten his nature. Without opening one new avenue to the understanding, they have succeeded in stopping up those that lead to the heart. They have perverted in themselves, and in those that attend to them, all the well-placed sympathies of the human breast.

This famous sermon of the Old Jewry breathes nothing but this spirit through all the political part. Plots, massacres, assassinations seem to some people a trivial price for obtaining a revolution. Cheap, bloodless reformation, a guiltless liberty appear flat and vapid to their taste. There must be a great change of scene; there must be a magnificent stage effect; there must be a grand spectacle to rouse the imagination grown torpid with the lazy enjoyment of sixty years' security and the still unanimating repose of public prosperity. The preacher found them all in the French Revolution. This inspires a juvenile warmth through his whole frame. His enthusiasm kindles as he advances; and when he arrives at his peroration it is in a full blaze. Then viewing, from the Pisgah of his pulpit, the free, moral, happy, flourishing and glorious state of France as in a bird's-eye landscape of a promised land, he breaks out into the following rapture: What an eventful period is this! I am *thankful* that I have lived to it; I could almost say, *Lord, now lettest thou thy servant depart in peace, for mine eyes have seen thy salvation.*—I have lived to see a diffusion of knowledge, which has undermined superstition and error.—I have lived to see *the rights of men* better understood than ever; and nations panting for liberty which seemed to have lost the idea of it.—I have lived to see *thirty millions of people,* indignant and resolute, spurning at slavery, and demanding liberty with an irresistible voice. *Their king led in triumph and an arbitrary monarch surrendering himself to his subjects.*[12]

Before I proceed further, I have to remark that Dr. Price seems rather to overvalue the great acquisitions of light which he has obtained and diffused in this age. The last century appears to me to have been quite as much enlightened. It had, though in a different place, a triumph as memorable as that of Dr. Price; and some of the great preachers of that period partook of it as eagerly as he has done in the triumph of France. On the trial of the Rev. Hugh Peters for high treason, it was deposed that, when King Charles was brought to London for his trial, the Apostle of Liberty in that day conducted the *triumph*. "I saw", says the witness, "his Majesty in the coach with six horses, and Peters riding before the king, *triumphing*". Dr. Price,

---

[12] Another of these reverend gentlemen, who was witness to some of the spectacles which Paris has lately exhibited, expresses himself thus:—"*A king dragged in submissive triumph by his conquering subjects,* is one of those appearances of grandeur which seldom rise in the prospect of human affairs, and which, during the remainder of my life, I shall think of with wonder and gratification". These gentlemen agree marvelously in their feelings.

when he talks as if he had made a discovery, only follows a precedent, for after the commencement of the king's trial this precursor, the same Dr. Peters, concluding a long prayer at the Royal Chapel at Whitehall (he had very triumphantly chosen his place), said, "I have prayed and preached these twenty years; and now I may say with old Simeon, *Lord, now lettest thou thy servant depart in peace, for mine eyes have seen thy salvation"*.[13] Peters had not the fruits of his prayer, for he neither departed so soon as he wished, nor in peace. He became (what I heartily hope none of his followers may be in this country) himself a sacrifice to the triumph which he led as pontiff.

They dealt at the Restoration, perhaps, too hardly with this poor good man.[xlii] But we owe it to his memory and his sufferings that he had as much illumination and as much zeal, and had as effectually undermined all *the superstition and error* which might impede the great business he was engaged in, as any who follow and repeat after him in this age, which would assume to itself an exclusive title to the knowledge of the rights of men and all the glorious consequences of that knowledge.

After this sally of the preacher of the Old Jewry, which differs only in place and time, but agrees perfectly with the spirit and letter of the rapture of 1648, the Revolution Society, the fabricators of governments, the heroic band of *cashierers of monarchs,* electors of sovereigns, and leaders of kings in triumph, strutting with a proud consciousness of the diffusion of knowledge of which every member had obtained so large a share in the donative, were in haste to make a generous diffusion of the knowledge they had thus gratuitously received. To make this bountiful communication, they adjourned from the church in the Old Jewry to the London Tavern, where the same Dr. Price, in whom the fumes of his oracular tripod were not entirely evaporated, moved and carried the resolution or address of congratulation transmitted by Lord Stanhope to the National Assembly of France.

I find a preacher of the gospel profaning the beautiful and prophetic ejaculation, commonly called *"nunc dimittis",* made on the first presentation of our Saviour in the Temple, and applying it with an inhuman and unnatural rapture to the most horrid, atrocious, and afflicting spectacle that perhaps ever was exhibited to the pity and indignation of mankind. This "leading in triumph", a thing in its best form unmanly and irreligious, which fills our preacher with such

[13] State Trials, vol. ii, pp. 360, 363.

unhallowed transports, must shock, I believe, the moral taste of every well-born mind. Several English were the stupefied and indignant spectators of that triumph. It was (unless we have been strangely deceived) a spectacle more resembling a procession of American savages, entering into Onondaga after some of their murders called victories and leading into hovels hung round with scalps their captives, overpowered with the scoffs and buffets of women as ferocious as themselves, much more than it resembled the triumphal pomp of a civilized martial nation—if a civilized nation, or any men who had a sense of generosity, were capable of a personal triumph over the fallen and afflicted.

THIS, MY DEAR SIR, was not the triumph of France. I must believe that, as a nation, it overwhelmed you with shame and horror. I must believe that the National Assembly find themselves in a state of the greatest humiliation in not being able to punish the authors of this triumph or the actors in it, and that they are in a situation in which any inquiry they may make upon the subject must be destitute even of the appearance of liberty or impartiality. The apology of that assembly is found in their situation; but when we approve what they *must* bear, it is in us the degenerate choice of a vitiated mind.

With a compelled appearance of deliberation, they vote under the dominion of a stern necessity. They sit in the heart, as it were, of a foreign republic: they have their residence in a city whose constitution has emanated neither from the charter of their king nor from their legislative power. There they are surrounded by an army not raised either by the authority of their crown or by their command, and which, if they should order to dissolve itself, would instantly dissolve them. There they sit, after a gang of assassins had driven away some hundreds of the members, whilst those who held the same moderate principles, with more patience or better hope, continued every day exposed to outrageous insults and murderous threats. There a majority, sometimes real, sometimes pretended, captive itself, compels a captive king to issue as royal edicts, at third hand, the polluted nonsense of their most licentious and giddy coffeehouses. It is notorious that all their measures are decided before they are debated. It is beyond doubt that, under the terror of the bayonet and the lamp-post and the torch to their houses, they are obliged to adopt all the crude and desperate measures suggested by clubs composed of a monstrous medley of all conditions, tongues, and nations. Among these are found persons, in comparison of whom Catiline would be thought scrupulous and Cethegus[xliii] a man of sobriety and moderation. Nor is it in these clubs alone that the public measures are deformed into monsters. They undergo a previous distortion in academies, intended as so many seminaries for these clubs, which are set up in all the places of public resort. In these meetings of all sorts every counsel, in proportion as it is daring and violent and perfidious, is taken for the mark of superior genius. Humanity and compassion are ridiculed as the fruits of superstition and ignorance. Tenderness to individuals is considered as treason to the public. Liberty is always to be estimated perfect, as property is rendered insecure. Amidst assassination, massacre, and confiscation, perpetrated or meditated, they are forming plans for the good order of future society. Embracing in their arms the carcasses of base criminals and promoting their relations on the title of their offences, they drive hundreds of virtuous persons to the same end, by forcing them to subsist by beggary or by crime.

The Assembly, their organ, acts before them the farce of deliberation with as little decency as liberty. They act like the comedians of a fair before a riotous audience; they act amidst the tumultuous cries of a mixed mob of ferocious men, and of women lost to shame, who, according to their insolent fancies, direct, control, applaud, explode them, and sometimes mix and take their seats amongst them, domineering over them with a strange mixture of servile petulance and proud, presumptuous authority. As they have inverted order in all things, the gallery is in the place of the house. This assembly, which overthrows kings and kingdoms, has not even the physiognomy and aspect of a grave legislative body—*nec color imperii, nec frons ulla senatûs.*[xliv] They have a power given to them, like that of the evil principle, to subvert and destroy, but none to construct, except such machines as may be fitted for further subversion and further destruction.

WHO is it that admires, and from the heart is attached to, national representative assemblies, but must turn with horror and disgust from such a profane burlesque, and abominable perversion of that sacred institute? Lovers of monarchy, lovers of republics must alike abhor it. The members of your assembly must themselves groan under the tyranny of which they have all the shame, none of the direction, and little of the profit. I am sure many of the members who compose even the majority of that body must feel as I do, notwith standing the applauses of the Revolution Society. Miserable king! miserable assembly! How must that assembly be silently scandalized with those of their members who could call a day which seemed to blot the sun out of heaven *"un beau jour!"*[14] How must they be inwardly indignant at hearing others who thought fit to declare to them "that the vessel of the state would fly forward in her course toward regeneration with more speed than ever", from the stiff gale of treason and murder which preceded our preacher's triumph! What must they have felt whilst, with outward patience and inward indignation, they heard, of the slaughter of innocent gentlemen in their houses, that "the blood spilled was not the most pure!" What must they have felt, when they were besieged by complaints of disorders which shook their country to its foundations, at being compelled coolly to tell the complainants that they were under the protection of the law, and that they would address the king (the captive king) to cause the laws to be enforced for their protection; when the enslaved ministers of that captive king had formally notified to them that there were neither law nor authority nor power left to protect? What must they have felt at being obliged, as a felicitation on the present new year, to request their captive king to forget the stormy period of the last, on account of the great good which *he* was likely to produce to his people; to the complete attainment of which good they adjourned the practical demonstrations of their loyalty, assuring him of their obedience when he should no longer possess any authority to command?

This address was made with much good nature and affection, to be sure. But among the revolutions in France must be reckoned a considerable revolution in their ideas of politeness. In England we are said to learn manners at second-hand from your side of the water, and that we dress our behavior in the frippery of France. If so, we are still in the old cut and have not so far conformed to the new Parisian mode of good breeding as to think it quite in the most refined strain of delicate compliment (whether in condolence or congratulation) to say, to the most humiliated creature that crawls upon the earth, that great public benefits are derived from the murder of his servants, the attempted assassination of himself and of his wife, and the mortification, disgrace, and degradation that he has personally suffered. It is a topic of consolation which our ordinary of Newgate[xlv] would be too humane to use to a criminal at the foot of the gallows. I should have

---

[14] 6th of October, 1789.

thought that the hangman of Paris, now that he is liberalized by the vote of the National Assembly and is allowed his rank and arms in the herald's college of the rights of men, would be too generous, too gallant a man, too full of the sense of his new dignity to employ that cutting consolation to any of the persons whom the *lèse nation*[xlvi] might bring under the administration of his *executive power.*

A man is fallen indeed when he is thus flattered. The anodyne draught of oblivion, thus drugged, is well calculated to preserve a galling wakefulness and to feed the living ulcer of a corroding memory. Thus to administer the opiate potion of amnesty, powdered with all the ingredients of scorn and contempt, is to hold to his lips, instead of "the balm of hurt minds",[xlvii] the cup of human misery full to the brim and to force him to drink it to the dregs.

Yielding to reasons at least as forcible as those which were so delicately urged in the compliment on the new year, the king of France will probably endeavor to forget these events and that compliment. But history, who keeps a durable record of all our acts and exercises her awful censure over the proceedings of all sorts of sovereigns, will not forget either those events or the era of this liberal refinement in the intercourse of mankind. History will record that on the morning of the 6th of October, 1789, the king and queen of France, after a day of confusion, alarm, dismay, and slaughter, lay down, under the pledged security of public faith, to indulge nature in a few hours of respite and troubled, melancholy repose. From this sleep the queen was first startled by the sentinel at her door, who cried out to her to save herself by flight—that this was the last proof of fidelity he could give—that they were upon him, and he was dead. Instantly he was cut down.[xlviii] A band of cruel ruffians and assassins, reeking with his blood, rushed into the chamber of the queen and pierced with a hundred strokes of bayonets and poniards the bed, from whence this persecuted woman had but just time to fly almost naked, and, through ways unknown to the murderers, had escaped to seek refuge at the feet of a king and husband not secure of his own life for a moment.

This king, to say no more of him, and this queen, and their infant children (who once would have been the pride and hope of a great and generous people) were then forced to abandon the sanctuary of the most splendid palace in the world, which they left swimming in blood, polluted by massacre and strewed with scattered limbs and mutilated carcasses. Thence they were conducted into the capital of their kingdom.

Two had been selected from the unprovoked, unresisted, promiscuous slaughter, which was made of the gentlemen of birth and family who composed the king's body guard. These two gentlemen, with all the parade of an execution of justice, were cruelly and publicly dragged to the block and beheaded in the great court of the palace. Their heads were stuck upon spears and led the procession, whilst the royal captives who followed in the train were slowly moved along, amidst the horrid yells, and shrilling screams, and frantic dances, and infamous contumelies, and all the unutterable abominations of the furies of hell in the abused shape of the vilest of women. After they had been made to taste, drop by drop, more than the bitterness of death in the slow torture of a journey of twelve miles, protracted to six hours, they were, under a guard composed of those very soldiers who had thus conducted them through this famous triumph, lodged in one of the old palaces of Paris, now converted into a bastille for kings.

Is this a triumph to be consecrated at altars? to be commemorated with grateful thanksgiving? to be offered to the divine humanity with fervent prayer and enthusiastic ejaculation?—These Theban and Thracian orgies, acted in France and applauded only in the Old Jewry, I assure you, kindle prophetic enthusiasm in the minds but of very few people in this kingdom, although a saint and apostle, who may have revelations of his own and who has so completely vanquished all the mean superstitions of the heart,[xlix] may incline to think it pious and decorous to compare it with the entrance into the world of the Prince of Peace, proclaimed in a holy temple by a venerable sage, and not long before not worse announced by the voice of angels to the quiet innocence of shepherds.

At first I was at a loss to account for this fit of unguarded transport. I knew, indeed, that the sufferings of monarchs make a delicious repast to some sort of palates. There were reflections which might serve to keep this appetite within some bounds of temperance. But when I took one circumstance into my consideration, I was obliged to confess that much allowance ought to be made for the Society, and that the temptation was too strong for common discretion—I mean, the circumstance of the *Io Paean* of the triumph, the animating cry which called "for *all* the BISHOPS to be hanged on the lampposts",[15] might well have brought forth a burst of enthusiasm on the foreseen consequences of this happy day. I allow to so much enthusiasm some

---

[15] *"Tous les Evêques à la lanterne"*.

little deviation from prudence. I allow this prophet to break forth into hymns of joy and thanksgiving on an event which appears like the precursor of the Millennium and the projected fifth monarchy in the destruction of all church establishments.

There was, however, (as in all human affairs there is) in the midst of this joy something to exercise the patience of these worthy gentlemen and to try the long-suffering of their faith. The actual murder of the king and queen, and their child, was wanting to the other auspicious circumstances of this "beautiful day". The actual murder of the bishops, though called for by so many holy ejaculations, was also wanting. A group of regicide and sacrilegious slaughter was indeed boldly sketched, but it was only sketched. It unhappily was left unfinished in this great history-piece of the massacre of innocents. What hardy pencil of a great master from the school of the rights of man will finish it is to be seen hereafter. The age has not yet the complete benefit of that diffusion of knowledge that has undermined superstition and error; and the king of France wants another object or two to consign to oblivion, in consideration of all the good which is to arise from his own sufferings and the patriotic crimes of an enlightened age.[16]

Although this work of our new light and knowledge did not go to the length that in all probability it was intended it should be carried, yet I must think that such treatment of any human creatures must be shocking to any but those who are made for accomplishing revolu-

---

[16] It is proper here to refer to a letter written upon this subject by an eye witness. That eye witness was one of the most honest, intelligent, and eloquent members of the National Assembly, one of the most active and zealous reformers of the state. He was obliged to secede from the Assembly; and he afterwards became a voluntary exile, on account of the horrors of this pious triumph and the dispositions of men who, profiting of crimes, if not causing them, have taken the lead in public affairs.
EXTRACT of M. de Lally Tollendal's Second Letter to a Friend.

"Parlons du parti que j'ai pris; il est bien justifié dans ma conscience.—Ni cette ville coupable, ni cette assemblée plus coupable encore, ne meritoient que je me justifie; mais j'ai à coeur que vous, et les personnes qui pensent comme vous, ne me condamnent pas.—Ma santé, je vous jure, me rendoit mes fonctions impossibles; mais même en les mettant de coté il a eté au-dessus de mes forces de supporter plus long-tems l'horreur que me causoit ce sang,—ces têtes.—cette reine *presque egorgée,*—ce roi,—amené *esclave,*—entrant à Paris, au milieu de ses assassins, et precedé des têtes de ses malheureux gardes.—Ces perfides jannissaires, ces assassins, ces femmes cannibales, ce cri de,

tions. But I cannot stop here. Influenced by the inborn feelings of my nature, and not being illuminated by a single ray of this new-sprung modern light, I confess to you, Sir, that the exalted rank of the persons suffering, and particularly the sex, the beauty, and the amiable qualities of the descendant of so many kings and emperors, with the tender age of royal infants, insensible only through infancy and innocence of the cruel outrages to which their parents were exposed, instead of being a subject of exultation, adds not a little to any sensibility on that most melancholy occasion.

I hear that the august person who was the principal object of our preacher's triumph, though he supported himself, felt much on that shameful occasion. As a man, it became him to feel for his wife and

---

TOUS LES EVEQUES A LA LANTERNE, dans le moment ou le roi entre sa capitale avec deux evêques de son conseil dans sa voiture. Un *coup de fusil,* que j'ai vu tirer dans un *des carosses de la reine.* M. Bailly appellant cela *un beau jour.* L'assemblée ayant declaré froidement le matin, qu'il n'étoit pas de sa dignité d'aller toute entiére environner le roi. M. Mirabeau disant impunement dans cette assemblée, que le vaisseau de l'état, loin d'être arrêté dans sa course, s'élanceroit avec plus de rapidité que jamais vers sa régénération. M. Barnave, riant avec lui, quand des flots de sang couloient autour de nous. Le vertueux Mounier* echappant par miracle à vingt assassins, qui avoient voulu faire de sa tête un trophée de plus.

"Voila ce qui me fit jurer de ne plus mettre le pied *dans cette caverne d'Antropophages* où je n'avois plus de force d'élever la voix, ou depuis six semaines je l'avois elevée en vain. Moi, Mounier, et tous les honnêtes gens, ont le dernier effort à faire pour le bien étoit *(sic)* d'en sortir. Aucune idée de crainte ne s'est approchée de moi. Je rougirois de m'en defendre. J'avois encore reçû sur la route de la part de ce peuple, moins coupable que ceux qui l'ont enivré de fureur, des acclamations, et des applaudissements, dont d'autres auroient été flattés, et qui m'ont fait fremir. C'est à l'indignation, c'est à l'horreur, c'est aux convulsions physiques, que se seul aspect du sang me fait eprouver que j'ai cedé. On brave une seule mort; on la brave plusieurs fois, quand elle peut être utile. Mais aucune puissance sous le Ciel, mais aucune opinion publique ou privée n'ont le droit de me condamner à souffrir inutilement mille supplices par minute, et à perir de désespoir, de rage, au milieu des *triomphes,* du crime que je n'ai pu arrêter. Ils me proscriront, ils confisqueront mes biens. Je labourerai la terre, et je ne les verrai plus.—Voilà ma justification. Vous pouvez la lire, la montrer, la laisser copier; tant pis pour ceux qui ne la comprendront pas; ce ne sera alors moi qui auroit eu tort de la leur donner".[1]

This military man had not so good nerves as the peaceable gentleman of the Old Jewry.—See Mons. Mounier's narrative of these transactions; a man also of honour and virtue, and talents, and therefore a fugitive.

*N.B. Mr. Mounier was then speaker of the National Assembly. He has since been obliged to live in exile, though one of the firmest assertors of liberty.

his children, and the faithful guards of his person that were massacred in cold blood about him; as a prince, it became him to feel for the strange and frightful transformation of his civilized subjects, and to be more grieved for them than solicitous for himself. It derogates little from his fortitude, while it adds infinitely to the honor of his humanity. I am very sorry to say it, very sorry indeed, that such personages are in a situation in which it is not unbecoming in us to praise the virtues of the great.

I hear, and I rejoice to hear, that the great lady, the other object of the triumph, has borne that day (one is interested that beings made for suffering should suffer well),[li] and that she bears all the succeeding days, that she bears the imprisonment of her husband, and her own captivity, and the exile of her friends, and the insulting adulation of addresses, and the whole weight of her accumulated wrongs, with a serene patience, in a manner suited to her rank and race, and becoming the offspring of a sovereign distinguished for her piety and her courage; that, like her, she has lofty sentiments; that she feels with the dignity of a Roman matron; that in the last extremity she will save herself from the last disgrace; and that, if she must fall, she will fall by no ignoble hand.[lii]

It is now sixteen or seventeen years since I saw the queen of France, then the dauphiness, at Versailles, and surely never lighted on this orb, which she hardly seemed to touch, a more delightful vision. I saw her just above the horizon, decorating and cheering the elevated sphere she just began to move in—glittering like the morning star, full of life and splendor and joy. Oh! what a revolution! and what a heart must I have to contemplate without emotion that elevation and that fall! Little did I dream when she added titles of veneration to those of enthusiastic, distant, respectful love, that she should ever be obliged to carry the sharp antidote against disgrace concealed in that bosom; little did I dream that I should have lived to see such disasters fallen upon her in a nation of gallant men, in a nation of men of honor and of cavaliers. I thought ten thousand swords must have leaped from their scabbards to avenge even a look that threatened her with insult. But the age of chivalry is gone. That of sophisters, economists; and calculators has succeeded; and the glory of Europe is extinguished forever. Never, never more shall we behold that generous loyalty to rank and sex, that proud submission, that dignified obedience, that subordination of the heart which kept alive, even in servitude itself, the spirit of an exalted freedom. The unbought grace

EDMUND BURKE

of life, the cheap defense of nations, the nurse of manly sentiment and heroic enterprise, is gone! It is gone, that sensibility of principle, that chastity of honor which felt a stain like a wound, which inspired courage whilst it mitigated ferocity, which ennobled whatever it touched, and under which vice itself lost half its evil by losing all its grossness.

THIS mixed system of opinion and sentiment had its origin in the ancient chivalry; and the principle, though varied in its appearance by the varying state of human affairs, subsisted and influenced through a long succession of generations even to the time we live in. If it should ever be totally extinguished, the loss I fear will be great. It is this which has given its character to modern Europe. It is this which has distinguished it under all its forms of government, and distinguished it to its advantage, from the states of Asia and possibly from those states which flourished in the most brilliant periods of the antique world. It was this which, without confounding ranks, had produced a noble equality and handed it down through all the gradations of social life. It was this opinion which mitigated kings into companions and raised private men to be fellows with kings. Without force or opposition, it subdued the fierceness of pride and power, it obliged sovereigns to submit to the soft collar of social esteem, compelled stern authority to submit to elegance, and gave a domination, vanquisher of laws, to be subdued by manners.

But now all is to be changed. All the pleasing illusions which made power gentle and obedience liberal, which harmonized the different shades of life, and which, by a bland assimilation, incorporated into politics the sentiments which beautify and soften private society, are to be dissolved by this new conquering empire of light and reason. All the decent drapery of life is to be rudely torn off. All the superadded ideas, furnished from the wardrobe of a moral imagination, which the heart owns and the understanding ratifies as necessary to cover the defects of our naked, shivering nature, and to raise it to dignity in our own estimation, are to be exploded as a ridiculous, absurd, and antiquated fashion.

On this scheme of things, a king is but a man, a queen is but a woman; a woman is but an animal, and an animal not of the highest order. All homage paid to the sex in general as such, and without distinct views, is to be regarded as romance and folly. Regicide, and parricide, and sacrilege are but fictions of superstition, corrupting

Whoa, this is a pretty off the wall declension

jurisprudence by destroying its simplicity. The murder of a king, or a queen, or a bishop, or a father are only common homicide; and if the people are by any chance or in any way gainers by it, a sort of homicide much the most pardonable, and into which we ought not to make too severe a scrutiny.

On the scheme of this barbarous philosophy, which is the offspring of cold hearts and muddy understandings, and which is as void of solid wisdom as it is destitute of all taste and elegance, laws are to be supported only by their own terrors and by the concern which each individual may find in them from his own private speculations or can spare to them from his own private interests. In the groves of *their* academy, at the end of every vista, you see nothing but the gallows. Nothing is left which engages the affections on the part of the commonwealth. On the principles of this mechanic philosophy, our institutions can never be embodied, if I may use the expression, in persons, so as to create in us love, veneration, admiration, or attachment. But that sort of reason which banishes the affections is incapable of filling their place. These public affections, combined with manners, are required sometimes as supplements, sometimes as correctives, always as aids to law. The precept given by a wise man, as well as a great critic, for the construction of poems is equally true as to states:—*Non satis est pulchra esse poemata, dulcia sunto.*[liii] There ought to be a system of manners in every nation which a well-informed mind would be disposed to relish. To make us love our country, our country ought to be lovely.

But power, of some kind or other, will survive the shock in which manners and opinions perish; and it will find other and worse means for its support. The usurpation which, in order to subvert ancient institutions, has destroyed ancient principles will hold power by arts similar to those by which it has acquired it. When the old feudal and chivalrous spirit of *fealty,* which, by freeing kings from fear, freed both kings and subjects from the precautions of tyranny, shall be extinct in the minds of men, plots and assassinations will be anticipated by preventive murder and preventive confiscation, and that long roll of grim and bloody maxims which form the political code of all power not standing on its own honor and the honor of those who are to obey it. Kings will be tyrants from policy when subjects are rebels from principle.

When ancient opinions and rules of life are taken away, the loss cannot possibly be estimated. From that moment we have no compass to govern us; nor can we know distinctly to what port we steer. Europe, undoubtedly, taken in a mass, was in a flourishing condition the day on which your revolution was completed. How much of that prosperous state was owing to the spirit of our old manners and opinions is not easy to say; but as such causes cannot be indifferent in their operation, we must presume that on the whole their operation was beneficial.

We are but too apt to consider things in the state in which we find them, without sufficiently adverting to the causes by which they have been produced and possibly may be upheld. Nothing is more certain than that our manners, our civilization, and all the good things which are connected with manners and with civilization have, in this European world of ours, depended for ages upon two principles and were, indeed, the result of both combined: I mean the spirit of a gentleman and the spirit of religion. The nobility and the clergy, the one by profession, the other by patronage, kept learning in existence, even in the midst of arms and confusions, and whilst governments were rather in their causes than formed. Learning paid back what it received to nobility and to priesthood, and paid it with usury, by enlarging their ideas and by furnishing their minds. Happy if they had all continued to know their indissoluble union and their proper place! Happy if learning, not debauched by ambition, had been satisfied to continue the instructor, and not aspired to be the master! Along with its natural protectors and guardians, learning will be cast into the mire and trodden down under the hoofs of a swinish[17] multitude.[liv]

If, as I suspect, modern letters owe more than they are always willing to own to ancient manners, so do other interests which we value full as much as they are worth. Even commerce and trade and manufacture, the gods of our economical politicians, are themselves perhaps but creatures, are themselves but effects which, as first causes, we choose to worship. They certainly grew under the same shade in which learning flourished. They, too, may decay with their natural protecting principles. With you, for the present at least, they all threaten to disappear together. Where trade and manufactures are wanting to a people, and the spirit of nobility and religion remains, sentiment supplies, and not always ill supplies, their place; but if

---

[17] See the fate of Bailly and Condorcet, supposed to be here particularly alluded to. Compare the circumstances of the trial and execution of the former with this prediction. [1803]

commerce and the arts should be lost in an experiment to try how well a state may stand without these old fundamental principles, what sort of a thing must be a nation of gross, stupid, ferocious, and, at the same time, poor and sordid barbarians, destitute of religion, honor, or manly pride, possessing nothing at present, and hoping for nothing hereafter?

I wish you may not be going fast, and by the shortest cut, to that horrible and disgustful situation. Already there appears a poverty of conception, a coarseness, and a vulgarity in all the proceedings of the Assembly and of all their instructors. Their liberty is not liberal. Their science is presumptuous ignorance. Their humanity is savage and brutal.

It is not clear whether in England we learned those grand and decorous principles and manners, of which considerable traces yet remain, from you or whether you took them from us. But to you, I think, we trace them best. You seem to me to be *gentis incunabula nostrae.*[iv] France has always more or less influenced manners in England; and when your fountain is choked up and polluted, the stream will not run long, or not run clear, with us or perhaps with any nation. This gives all Europe, in my opinion, but too close and connected a concern in what is done in France. Excuse me, therefore, if I have dwelt too long on the atrocious spectacle of the 6th of October, 1789, or have given too much scope to the reflections which have arisen in my mind on occasion of the most important of all revolutions, which may be dated from that day—I mean a revolution in sentiments, manners, and moral opinions. As things now stand, with everything respectable destroyed without us, and an attempt to destroy within us every principle of respect, one is almost forced to apologize for harboring the common feelings of men.

WHY do I feel so differently from the Reverend Dr. Price and those of his lay flock who will choose to adopt the sentiments of his discourse?—For this plain reason: because it is *natural* I should; because we are so made as to be affected at such spectacles with melancholy sentiments upon the unstable condition of mortal prosperity and the tremendous uncertainty of human greatness; because in those natural feelings we learn great lessons; because in events like these our passions instruct our reason; because when kings are hurled from their thrones by the Supreme Director of this great drama and become the objects of insult to the base and of pity to the good, we behold such disasters in the moral as we should behold a miracle in the physical order of things. We are alarmed into reflection; our minds (as it has long since been observed) are purified by terror and pity, our weak, unthinking pride is humbled under the dispensations of a mysterious wisdom. Some tears might be drawn from me if such a spectacle were exhibited on the stage. I should be truly ashamed of finding in myself that superficial, theatric sense of painted distress whilst I could exult over it in real life. With such a perverted mind I could never venture to show my face at a tragedy. People would think the tears that Garrick formerly, or that Siddons not long since, have extorted from me were the tears of hypocrisy; I should know them to be the tears of folly.

Indeed, the theatre is a better school of moral sentiments than churches, where the feelings of humanity are thus outraged. Poets who have to deal with an audience not yet graduated in the school of the rights of men and who must apply themselves to the moral constitution of the heart would not dare to produce such a triumph as a matter of exultation. There, where men follow their natural impulses, they would not bear the odious maxims of a Machiavellian policy, whether applied to the attainments of monarchical or democratic tyranny. They would reject them on the modern as they once did on the ancient stage, where they could not bear even the hypothetical proposition of such wickedness in the mouth of a personated tyrant, though suitable to the character he sustained. No theatric audience in Athens would bear what has been borne in the midst of the real tragedy of this triumphal day: a principal actor weighing, as it were, in scales hung in a shop of horrors, so much actual crime against so much contingent advantage; and after putting in and out weights, declaring that the balance was on the side of the advantages. They would not bear to see the crimes of new democracy posted as in a ledger against the crimes of old despotism, and the book-keepers of politics finding democracy still in debt, but by no means unable or unwilling to pay the balance. In the theater, the first intuitive glance, without any elaborate process of reasoning, will show that this method of political computation would justify every extent of crime. They would see that on these principles, even where the very worst acts were not perpetrated, it was owing rather to the fortune of the conspirators than to their parsimony in the expenditure of treachery and blood. They would soon see that criminal means once tolerated are

71

soon preferred. They present a shorter cut to the object than through the highway of the moral virtues. Justifying perfidy and murder for public benefit, public benefit would soon become the pretext, and perfidy and murder the end, until rapacity, malice, revenge, and fear more dreadful than revenge could satiate their insatiable appetites. Such must be the consequences of losing, in the splendor of these triumphs of the rights of men, all natural sense of wrong and right.

But the reverend pastor exults in this "leading in triumph", because truly Louis the Sixteenth was "an arbitrary monarch"; that is, in other words, neither more nor less than because he was Louis the Sixteenth, and because he had the misfortune to be born king of France, with the prerogatives of which a long line of ancestors and a long acquiescence of the people, without any act of his, had put him in possession. A misfortune it has indeed turned out to him that he was born king of France. But misfortune is not crime, nor is indiscretion always the greatest guilt. I shall never think that a prince the acts of whose whole reign was a series of concessions to his subjects, who was willing to relax his authority, to remit his prerogatives, to call his people to a share of freedom not known, perhaps not desired, by their ancestors—such a prince, though he should be subjected to the common frailties attached to men and to princes, though he should have once thought it necessary to provide force against the desperate designs manifestly carrying on against his person and the remnants of his authority—though all this should be taken into consideration, I shall be led with great difficulty to think he deserves the cruel and insulting triumph of Paris and of Dr. Price. I tremble for the cause of liberty from such an example to kings. I tremble for the cause of humanity in the unpunished outrages of the most wicked of mankind. But there are some people of that low and degenerate fashion of mind, that they look up with a sort of complacent awe and admiration to kings who know to keep firm in their seat, to hold a strict hand over their subjects, to assert their prerogative, and, by the awakened vigilance of a severe despotism, to guard against the very first approaches to freedom. Against such as these they never elevate their voice. Deserters from principle, listed[lvi] with fortune, they never see any good in suffering virtue, nor any crime in prosperous usurpation.

If it could have been made clear to me that the king and queen of France (those I mean who were such before the triumph) were inexorable and cruel tyrants, that they had formed a deliberate scheme for massacring the National Assembly (I think I have seen something like the latter insinuated in certain publications), I should think their captivity just. If this be true, much more ought to have been done, but done, in my opinion, in another manner. The punishment of real tyrants is a noble and awful act of justice; and it has with truth been said to be consolatory to the human mind. But if I were to punish a wicked king, I should regard the dignity in avenging the crime. Justice is grave and decorous, and in its punishments rather seems to submit to a necessity than to make a choice. Had Nero, or Agrippina, or Louis the Eleventh, or Charles the Ninth been the subject; if Charles the Twelfth of Sweden, after the murder of Patkul, or his predecessor Christina, after the murder of Monaldeschi, had fallen into your hands, Sir, or into mine, I am sure our conduct would have been different.[lvii]

If the French king, or king of the French (or by whatever name he is known in the new vocabulary of your constitution), has in his own person and that of his queen really deserved these unavowed, but unavenged, murderous attempts and those frequent indignities more cruel than murder, such a person would ill deserve even that subordinate executory trust which I understand is to be placed in him, nor is he fit to be called chief in a nation which he has outraged and oppressed. A worse choice for such an office in a new commonwealth than that of a deposed tyrant could not possibly be made. But to degrade and insult a man as the worst of criminals and afterwards to trust him in your highest concerns as a faithful, honest, and zealous servant is not consistent to reasoning, nor prudent in policy, nor safe in practice. Those who could make such an appointment must be guilty of a more flagrant breach of trust than any they have yet committed against the people. As this is the only crime in which your leading politicians could have acted inconsistently, I conclude that there is no sort of ground for these horrid insinuations. I think no better of all the other calumnies.

IN ENGLAND, we give no credit to them. We are generous enemies; we are faithful allies. We spurn from us with disgust and indignation the slanders of those who bring us their anecdotes with the attestation of the flower-de-luce on their shoulder.[lviii] We have Lord George Gordon[lix] fast in Newgate; and neither his being a public proselyte to Judaism, nor his having, in his zeal against Catholic priests and all sorts of ecclesiastics, raised a mob (excuse the term, it is still in use

73

here) which pulled down all our prisons, have preserved to him a liberty of which he did not render himself worthy by a virtuous use of it. We have rebuilt Newgate and tenanted the mansion. We have prisons almost as strong as the Bastille for those who dare to libel the queens of France. In this spiritual retreat, let the noble libeller remain. Let him there meditate on his Talmud until he learns a conduct more becoming his birth and parts, and not so disgraceful to the ancient religion to which he has become a proselyte; or until some persons from your side of the water, to please your new Hebrew brethren, shall ransom him. He may then be enabled to purchase with the old boards of the synagogue and a very small poundage on the long compound interest of the thirty pieces of silver (Dr. Price has shown us what miracles compound interest will perform in 1790 years,[ix]), the lands which are lately discovered to have been usurped by the Gallican church. Send us your Popish archbishop of Paris, and we will send you our Protestant Rabbin. We shall treat the person you send us in exchange like a gentleman and an honest man, as he is; but pray let him bring with him the fund of his hospitality, bounty, and charity, and, depend upon it, we shall never confiscate a shilling of that honorable and pious fund, nor think of enriching the treasury with the spoils of the poor-box.

To tell you the truth, my dear Sir, I think the honor of our nation to be somewhat concerned in the disclaimer of the proceedings of this society of the Old Jewry and the London Tavern. I have no man's proxy. I speak only for myself when I disclaim, as I do with all possible earnestness, all communion with the actors in that triumph or with the admirers of it. When I assert anything else as concerning the people of England, I speak from observation, not from authority, but I speak from the experience I have had in a pretty extensive and mixed communication with the inhabitants of this kingdom, of all descriptions and ranks, and after a course of attentive observations begun early in life and continued for nearly forty years. I have often been astonished, considering that we are divided from you but by a slender dyke of about twenty-four miles, and that the mutual intercourse between the two countries has lately been very great, to find how little you seem to know of us. I suspect that this is owing to your forming a judgment of this nation from certain publications which do very erroneously, if they do at all, represent the opinions and dispositions generally prevalent in England. The vanity, restlessness, petulance, and spirit of intrigue, of several petty cabals, who attempt to hide their total want of consequence in bustle and noise, and puffing, and mutual quotation of each other, makes you imagine that our contemptuous neglect of their abilities is a mark of general acquiescence in their opinions. No such thing, I assure you. Because half a dozen grasshoppers under a fern make the field ring with their importunate chink, whilst thousands of great cattle, reposed beneath the shadow of the British oak, chew the cud and are silent, pray do not imagine that those who make the noise are the only inhabitants of the field; that, of course, they are many in number, or that, after all, they are other than the little, shrivelled, meager, hopping, though loud and troublesome, insects of the hour.

I almost venture to affirm that not one in a hundred amongst us participates in the "triumph" of the Revolution Society. If the king and queen of France, and their children, were to fall into our hands by the chance of war, in the most acrimonious of all hostilities (I deprecate such an event, I deprecate such hostility), they would be treated with another sort of triumphal entry into London. We formerly have had a king of France in that situation; you have read how he was treated by the victor in the field, and in what manner he was afterwards received in England. Four hundred years have gone over us, but I believe we are not materially changed since that period. Thanks to our sullen resistance to innovation, thanks to the cold sluggishness of our national character, we still bear the stamp of our forefathers. We have not (as I conceive) lost the generosity and dignity of thinking of the fourteenth century, nor as yet have we subtilized ourselves into savages. We are not the converts of Rousseau; we are not the disciples of Voltaire; Helvetius has made no progress amongst us. Atheists are not our preachers; madmen are not our lawgivers. We know that *we* have made no discoveries, and we think that no discoveries are to be made in morality, nor many in the great principles of government, nor in the ideas of liberty, which were understood long before we were born, altogether as well as they will be after the grace has heaped its mold upon our presumption and the silent tomb shall have imposed its law on our pert loquacity. In England we have not yet been completely embowelled of our natural entrails; we still feel within us, and we cherish and cultivate, those inbred sentiments which are the faithful guardians, the active monitors of our duty, the true supporters of all liberal and manly morals. We have not been drawn and trussed, in order that we may be filled, like stuffed birds in a museum, with chaff and rags and paltry blurred shreds of paper about the rights of men. We preserve the whole of our feelings still native and entire, unsophisticated by pedantry and infidelity. We have real hearts of flesh and blood beating in our bosoms. We fear God; we look up with awe to kings, with affection to parliaments, with duty to magistrates, with reverence to priests, and with respect to nobility.[18] Why? Because when such ideas are brought before our minds, it is *natural* to be so affected; because all other feelings are false and spurious and tend to corrupt our minds, to vitiate our primary morals, to render us unfit for rational liberty, and, by teaching us a servile, licentious, and abandoned insolence, to be our low sport for a few holidays, to make us perfectly fit for, and justly deserving of, slavery through the whole course of our lives.

YOU see, Sir, that in this enlightened age I am bold enough to confess that we are generally men of untaught feelings, that, instead of casting away all our old prejudices, we cherish them to a very considerable degree, and, to take more shame to ourselves, we cherish them because they are prejudices; and the longer they have lasted and the more generally they have prevailed, the more we cherish them. We are afraid to put men to live and trade each on his own private stock of reason, because we suspect that this stock in each man is small, and that the individuals would do better to avail themselves of the general bank and capital of nations and of ages. Many of our men of speculation, instead of exploding general prejudices, employ their sagacity to discover the latent wisdom which prevails in them. If they find what they seek, and they seldom fail, they think it more wise to continue the prejudice, with the reason involved, than to cast away the coat of prejudice and to leave nothing but the naked reason; because prejudice, with its reason, has a motive to give action to that reason, and an affection which will give it permanence. Prejudice is of ready application in the emergency; it previously engages the mind in a steady course of wisdom and virtue and does not leave the man hesitating in the moment of decision skeptical, puzzled, and unresolved. Prejudice renders a man's virtue his habit, and not a series of

[18] The English are, I conceive, misrepresented in a letter published in one of the papers, by a gentleman thought to be a dissenting minister.—When writing to Dr. Price of the spirit which prevails at Paris, he says: "The spirit of the people in this place has abolished all the proud *distinctions* which the *king* and *nobles* had usurped in their minds; whether they talk of *the king, the noble, or the priest,* their whole language is that of the most *enlightened and liberal amongst the English".* If this gentleman means to confine the terms "enlightened" *and* "liberal" to one set of men in England, it may be true. It is not generally so.

unconnected acts. Through just prejudice, his duty becomes a part of his nature.

Your literary men and your politicians, and so do the whole clan of the enlightened among us, essentially differ in these points. They have no respect for the wisdom of others, but they pay it off by a very full measure of confidence in their own. With them it is a sufficient motive to destroy an old scheme of things because it is an old one. As to the new, they are in no sort of fear with regard to the duration of a building run up in haste, because duration is no object to those who think little or nothing has been done before their time, and who place all their hopes in discovery. They conceive, very systematically, that all things which give perpetuity are mischievous, and therefore they are at inexpiable war with all establishments. They think that government may vary like modes of dress, and with as little ill effect; that there needs no principle of attachment, except a sense of present convenience, to any constitution of the state. They always speak as if they were of opinion that there is a singular species of compact between them and their magistrates which binds the magistrate, but which has nothing reciprocal in it, but that the majesty of the people has a right to dissolve it without any reason but its will. Their attachment to their country itself is only so far as it agrees with some of their fleeting projects; it begins and ends with that scheme of polity which falls in with their momentary opinion.

These doctrines, or rather sentiments, seem prevalent with your new statesmen. But they are wholly different from those on which we have always acted in this country.

I hear it is sometimes given out in France that what is doing among you is after the example of England. I beg leave to affirm that scarcely anything done with you has originated from the practice or the prevalent opinions of this people, either in the act or in the spirit of the proceeding. Let me add that we are as unwilling to learn these lessons from France as we are sure that we never taught them to that nation. The cabals here who take a sort of share of your transactions as yet consist of but a handful of people. If, unfortunately, by their intrigues, their sermons, their publications, and by a confidence derived from an expected union with the counsels and forces of the French nation, they should draw considerable numbers into their faction, and in consequence should seriously attempt anything here in imitation of what has been done with you, the event, I dare venture to prophesy, will be that, with some trouble to their country, they will soon accomplish their own destruction. This people refused to change their law in remote ages from respect to the infallibility of popes, and they will not now alter it from a pious implicit faith in the dogmatism of philosophers, though the former was armed with the anathema and crusade, and though the latter should act with the libel and the lamp-iron.

Formerly, your affairs were your own concern only. We felt for them as men, but we kept aloof from them because we were not citizens of France. But when we see the model held up to ourselves, we must feel as Englishmen, and feeling, we must provide as Englishmen. Your affairs, in spite of us, are made a part of our interest, so far at least as to keep at a distance your panacea, or your plague. If it be a panacea, we do not want it. We know the consequences of unnecessary physic. If it be a plague, it is such a plague that the precautions of the most severe quarantine ought to be established against it.

I hear on all hands that a cabal calling itself philosophic receives the glory of many of the late proceedings, and that their opinions and systems are the true actuating spirit of the whole of them. I have heard of no party in England, literary or political, at any time, known by such a description. It is not with you composed of those men, is it, whom the vulgar in their blunt, homely style commonly call atheists and infidels? If it be, I admit that we, too, have had writers of that description who made some noise in their day. At present they repose in lasting oblivion. Who, born within the last forty years, has read one word of Collins, and Toland, and Tindal, and Chubb, and Morgan, and that whole race who called themselves Freethinkers?[lxi] Who now reads Bolingbroke? Who ever read him through? Ask the booksellers of London what is become of all these lights of the world. In as few years their few successors will go to the family vault of "all the Capulets". But whatever they were, or are, with us, they were and are wholly unconnected individuals. With us they kept the common nature of their kind and were not gregarious. They never acted in corps or were known as a faction in the state, nor presumed to influence in that name or character, or for the purposes of such a faction, on any of our public concerns. Whether they ought so to exist and so be permitted to act is another question. As such cabals have not existed in England, so neither has the spirit of them had any influence in establishing the original frame of our constitution or in any one of the several reparations and improvements it has undergone. The whole has been done under the auspices, and is confirmed by the sanctions, of religion and piety. The whole has emanated from the simplicity of our national character and from a sort of native plainness and directness of understanding, which for a long time characterized those men who have successively obtained authority amongst us. This disposition still remains, at least in the great body of the people.

WE KNOW, AND WHAT IS BETTER, we feel inwardly, that religion is the basis of civil society and the source of all good and of all comfort.[19] In England we are so convinced of this, that there is no rust of superstition with which the accumulated absurdity of the human mind might have crusted it over in the course of ages, that ninety-nine in a hundred of the people of England would not prefer to impiety. We shall never be such fools as to call in an enemy to the substance of any system to remove its corruptions, to supply its defects, or to perfect its construction. If our religious tenets should ever want a further elucidation, we shall not call on atheism to explain them. We shall not light up our temple from that unhallowed fire. It will be illuminated with other lights. It will be perfumed with other incense than the infectious stuff which is imported by the smugglers of adulterated metaphysics. If our ecclesiastical establishment should want a revision, it is not avarice or rapacity, public or private, that we shall employ for the audit, or receipt, or application of its consecrated revenue. Violently condemning neither the Greek nor the Armenian, nor, since heats are subsided, the Roman system of religion, we prefer the Protestant, not because we think it has less of the Christian religion in it, but because, in our judgment, it has more. We are

[19] Sit igitur hoc ab initio persuasum civibus, dominos esse omnium rerum ac moderatores, deos; eaque, quae gerantur, eorum geri vi, ditione, ac numine; eosdemque optime de genere hominum mereri; et qualis quisque sit, quid agat, quid in se admittat, qua mente, qua pietate colat religiones intueri; piorum et impiorum habere rationem. His enim rebus imbutae mentes haud sane abhorrebunt ab utili et a vera sententia. Cic. *de Legibus,* 1. 2. ["So let our citizens be convinced of this at the outset: that the gods are the lords and rulers of all things, that all that is done is done by their might, dominion, and authority, and that they have treated mankind very well; that they also observe what sort of man each individual is, what he does, of what wrong he is guilty, with what intention, with what piety, he keeps ritual observances; and that they take cognizance of the pious and the impious. For minds imbued with these beliefs will surely not reject useful or true doctrine".—Cicero, *Of the Laws,* Bk. 2.]

Protestants, not from indifference, but from zeal.

We know, and it is our pride to know, that man is by his constitution a religious animal; that atheism is against, not only our reason, but our instincts; and that it cannot prevail long. But if, in the moment of riot and in a drunken delirium from the hot spirit drawn out of the alembic of hell, which in France is now so furiously boiling, we should uncover our nakedness by throwing off that Christian religion which has hitherto been our boast and comfort, and one great source of civilization amongst us and amongst many other nations, we are apprehensive (being well aware that the mind will not endure a void) that some uncouth, pernicious, and degrading superstition might take place of it.

For that reason, before we take from our establishment the natural, human means of estimation and give it up to contempt, as you have done, and in doing it have incurred the penalties you well deserve to suffer, we desire that some other may be presented to us in the place of it. We shall then form our judgment.

On these ideas, instead of quarrelling with establishments, as some do who have made a philosophy and a religion of their hostility to such institutions, we cleave closely to them. We are resolved to keep an established church, an established monarchy, an established aristocracy, and an established democracy, each in the degree it exists, and in no greater. I shall show you presently how much of each of these we possess.

It has been the misfortune (not, as these gentlemen think it, the glory) of this age that everything is to be discussed as if the constitution of our country were to be always a subject rather of altercation than enjoyment. For this reason, as well as for the satisfaction of those among you (if any such you have among you) who may wish to profit of examples, I venture to trouble you with a few thoughts upon each of these establishments. I do not think they were unwise in ancient Rome who, when they wished to new-model their laws, set commissioners to examine the best constituted republics within their reach.

First, I beg leave to speak of our church establishment, which is the first of our prejudices, not a prejudice destitute of reason, but involving in it profound and extensive wisdom. I speak of it first. It is first and last and midst in our minds. For, taking ground on that religious system of which we are now in possession, we continue to act on the early received and uniformly continued sense of mankind. That sense not only, like a wise architect, hath built up the august fabric of states, but, like a provident proprietor, to preserve the structure from profanation and ruin, as a sacred temple purged from all the impurities of fraud and violence and injustice and tyranny, hath solemnly and forever consecrated the commonwealth and all that officiate in it. This consecration is made that all who administer the government of men, in which they stand in the person of God himself, should have high and worthy notions of their function and destination, that their hope should be full of immortality, that they should not look to the paltry pelf of the moment nor to the temporary and transient praise of the vulgar, but to a solid, permanent existence in the permanent part of their nature, and to a permanent fame and glory in the example they leave as a rich inheritance to the world.

Such sublime principles ought to be infused into persons of exalted situations, and religious establishments provided that may continually revive and enforce them. Every sort of moral, every sort of civil, every sort of politic institution, aiding the rational and natural ties that connect the human understanding and affections to the divine, are not more than necessary in order to build up that wonderful structure Man, whose prerogative it is to be in a great degree a creature of his own making, and who, when made as he ought to be made, is destined to hold no trivial place in the creation. But whenever man is put over men, as the better nature ought ever to preside, in that case more particularly, he should as nearly as possible be approximated to his perfection.

The consecration of the state by a state religious establishment is necessary, also, to operate with a wholesome awe upon free citizens, because, in order to secure their freedom, they must enjoy some determinate portion of power. To them, therefore, a religion connected with the state, and with their duty toward it, becomes even more necessary than in such societies where the people, by the terms of their subjection, are confined to private sentiments and the management of their own family concerns. All persons possessing any portion of power ought to be strongly and awfully impressed with an idea that they act in trust, and that they are to account for their conduct in that trust to the one great Master, Author, and Founder of society.

This principle ought even to be more strongly impressed upon the minds of those who compose the collective sovereignty than upon those of single princes. Without instruments, these princes can do nothing. Whoever uses instruments, in finding helps, finds also impediments. Their power is, therefore, by no means complete, nor are they safe in extreme abuse. Such persons, however elevated by flattery, arrogance, and self-opinion, must be sensible that, whether covered or not by positive law, in some way or other they are accountable even here for the abuse of their trust. If they are not cut off by a rebellion of their people, they may be strangled by the very janissaries kept for their security against all other rebellion. Thus we have seen the king of France sold by his soldiers for an increase of pay. But where popular authority is absolute and unrestrained, the people have an infinitely greater, because a far better founded, confidence in their own power. They are themselves, in a great measure, their own instruments. They are nearer to their objects. Besides, they are less under responsibility to one of the greatest controlling powers on the earth, the sense of fame and estimation. The share of infamy that is likely to fall to the lot of each individual in public acts is small indeed, the operation of opinion being in the inverse ratio to the number of those who abuse power. Their own approbation of their own acts has to them the appearance of a public judgment in their favor. A perfect democracy is, therefore, the most shameless thing in the world. As it is the most shameless, it is also the most fearless. No man apprehends in his person that he can be made subject to punishment. Certainly the people at large never ought, for as all punishments are for example toward the conservation of the people at large, the people at large can never become the subject of punishment by any human hand.[20] It is therefore of infinite importance that they should not be suffered to imagine that their will, any more than that of kings, is the standard of right and wrong. They ought to be persuaded that they are full as little entitled, and far less qualified with safety to themselves, to use any arbitrary power whatsoever; that therefore they are not, under a false show of liberty, but in truth to exercise an unnatural, inverted domination, tyrannically to exact from those who officiate in the state not an entire devotion to their interest, which is their right, but an abject submission to their occasional will, extinguishing thereby in all those who serve them all moral principle, all sense of dignity, all use of judgment, and all consistency of character; whilst by the very same process they give themselves up a proper, a suitable, but a most contemptible prey to

[20] *Quicquid multis peccatur inultum.* [Lucan, *Pharsalia* V. 260. "Whatever wrong is committed by the many goes unpunished".]

the servile ambition of popular sycophants or courtly flatterers.[lxii]

When the people have emptied themselves of all the lust of selfish will, which without religion it is utterly impossible they ever should, when they are conscious that they exercise, and exercise perhaps in a higher link of the order of delegation, the power, which to be legitimate must be according to that eternal, immutable law in which will and reason are the same, they will be more careful how they place power in base and incapable hands. In their nomination to office, they will not appoint to the exercise of authority as to a pitiful job, but as to a holy function, not according to their sordid, selfish interest, nor to their wanton caprice, nor to their arbitrary will, but they will confer that power (which any man may well tremble to give or to receive) on those only in whom they may discern that predominant proportion of active virtue and wisdom, taken together and fitted to the charge, such as in the great and inevitable mixed mass of human imperfections and infirmities is to be found.

When they are habitually convinced that no evil can be acceptable, either in the act or the permission, to him whose essence is good, they will be better able to extirpate out of the minds of all magistrates, civil, ecclesiastical, or military, anything that bears the least resemblance to a proud and lawless domination.

But one of the first and most leading principles on which the commonwealth and the laws are consecrated is, lest the temporary possessors and life-renters in it, unmindful of what they have received from their ancestors or of what is due to their posterity, should act as if they were the entire masters, that they should not think it among their rights to cut off the entail or commit waste on the inheritance by destroying at their pleasure the whole original fabric of their society, hazarding to leave to those who come after them a ruin instead of an habitation—and teaching these successors as little to respect their contrivances as they had themselves respected the institutions of their forefathers. By this unprincipled facility of changing the state as often, and as much, and in as many ways as there are floating fancies or fashions, the whole chain and continuity of the commonwealth would be broken. No one generation could link with the other. Men would become little better than the flies of a summer.

And first of all, the science of jurisprudence, the pride of the human intellect, which with all its defects, redundancies, and errors is the collected reason of ages, combining the principles of original justice with the infinite variety of human concerns, as a heap of old exploded errors, would be no longer studied. Personal self-sufficiency and arrogance (the certain attendants upon all those who have never experienced a wisdom greater than their own) would usurp the tribunal. Of course, no certain laws, establishing invariable grounds of hope and fear, would keep the actions of men in a certain course or direct them to a certain end. Nothing stable in the modes of holding property or exercising function could form a solid ground on which any parent could speculate in the education of his offspring or in a choice for their future establishment in the world. No principles would be early worked into the habits. As soon as the most able instructor had completed his laborious course of institution, instead of sending forth his pupil, accomplished in a virtuous discipline, fitted to procure him attention and respect in his place in society, he would find everything altered, and that he had turned out a poor creature to the contempt and derision of the world, ignorant of the true grounds of estimation. Who would insure a tender and delicate sense of honor to beat almost with the first pulses of the heart when no man could know what would be the test of honor in a nation continually varying the standard of its coin? No part of life would retain its acquisitions. Barbarism with regard to science and literature, unskilfulness with regard to arts and manufactures, would infallibly succeed to the want of a steady education and settled principle; and thus the commonwealth itself would, in a few generations, crumble away, be disconnected into the dust and powder of individuality, and at length dispersed to all the winds of heaven.

To avoid, therefore, the evils of inconstancy and versatility, ten thousand times worse than those of obstinacy and the blindest prejudice, we have consecrated the state, that no man should approach to look into its defects or corruptions but with due caution, that he should never dream of beginning its reformation by its subversion, that he should approach to the faults of the state as to the wounds of a father, with pious awe and trembling solicitude. By this wise prejudice we are taught to look with horror on those children of their country who are prompt rashly to hack that aged parent in pieces and put him into the kettle of magicians, in hopes that by their poisonous weeds and wild incantations they may regenerate the paternal constitution and renovate their father's life.

SOCIETY is indeed a contract. Subordinate contracts for objects of mere occasional interest may be dissolved at pleasure—but the state ought not to be considered as nothing better than a partnership

CONTRACT   84

agreement in a trade of pepper and coffee, calico, or tobacco, or some
other such low concern, to be taken up for a little temporary interest,
and to be dissolved by the fancy of the parties. It is to be looked on
with other reverence, because it is not a partnership in things subservient only to the gross animal existence of a temporary and perish-
able nature. It is a partnership in all science; a partnership in all art; a
partnership in every virtue and in all perfection. As the ends of such
a partnership cannot be obtained in many generations, it becomes a
partnership not only between those who are living, but between those
who are living, those who are dead, and those who are to be born.
Each contract of each particular state is but a clause in the great
primeval contract of eternal society, linking the lower with the higher
natures, connecting the visible and invisible world, according to a
fixed compact sanctioned by the inviolable oath which holds all
physical and all moral natures, each in their appointed place. This
law is not subject to the will of those who by an obligation above
them, and infinitely superior, are bound to submit their will to that
law. The municipal corporations of that universal kingdom are not
morally at liberty at their pleasure, and on their speculations of a
contingent improvement, wholly to separate and tear asunder the
bands of their subordinate community and to dissolve it into an
unsocial, uncivil, unconnected chaos of elementary principles. It is
the first and supreme necessity only, a necessity that is not chosen but
chooses, a necessity paramount to deliberation, that admits no discussion and demands no evidence, which alone can justify a resort to
anarchy. This necessity is no exception to the rule, because this necessity itself is a part, too, of that moral and physical disposition of
things to which man must be obedient by consent or force; but if that
which is only submission to necessity should be made the object of
choice, the law is broken, nature is disobeyed, and the rebellious are
outlawed, cast forth, and exiled from this world of reason, and order,
and peace, and virtue, and fruitful penitence, into the antagonist
world of madness, discord, vice, confusion, and unavailing sorrow.

These, my dear Sir, are, were, and, I think, long will be the sentiments
of not the least learned and reflecting part of this kingdom. They who
are included in this description form their opinions on such grounds
as such persons ought to form them. The less inquiring receive them
from an authority which those whom Providence dooms to live on
trust need not be ashamed to rely on. These two sorts of men move
in the same direction, though in a different place. They both move

with the order of the universe. They all know or feel this great ancient truth: *Quod illi principi et praepotenti Deo qui omnem hunc mundum regit, nihil eorum quae quidem fiant in terris acceptius quam concilia et coetus hominum jure sociati quae civitates appellantur.*[lxiii] They take this tenet of the head and heart, not from the great name which it immediately bears, nor from the greater from whence it is derived, but from that which alone can give true weight and sanction to any learned opinion, the common nature and common relation of men. Persuaded that all things ought to be done with reference, and referring all to the point of reference to which all should be directed, they think themselves bound, not only as individuals in the sanctuary of the heart or as congregated in that personal capacity, to renew the memory of their high origin and cast, but also in their corporate character to perform their national homage to the institutor and author and protector of civil society; without which civil society man could not by any possibility arrive at the perfection of which his nature is capable, nor even make a remote and faint approach to it. They conceive that He who gave our nature to be perfected by our virtue willed also the necessary means of its perfection. He willed therefore the state—He willed its connection with the source and original archetype of all perfection. They who are convinced of this His will, which is the law of laws and the sovereign of sovereigns, cannot think it reprehensible that this our corporate fealty and homage, that this our recognition of a seigniory paramount, I had almost said this oblation of the state itself as a worthy offering on the high altar of universal praise, should be performed as all public, solemn acts are performed, in buildings, in music, in decoration, in speech, in the dignity of persons, according to the customs of mankind taught by their nature; that is, with modest splendor and unassuming state, with mild majesty and sober pomp. For those purposes they think some part of the wealth of the country is as usefully employed as it can be in fomenting the luxury of individuals. It is the public ornament. It is the public consolation. It nourishes the public hope. The poorest man finds his own importance and dignity in it, whilst the wealth and pride of individuals at every moment makes the man of humble rank and fortune sensible of his inferiority and degrades and vilifies his condition. It is for the man in humble life, and to raise his nature and to put him in mind of a state in which the privileges of opulence will cease, when he will be equal by nature, and may be more than equal by virtue, that this portion of the general wealth of his country is employed and sanctified.

I assure you I do not aim at singularity. I give you opinions which have been accepted amongst us, from very early times to this moment, with a continued and general approbation, and which indeed are worked into my mind that I am unable to distinguish what I have learned from others from the results of my own meditation.

It is on some such principles that the majority of the people of England, far from thinking a religious national establishment unlawful, hardly think it lawful to be without one. In France you are wholly mistaken if you do not believe us above all other things attached to it, and beyond all other nations; and when this people has acted unwisely and unjustifiably in its favor (as in some instances they have done most certainly), in their very errors you will at least discover their zeal.

This principle runs through the whole system of their polity. They do not consider their church establishment as convenient, but as essential to their state, not as a thing heterogeneous and separable, something added for accommodation, what they may either keep or lay aside according to their temporary ideas of convenience. They consider it as the foundation of their whole constitution, with which, and with every part of which, it holds an indissoluble union. Church and state are ideas inseparable in their minds, and scarcely is the one ever mentioned without mentioning the other.

Our education is so formed as to confirm and fix this impression. Our education is in a manner wholly in the hands of ecclesiastics, and in all stages from infancy to manhood. Even when our youth, leaving schools and universities, enter that most important period of life which begins to link experience and study together, and when with that view they visit other countries, instead of old domestics whom we have seen as governors to principal men from other parts, three-fourths of those who go abroad with our young nobility and gentlemen are ecclesiastics, not as austere masters, nor as mere followers, but as friends and companions of a graver character, and not seldom persons as well-born as themselves. With them, as relations, they most constantly keep a close connection through life. By this connection we conceive that we attach our gentlemen to the church, and we liberalize the church by an intercourse with the leading characters of the country.

So tenacious are we of the old ecclesiastical modes and fashions of institution that very little alteration has been made in them since the fourteenth or fifteenth century; adhering in this particular, as in all things else, to our old settled maxim, never entirely nor at once to depart from antiquity. We found these old institutions, on the whole, favorable to morality and discipline, and we thought they were susceptible of amendment without altering the ground. We thought that they were capable of receiving and meliorating, and above all of preserving, the accessions of science and literature, as the order of Providence should successively produce them. And after all, with this Gothic and monkish education (for such it is in the groundwork) we may put in our claim to as ample and as early a share in all the improvements in science, in arts, and in literature which have illuminated and adorned the modern world, as any other nation in Europe.[lxiv] We think one main cause of this improvement was our not despising the patrimony of knowledge which was left us by our forefathers.

It is from our attachment to a church establishment that the English nation did not think it wise to entrust that great, fundamental interest of the whole to what they trust no part of their civil or military public service, that is, to the unsteady and precarious contribution of individuals. They go further. They certainly never have suffered, and never will suffer, the fixed estate of the church to be converted into a pension, to depend on the treasury and to be delayed, withheld, or perhaps to be extinguished by fiscal difficulties, which difficulties may sometimes be pretended for political purposes, and are in fact often brought on by the extravagance, negligence, and rapacity of politicians. The people of England think that they have constitutional motives, as well as religious, against any project of turning their independent clergy into ecclesiastical pensioners of state. They tremble for their liberty, from the influence of a clergy dependent on the crown; they tremble for the public tranquillity from the disorders of a factious clergy, if it were made to depend upon any other than the crown. They therefore made their church, like their king and their nobility, independent.

From the united considerations of religion and constitutional policy, from their opinion of a duty to make sure provision for the consolation of the feeble and the instruction of the ignorant, they have incorporated and identified the estate of the church with the mass of *private property*, of which the state is not the proprietor, either for use or dominion, but the guardian only and the regulator. They have ordained that the provision of this establishment might be as stable as the earth on which it stands, and should not fluctuate with the Euripus of funds and actions.[lxv]

The men of England, the men, I mean, of light and leading in England, whose wisdom (if they have any) is open and direct, would be ashamed, as of a silly deceitful trick, to profess any religion in name which, by their proceedings, they appear to contemn. If by their conduct (the only language that rarely lies) they seemed to regard the great ruling principle of the moral and the natural world as a mere invention to keep the vulgar in obedience, they apprehend that by such a conduct they would defeat the politic purpose they have in view. They would find it difficult to make others believe in a system to which they manifestly give no credit themselves. The Christian statesmen of this land would indeed first provide for the *multitude,* because it is the *multitude,* and is therefore, as such, the first object in the ecclesiastical institution, and in all institutions. They have been taught that the circumstance of the gospel's being preached to the poor was one of the great tests of its true mission. They think, therefore, that those do not believe it who do not take care it should be preached to the poor. But as they know that charity is not confined to any one description, but ought to apply itself to all men who have wants, they are not deprived of a due and anxious sensation of pity to the distresses of the miserable great. They are not repelled through a fastidious delicacy, at the stench of their arrogance and presumption, from a medicinal attention to their mental blotches and running sores. They are sensible that religious instruction is of more consequence to them than to any others—from the greatness of the temptation to which they are exposed; from the important consequences that attend their faults; from the contagion of their ill example; from the necessity of bowing down the stubborn neck of their pride and ambition to the yoke of moderation and virtue; from a consideration of the fat stupidity and gross ignorance concerning what imports men most to know, which prevails at courts, and at the head of armies, and in senates as much as at the loom and in the field.

The English people are satisfied that to the great the consolations of religion are as necessary as its instructions. They, too, are among the unhappy. They feel personal pain and domestic sorrow. In these they have no privilege, but are subject to pay their full contingent to the contributions levied on mortality. They want this sovereign balm under their gnawing cares and anxieties, which, being less conversant about the limited wants of animal life, range without limit, and are diversified by infinite combinations, in the wild and unbounded regions of imagination. Some charitable dole is wanting to these our often very unhappy brethren to fill the gloomy void that reigns in minds which have nothing on earth to hope or fear; something to relieve in the killing languor and overlabored lassitude of those who have nothing to do; something to excite an appetite to existence in the palled satiety which attends on all pleasures which may be bought where nature is not left to her own process, where even desire is anticipated, and therefore fruition defeated by meditated schemes and contrivances of delight; and no interval, no obstacle, is interposed between the wish and the accomplishment.[lxvi]

The people of England know how little influence the teachers of religion are likely to have with the wealthy and powerful of long standing, and how much less with the newly fortunate, if they appear in a manner no way assorted to those with whom they must associate, and over whom they must even exercise, in some cases, something like an authority. What must they think of that body of teachers if they see it in no part above the establishment of their domestic servants? If the poverty were voluntary, there might be some difference. Strong instances of self-denial operate powerfully on our minds, and a man who has no wants has obtained great freedom and firmness and even dignity. But as the mass of any description of men are but men, and their poverty cannot be voluntary, that disrespect which attends upon all lay poverty will not depart from the ecclesiastical. Our provident constitution has therefore taken care that those who are to instruct presumptuous ignorance, those who are to be censors over insolent vice, should neither incur their contempt nor live upon their alms, nor will it tempt the rich to a neglect of the true medicine of their minds. For these reasons, whilst we provide first for the poor, and with a parental solicitude, we have not relegated religion (like something we were ashamed to show) to obscure municipalities or rustic villages. No! we will have her to exalt her mitred front in courts and parliaments. We will have her mixed throughout the whole mass of life and blended with all the classes of society. The people of England will show to the haughty potentates of the world, and to their talking sophisters, that a free, a generous, an informed nation honors the high magistrates of its church; that it will not suffer the insolence of wealth and titles, or any other species of proud pretension, to look down with scorn upon what they looked up to with reverence; nor presume to trample on that acquired personal nobility which they intend always to be, and which often is, the fruit, not the reward (for what can be the reward?) of learning, piety, and virtue. They can see, without pain or grudging, an archbishop precede a duke. They can see a bishop of Durham, or a bishop of Winchester, in possession of ten thousand pounds a year, and cannot conceive why it is in worse hands than estates to the like amount in the hands of this earl or that squire, although it may be true that so many dogs and horses are not kept by the former and fed with the victuals which ought to nourish the children of the people. It is true, the whole church revenue is not always employed, and to every shilling, in charity, nor perhaps ought it, but something is generally employed. It is better to cherish virtue and humanity by leaving much to free will, even with some loss to the object, than to attempt to make men mere machines and instruments of a political benevolence. The world on the whole will gain by a liberty without which virtue cannot exist.

When once the commonwealth has established the estates of the church as property, it can, consistently, hear nothing of the more or the less. "Too much" and "too little" are treason against property. What evil can arise from the quantity in any hand whilst the supreme authority has the full, sovereign superintendence over this, as over all property, to prevent every species of abuse, and, whenever it notably deviates, to give to it a direction agreeable to the purposes of its institution?

In England most of us conceive that it is envy and malignity toward those who are often the beginners of their own fortune, and not a love of the self-denial and mortification of the ancient church, that makes some look askance at the distinctions, and honors, and revenues which, taken from no person, are set apart for virtue. The ears of the people of England are distinguishing. They hear these men speak broad. Their tongue betrays them. Their language is in the *patois* of fraud, in the cant and gibberish of hypocrisy. The people of England must think so when these praters affect to carry back the clergy to that primitive, evangelic poverty which, in the spirit, ought always to exist in them (and in us, too, however we may like it), but in the thing must be varied when the relation of that body to the state is altered—when manners, when modes of life, when indeed the whole order of human affairs has undergone a total revolution. We shall believe those reformers, then, to be honest enthusiasts, not, as now we think them, cheats and deceivers, when we see them throwing their own goods into common and submitting their own persons to the austere discipline of the early church.

With these ideas rooted in their minds, the commons of Great

Britain, in the national emergencies, will never seek their resource from the confiscation of the estates of the church and poor. Sacrilege and proscription are not among the ways and means of our committee of supply. The Jews in Change Alley have not yet dared to hint their hopes of a mortgage on the revenues belonging to the see of Canterbury. I am not afraid that I shall be disavowed when I assure you that there is not *one* public man in this kingdom whom you would wish to quote, no, not one, of any party or description, who does not reprobate the dishonest, perfidious, and cruel confiscation which the National Assembly has been compelled to make of that property which it was their first duty to protect.

It is with the exultation of a little national pride I tell you that those amongst us who have wished to pledge the societies of Paris in the cup of their abominations have been disappointed. The robbery of your church has proved a security to the possession of ours. It has roused the people. They see with horror and alarm that enormous and shameless act of proscription. It has opened, and will more and more open, their eyes upon the selfish enlargement of mind and the narrow liberality of sentiment of insidious men, which, commencing in close hypocrisy and fraud, have ended in open violence and rapine. At home we behold similar beginnings. We are on our guard against similar conclusions.

I HOPE WE SHALL NEVER be so totally lost to all sense of the duties imposed upon us by the law of social union as, upon any pretext of public service, to confiscate the goods of a single unoffending citizen. Who but a tyrant (a name expressive of everything which can vitiate and degrade human nature) could think of seizing on the property of men unaccused, unheard, untried, by whole descriptions, by hundreds and thousands together? Who that had not lost every trace of humanity could think of casting down men of exalted rank and sacred function, some of them of an age to call at once for reverence and compassion, of casting them down from the highest situation in the commonwealth, wherein they were maintained by their own landed property, to a state of indigence, depression, and contempt?

The confiscators truly have made some allowance to their victims from the scraps and fragments of their own tables from which they have been so harshly driven, and which have been so bountifully spread for a feast to the harpies of usury. But to drive men from independence to live on alms is itself great cruelty. That which might be a tolerable condition to men in one state of life, and not habituated to other things, may, when all these circumstances are altered, be a dreadful revolution, and one to which a virtuous mind would feel pain in condemning any guilt except that which would demand the life of the offender. But to many minds this punishment of *degradation* and *infamy* is worse than death. Undoubtedly it is an infinite aggravation of this cruel suffering that the persons who were taught a double prejudice in favor of religion, by education and by the place they held in the administration of its functions, are to receive the remnants of their property as alms from the profane and impious hands of those who had plundered them of all the rest; to receive (if they are at all to receive), not from the charitable contributions of the faithful but from the insolent tenderness of known and avowed atheism, the maintenance of religion measured out to them on the standard of the contempt in which it is held, and for the purpose of rendering those who receive the allowance vile and of no estimation in the eyes of mankind.

But this act of seizure of property, it seems, is a judgment in law, and not a confiscation. They have, it seems, found out in the academies of the *Palais Royal* and the *Jacobins* that certain men had no right to the possessions which they held under law, usage, the decisions of courts, and the accumulated prescription of a thousand years. They say that ecclesiastics are fictitious persons, creatures of the state, whom at pleasure they may destroy, and of course limit and modify in every particular; that the goods they possess are not properly theirs but belong to the state which created the fiction; and we are therefore not to trouble ourselves with what they may suffer in their natural feelings and natural persons on account of what is done toward them in this their constructive character. Of what import is it under what names you injure men and deprive them of the just emoluments of a profession, in which they were not only permitted but encouraged by the state to engage, and upon the supposed certainty of which emoluments they had formed the plan of their lives, contracted debts, and led multitudes to an entire dependence upon them?

You do not imagine, Sir, that I am going to compliment this miserable distinction of persons with any long discussion. The arguments of tyranny are as contemptible as its force is dreadful. Had not your confiscators, by their early crimes, obtained a power which secures indemnity to all the crimes of which they have since been guilty or that they can commit, it is not the syllogism of the logician, but the lash of the executioner, that would have refuted a sophistry which becomes an accomplice of theft and murder. The sophistic tyrants of Paris are loud in their declamations against the departed regal tyrants, who in former ages have vexed the world. They are thus bold, because they are safe from the dungeons and iron cages of their old masters. Shall we be more tender of the tyrants of our own time, when we see them acting worse tragedies under our eyes? Shall we not use the same liberty that they do, when we can use it with the same safety—when to speak honest truth only requires a contempt of the opinions of those whose actions we abhor?

This outrage on all the rights of property was at first covered with what, on the system of their conduct, was the most astonishing of all pretexts—a regard to national faith. The enemies to property at first pretended a most tender, delicate, and scrupulous anxiety for keeping the king's engagements with the public creditor. These professors of the rights of men are so busy in teaching others that they have not leisure to learn anything themselves; otherwise they would have known that it is to the property of the citizen, and not to the demands of the creditor of the state, that the first and original faith of civil society is pledged. The claim of the citizen is prior in time, paramount in title, superior in equity. The fortunes of individuals, whether possessed by acquisition or by descent or in virtue of a participation in the goods of some community, were no part of the creditor's security, expressed or implied. They never so much as entered into his head when he made his bargain. He well knew that the public, whether represented by a monarch or by a senate, can pledge nothing but the public estate; and it can have no public estate except in what it derives from a just and proportioned imposition upon the citizens at large. This was engaged, and nothing else could be engaged, to the public creditor. No man can mortgage his injustice as a pawn for his fidelity.

It is impossible to avoid some observation on the contradictions caused by the extreme rigor and the extreme laxity of this new public faith which influenced in this transaction, and which influenced not according to the nature of the obligation, but to the description of the persons to whom it was engaged. No acts of the old government of the kings of France are held valid in the National Assembly except its pecuniary engagements: acts of all others of the most ambiguous legality. The rest of the acts of that royal government are considered in so odious a light that to have a claim under its authority is looked on as a sort of crime. A pension, given as a reward for service to the state, is surely as good a ground of property as any security for money advanced to the state. It is better; for money is paid, and well paid, to obtain that service. We have, however, seen multitudes of people under this description in France who never had been deprived of their allowances by the most arbitrary ministers in the most arbitrary times, by this assembly of the rights of men robbed without mercy. They were told, in answer to their claim to the bread earned with their blood, that their services had not been rendered to the country that now exists.

This laxity of public faith is not confined to those unfortunate persons. The Assembly, with perfect consistency it must be owned, is engaged in a respectable deliberation how far it is bound by the treaties made with other nations under the former government, and their committee is to report which of them they ought to ratify, and which not. By this means they have put the external fidelity of this virgin state on a par with its internal.

It is not easy to conceive upon what rational principle the royal government should not, of the two, rather have possessed the power of rewarding service and making treaties, in virtue of its prerogative, than that of pledging to creditors the revenue of the state, actual and possible. The treasure of the nation, of all things, has been the least allowed to the prerogative of the king of France or to the prerogative of any king in Europe. To mortgage the public revenue implies the sovereign dominion, in the fullest sense, over the public purse. It goes far beyond the trust even of a temporary and occasional taxation. The acts, however, of that dangerous power (the distinctive mark of a boundless despotism) have been alone held sacred. Whence arose this preference given by a democratic assembly to a body of property deriving its title from the most critical and obnoxious of all the exertions of monarchical authority? Reason can furnish nothing to reconcile inconsistency, nor can partial favor be accounted for upon equitable principles. But the contradiction and partiality which admit no justification are not the less without an adequate cause; and that cause I do not think it difficult to discover.

By the vast debt of France a great monied interest had insensibly grown up, and with it a great power. By the ancient usages which prevailed in that kingdom, the general circulation of property, and in particular the mutual convertibility of land into money, and of money into land, had always been a matter of difficulty. Family settlements, rather more general and more strict than they are in England, the *jus retractus,*[lxvii] the great mass of landed property held by the crown, and, by a maxim of the French law, held unalienably, the vast estates of the ecclesiastical corporations—all these had kept the landed and monied interests more separated in France, less miscible, and the owners of the two distinct species of property not so well disposed to each other as they are in this country.

The monied property was long looked on with rather an evil eye by the people. They saw it connected with their distresses, and aggravating them. It was no less envied by the old landed interests, partly for the same reasons that rendered it obnoxious to the people, but much more so as it eclipsed, by the splendor of an ostentatious luxury, the unendowed pedigrees and naked titles of several among the nobility. Even when the nobility which represented the more permanent landed interest united themselves by marriage (which sometimes was the case) with the other description, the wealth which saved the family from ruin was supposed to contaminate and degrade it. Thus the enmities and heartburnings of these parties were increased even by the usual means by which discord is made to cease and quarrels are turned into friendship. In the meantime, the pride of the wealthy men, not noble or newly noble, increased with its cause. They felt with resentment an inferiority, the grounds of which they did not acknowledge. There was no measure to which they were not willing to lend themselves in order to be revenged of the outrages of this rival pride and to exalt their wealth to what they considered as its natural rank and estimation. They struck at the nobility through the crown and the church. They attacked them particularly on the side on which they thought them the most vulnerable, that is, the possessions of the church, which, through the patronage of the crown, generally devolved upon the nobility. The bishoprics and the great commendatory abbeys were, with few exceptions, held by that order.

In this state of real, though not always perceived, warfare between the noble ancient landed interest and the new monied interest, the greatest, because the most applicable, strength was in the hands of the latter. The monied interest is in its nature more ready for any adventure, and its possessors more disposed to new enterprises of any kind. Being of a recent acquisition, it falls in more naturally with any novelties. It is therefore the kind of wealth which will be resorted to by all who wish for change.

Along with the monied interest, a new description of men had grown

EDMUND BURKE

up with whom that interest soon formed a close and marked union—
I mean the political men of letters. Men of letters, fond of distinguishing themselves, are rarely averse to innovation. Since the decline of the life and greatness of Louis the Fourteenth, they were not
so much cultivated, either by him or by the regent or the successors
to the crown, nor were they engaged to the court by favors and
emoluments so systematically as during the splendid period of that
ostentatious and not impolitic reign. What they lost in the old court
protection, they endeavored to make up by joining in a sort of
incorporation of their own; to which the two academies of France,
and afterwards the vast undertaking of the *Encyclopedia,* carried on
by a society of these gentlemen, did not a little contribute.

The literary cabal had some years ago formed something like a
regular plan for the destruction of the Christian religion. This object
they pursued with a degree of zeal which hitherto had been discovered only in the propagators of some system of piety. They were
possessed with a spirit of proselytism in the most fanatical degree;
and from thence, by an easy progress, with the spirit of persecution
according to their means.[21] What was not to be done toward their
great end by any direct or immediate act might be wrought by a
longer process through the medium of opinion. To command that
opinion, the first step is to establish a dominion over those who
direct it. They contrived to possess themselves, with great method
and perseverance, of all the avenues to literary fame. Many of them
indeed stood high in the ranks of literature and science. The world
had done them justice and in favor of general talents forgave the evil
tendency of their peculiar principles. This was true liberality, which
they returned by endeavoring to confine the reputation of sense,
learning, and taste to themselves or their followers. I will venture to
say that this narrow, exclusive spirit has not been less prejudicial to
literature and to taste than to morals and true philosophy. These
atheistical fathers have a bigotry of their own, and they have learned
to talk against monks with the spirit of a monk. But in some things
they are men of the world. The resources of intrigue are called in to
supply the defects of argument and wit. To this system of literary
monopoly was joined an unremitting industry to blacken and discredit in every way, and by every means, all those who did not hold to

[21] This (down to the end of the first sentence in the next paragraph) and some
other parts here and there were inserted, on his reading the manuscript, by
my lost Son. [1803]

their faction. To those who have observed the spirit of their conduct it has long been clear that nothing was wanted but the power of carrying the intolerance of the tongue and of the pen into a persecution which would strike at property, liberty, and life.

The desultory and faint persecution carried on against them, more from compliance with form and decency than with serious resentment, neither weakened their strength nor relaxed their efforts. The issue of the whole was that, what with opposition, and what with success, a violent and malignant zeal, of a kind hitherto unknown in the world, had taken an entire possession of their minds and rendered their whole conversation, which otherwise would have been pleasing and instructive, perfectly disgusting. A spirit of cabal, intrigue, and proselytism pervaded all their thoughts, words, and actions. And as controversial zeal soon turns its thoughts on force, they began to insinuate themselves into a correspondence with foreign princes, in hopes through their authority, which at first they flattered, they might bring about the changes they had in view. To them it was indifferent whether these changes were to be accomplished by the thunderbolt of despotism or by the earthquake of popular commotion. The correspondence between this cabal and the late king of Prussia will throw no small light upon the spirit of all their proceedings.[22] For the same purpose for which they intrigued with princes, they cultivated, in a distinguished manner, the monied interest of France; and partly through the means furnished by those whose peculiar offices gave them the most extensive and certain means of communication, they carefully occupied all the avenues to opinion.

Writers, especially when they act in a body and with one direction, have great influence on the public mind; the alliance, therefore, of these writers with the monied interest[23] had no small effect in removing the popular odium and envy which attended that species of wealth. These writers, like the propagators of all novelties, pretended to a great zeal for the poor and the lower orders, whilst in their satires they rendered hateful, by every exaggeration, the faults of courts, of nobility, and of priesthood. They became a sort of demagogues. They served as a link to unite, in favor of one object, obnoxious wealth to restless and desperate poverty.

---

[22] I do not choose to shock the feeling of the moral reader with any quotation of their vulgar, base, and profane language.

[23] Their connection with Turgot and almost all the people of the finance. [1803]

As these two kinds of men appear principal leaders in all the late transactions, their junction and politics will serve to account, not upon any principles of law or of policy, but as a *cause,* for the general fury with which all the landed property of ecclesiastical corporations has been attacked; and the great care which, contrary to their pretended principles, has been taken of a monied interest originating from the authority of the crown. All the envy against wealth and power was artificially directed against other descriptions of riches. On what other principle than that which I have stated can we account for an appearance so extraordinary and unnatural as that of the ecclesiastical possessions, which had stood so many successions of ages and shocks of civil violences, and were girded at once by justice and by prejudice, being applied to the payment of debts comparatively recent, invidious, and contracted by a decried and subverted government?

WAS the public estate a sufficient stake for the public debts? Assume that it was not, and that a loss *must* be incurred somewhere.—When the only estate lawfully possessed, and which the contracting parties had in contemplation at the time in which their bargain was made, happens to fail, who according to the principles of natural and legal equity ought to be the sufferer? Certainly it ought to be either the party who trusted or the party who persuaded him to trust, or both, and not third parties who had no concern with the transaction. Upon any insolvency they ought to suffer who are weak enough to lend upon bad security, or they who fraudulently held out a security that was not valid. Laws are acquainted with no other rules of decision. But by the new institute of the rights of men, the only persons who in equity ought to suffer are the only persons who are to be saved harmless: those are to answer the debt who neither were lenders nor borrowers, mortgagers nor mortgagees.

What had the clergy to do with these transactions? What had they to do with any public engagement further than the extent of their own debt? To that, to be sure, their estates were bound to the last acre. Nothing can lead more to the true spirit of the Assembly, which sits for public confiscation, with its new equity and its new morality, than an attention to their proceeding with regard to this debt of the clergy. The body of confiscators, true to that monied interest for which they were false to every other, have found the clergy competent to incur a legal debt. Of course, they declared them legally entitled to the property which their power of incurring the debt and mortgaging

99

the estate implied, recognizing the rights of those persecuted citizens in the very act in which they were thus grossly violated.

If, as I said, any persons are to make good deficiencies to the public creditor, besides the public at large, they must be those who managed the agreement. Why, therefore, are not the estates of all the comptrollers-general confiscated?[24] Why not those of the long succession of ministers, financiers, and bankers who have been enriched whilst the nation was impoverished by their dealings and their counsels? Why is not the estate of M. Laborde declared forfeited rather than of the archbishop of Paris, who has had nothing to do in the creation or in the jobbing of the public funds? Or, if you must confiscate old landed estates in favor of the money-jobbers, why is the penalty confined to one description? I do not know whether the expenses of the Duke de Choiseul have left anything of the infinite sums which he had derived from the bounty of his master during the transactions of a reign which contributed largely by every species of prodigality in war and peace to the present debt of France. If any such remains, why is not this confiscated? I remember to have been in Paris during the time of the old government. I was there just after the Duke d'Aiguillon had been snatched (as it was generally thought) from the block by the hand of a protecting despotism.[lxviii] He was a minister and had some concern in the affairs of that prodigal period. Why do I not see his estate delivered up to the municipalities in which it is situated? The noble family of Noailles have long been servants (meritorious servants I admit) to the crown of France, and have had, of course, some share in its bounties. Why do I hear nothing of the application of their estates to the public debt? Why is the estate of the Duke de Rochefoucault more sacred than that of the Cardinal de Rochefoucault? The former is, I doubt not, a worthy person, and (if it were not a sort of profaneness to talk of the use, as affecting the title to the property) he makes a good use of his revenues; but it is no disrespect to him to say, what authentic information well warrants me in saying, that the use made of a property equally valid by his brother,[25] the cardinal archbishop of Rouen, was far more laudable and far more public-spirited. Can one hear of the proscription of such persons and the confiscation of their effects without indignation and horror? He is not a man who does not feel

---

[24] All have been confiscated in their turn. [1803]
[25] Not his brother nor any near relation; but this mistake does not affect the argument. [1803]

such emotions on such occasions. He does not deserve the name of a freeman who will not express them.

Few barbarous conquerors have ever made so terrible a revolution in property. None of the heads of the Roman factions, when they established *crudelem illam hastam*[lxix] in all their auctions of rapine, have ever set up to sale the goods of the conquered citizen to such an enormous amount. It must be allowed in favor of those tyrants of antiquity that what was done by them could hardly be said to be done in cold blood. Their passions were inflamed, their tempers soured, their understandings confused with the spirit of revenge, with the innumerable reciprocated and recent inflictions and retaliations of blood and rapine. They were driven beyond all bounds of moderation by the apprehension of the return of power, with the return of property, to the families of those they had injured beyond all hope of forgiveness.

These Roman confiscators, who were yet only in the elements of tyranny, and were not instructed in the rights of men to exercise all sorts of cruelties on each other without provocation, thought it necessary to spread a sort of color over their injustice. They considered the vanquished party as composed of traitors who had borne arms, or otherwise had acted with hostility, against the commonwealth. They regarded them as persons who had forfeited their property by their crimes. With you, in your improved state of the human mind, there was no such formality. You seized upon five millions sterling of annual rent and turned forty or fifty thousand human creatures out of their houses, because "such was your pleasure". The tyrant Harry the Eighth of England, as he was not better enlightened than the Roman Mariuses and Sullas, and had not studied in your new schools, did not know what an effectual instrument of despotism was to be found in that grand magazine of offensive weapons, the rights of men. When he resolved to rob the abbeys, as the club of the Jacobins have robbed all the ecclesiastics, he began by setting on foot a commission to examine into the crimes and abuses which prevailed in those communities. As it might be expected, his commission reported truths, exaggerations, and falsehoods. But truly or falsely, it reported abuses and offenses. However, as abuses might be corrected, as every crime of persons does not infer a forfeiture with regard to communities, and as property, in that dark age, was not discovered to be a creature of prejudice, all those abuses (and there were enough of them) were hardly thought sufficient ground for such a confiscation as it was for his purpose to make. He, therefore, procured the formal surrender of these estates. All these operose proceedings were adopted by one of the most decided tyrants in the rolls of history as necessary preliminaries before he could venture, by bribing the members of his two servile houses with a share of the spoil and holding out to them an eternal immunity from taxation, to demand a confirmation of his iniquitous proceedings by an act of Parliament. Had fate reserved him to our times, four technical terms would have done his business and saved him all this trouble; he needed nothing more than one short form of incantation—"Philosophy, Light, Liberality, the Rights of Men".

I can say nothing in praise of those acts of tyranny which no voice has hitherto ever commended under any of their false colors, yet in these false colors an homage was paid by despotism to justice. The power which was above all fear and all remorse was not set above all shame. Whilst shame keeps its watch, virtue is not wholly extinguished in the heart, nor will moderation be utterly exiled from the minds of tyrants.

I believe every honest man sympathizes in his reflections with our political poet on that occasion, and will pray to avert the omen whenever these acts of rapacious despotism present themselves to his view or his imagination:

> —May no such storm
> Fall on our times, where ruin must reform.
> Tell me (my Muse) what monstrous dire offense,
> What crimes could any Christian king incense
> To such a rage? Was't luxury, or lust?
> Was *he* so temperate, so chaste, so just?
> Were these their crimes? they were his own much more,
> But wealth is crime enough to him that's poor.[26]

---

[26] The rest of the passage is this—

> "Who having spent the treasures of his crown,
> Condemns their luxury to feed his own.
> And yet this act, to varnish o'er the shame
> Of sacrilege, must bear devotion's name.
> No crime so bold, but would be understood
> A real, or at least a seeming good;
> Who fears not to do ill, yet fears the name,
> And, free from conscience, is a slave to fame.
> Thus he the church at once protects, and spoils;
> But princes' swords are sharper than their styles.

This same wealth, which is at all times treason and *lèse nation* to indigent and rapacious despotism, under all modes of polity, was your temptation to violate property, law, and religion, united in one object. But was the state of France so wretched and undone that no other recourse but rapine remained to preserve its existence? On this point I wish to receive some information. When the states met, was the condition of the finances of France such that, after economizing on principles of justice and mercy through all departments, no fair repartition of burdens upon all the orders could possibly restore them? If such an equal imposition would have been sufficient, you well know it might easily have been made. M. Necker, in the budget which he laid before the orders assembled at Versailles, made a detailed exposition of the state of the French nation.[27]

If we give credit to him, it was not necessary to have recourse to any new impositions whatsoever to put the receipts of France on a balance with its expenses. He stated the permanent charges of all descriptions, including the interest of a new loan of four hundred millions, at 531,444,000 livres; the fixed revenue at 475,294,000,

> And thus to th' ages past he makes amends,
> Their charity destroys, their faith defends.
> Then did religion in a lazy cell,
> In empty aery contemplation dwell;
> And, like the block, unmoved lay; but ours,
> As much too active, like the stork devours.
> Is there no temperate region can be known,
> Betwixt their frigid and our torrid zone?
> Could we not wake from that lethargic dream,
> But to be restless in a worse extreme?
> And for that lethargy was there no cure,
> But to be cast into a calenture?
> Can knowledge have no bound, but must advance
> So far, to make us wish for ignorance?
> And rather in the dark to grope our way,
> Than, led by a false guide, to err by day?
> Who sees these dismal heaps, but would demand,
> What barbarous invader sacked the land?
> But when he hears, no Goth, no Turk did bring
> This desolation, but a Christian king;
> When nothing, but the name of zeal, appears
> 'Twixt our best actions and the worst of theirs,
> What does he think our sacrilege would spare,
> When such th' effects of our devotion are?"
> COOPER'S HILL, by SIR JOHN DENHAM.

[27] *Rapport de Mous. le Directeur-Général des Finances, fait par ordre du Roi à Versailles, Mai 5, 1789.*

making the deficiency 56,150,000, or short of £2,200,000 sterling. But to balance it, he brought forward savings and improvements of revenue (considered as entirely certain) to rather more than the amount of that deficiency; and he concludes with these emphatical words (p. 39), *"Quel pays, Messieurs, que celui, où, sans impôts et avec de simples objets inapperçus, on peut faire disparoître un deficit qui a fait tant de bruit en Europe"*.[lxx] As to the reimbursement, the sinking of debt, and the other great objects of public credit and political arrangement indicated in Mons. Necker's speech, no doubt could be entertained but that a very moderate and proportioned assessment on the citizens without distinction would have provided for all of them to the fullest extent of their demand.

If this representation of Mons. Necker was false, then the Assembly are in the highest degree culpable for having forced the king to accept as his minister and, since the king's deposition, for having employed as *their* minister a man who had been capable of abusing so notoriously the confidence of his master and their own, in a matter, too, of the highest moment and directly appertaining to his particular office. But if the representation was exact (as having always, along with you, conceived a high degree of respect for M. Necker, I make no doubt it was), then what can be said in favor of those who, instead of moderate, reasonable, and general contribution, have in cold blood, and impelled by no necessity, had recourse to a partial and cruel confiscation?

Was that contribution refused on a pretext of privilege, either on the part of the clergy or on that of the nobility? No, certainly. As to the clergy, they even ran before the wishes of the third order. Previous to the meeting of the states, they had in all their instructions expressly directed their deputies to renounce every immunity which put them upon a footing distinct from the condition of their fellow subjects. In this renunciation the clergy were even more explicit than the nobility.

But let us suppose that the deficiency had remained at the fifty-six millions (or £2,200,000 sterling), as at first stated by M. Necker. Let us allow that all the resources he opposed to that deficiency were impudent and groundless fictions, and that the Assembly (or their lords of articles[28] at the Jacobins) were from thence justified in laying

---

[28] In the constitution of Scotland, during the Stuart reigns, a committee sat for preparing bills; and none could pass but those previously approved by them. The committee was called "Lords of Articles".

the whole burden of that deficiency on the clergy—yet allowing all this, a necessity of £2,200,000 sterling will not support a confiscation to the amount of five millions. The imposition of £2,200,000 on the clergy, as partial, would have been oppressive and unjust, but it would not have been altogether ruinous to those on whom it was imposed, and therefore it would not have answered the real purpose of the managers.

Perhaps persons unacquainted with the state of France, on hearing the clergy and the noblesse were privileged in point of taxation, may be led to imagine that, previous to the Revolution, these bodies had contributed nothing to the state. This is a great mistake. They certainly did not contribute equally with each other, nor either of them equally with the commons. They both, however, contributed largely. Neither nobility nor clergy enjoyed any exemption from the excise on consumable commodities, from duties of custom, or from any of the other numerous *indirect* impositions, which in France, as well as here, make so very large a proportion of all payments to the public. The noblesse paid the capitation. They paid also a land-tax, called the twentieth penny, to the height sometimes of three, sometimes of four, shillings in the pound—both of them *direct* impositions of no light nature and no trivial produce. The clergy of the provinces annexed by conquest to France (which in extent make about an eighth part of the whole, but in wealth a much larger proportion) paid likewise to the capitation and the twentieth penny, at the rate paid by the nobility. The clergy in the old provinces did not pay the capitation, but they had redeemed themselves at the expense of about 24 millions, or a little more than a million sterling. They were exempted from the twentieths; but then they made free gifts, they contracted debts for the state, and they were subject to some other charges, the whole computed at about a thirteenth part of their clear income. They ought to have paid annually about forty thousand pounds more to put them on a par with the contribution of the nobility.

When the terrors of this tremendous proscription hung over the clergy, they made an offer of a contribution through the archbishop of Aix, which, for its extravagance, ought not to have been accepted. But it was evidently and obviously more advantageous to the public creditor than anything which could rationally be promised by the confiscation. Why was it not accepted? The reason is plain: there was no desire that the church should be brought to serve the state. The service of the state was made a pretext to destroy the church. In their way to the destruction of the church they would not scruple to destroy their country; and they have destroyed it. One great end in the project would have been defeated if the plan of extortion had been adopted in lieu of the scheme of confiscation. The new landed interest connected with the new republic, and connected with it for its very being, could not have been created. This was among the reasons why that extravagant ransom was not accepted.

THE madness of the project of confiscation, on the plan that was first pretended, soon became apparent. To bring this unwieldy mass of landed property, enlarged by the confiscation of all the vast landed domain of the crown, at once into market was obviously to defeat the profits proposed by the confiscation by depreciating the value of those lands and, indeed, of all the landed estates throughout France. Such a sudden diversion of all its circulating money from trade to land must be an additional mischief. What step was taken? Did the Assembly, on becoming sensible of the inevitable ill effects of their projected sale, revert to the offers of the clergy? No distress could oblige them to travel in a course which was disgraced by any appearance of justice. Giving over all hopes from a general immediate sale, another project seems to have succeeded. They proposed to take stock in exchange for the church lands. In that project great difficulties arose in equalizing the objects to be exchanged. Other obstacles also presented themselves, which threw them back again upon some project of sale. The municipalities had taken an alarm. They would not hear of transferring the whole plunder of the kingdom to the stockholders in Paris. Many of those municipalities had been (upon system) reduced to the most deplorable indigence. Money was nowhere to be seen. They were, therefore, led to the point that was so ardently desired. They panted for a currency of any kind which might revive their perishing industry. The municipalities were then to be admitted to a share in the spoil, which evidently rendered the first scheme (if ever it had been seriously entertained) altogether impracticable. Public exigencies pressed upon all sides. The minister of finance reiterated his call for supply with a most urgent, anxious, and boding voice. Thus pressed on all sides, instead of the first plan of converting their bankers into bishops and abbots, instead of paying the old debt, they contracted a new debt at 3 per cent, creating a new paper currency founded on an eventual sale of the church lands. They issued this paper currency to satisfy in the first instance chiefly the demands made upon them by the *bank of discount,* the great machine, or paper-mill, of their fictitious wealth.

The spoil of the church was now become the only resource of all their operations in finance, the vital principle of all their politics, the sole security for the existence of their power. It was necessary by all, even the most violent means, to put every individual on the same bottom, and to bind the nation in one guilty interest to uphold this act and the authority of those by whom it was done. In order to force the most reluctant into a participation of their pillage, they rendered their paper circulation compulsory in all payments. Those who consider the general tendency of their schemes to this one object as a center, and a center from which afterwards all their measures radiate, will not think that I dwell too long upon this part of the proceedings of the National Assembly.

To cut off all appearance of connection between the crown and public justice, and to bring the whole under implicit obedience to the dictators in Paris, the old independent judicature of the parliaments, with all its merits and all its faults, was wholly abolished. Whilst the parliaments existed, it was evident that the people might some time or other come to resort to them and rally under the standard of their ancient laws. It became, however, a matter of consideration that the magistrates and officers, in the courts now abolished, *had purchased their places* at a very high rate, for which, as well as for the duty they performed, they received but a very low return of interest. Simple confiscation is a boon only for the clergy; to the lawyers some appearances of equity are to be observed, and they are to receive compensation to an immense amount. Their compensation becomes part of the national debt, for the liquidation of which there is the one exhaustless fund. The lawyers are to obtain their compensation in the new church paper, which is to march with the new principles of judicature and legislature. The dismissed magistrates are to take their share of martyrdom with the ecclesiastics, or to receive their own property from such a fund, and in such a manner, as all those who have been seasoned with the ancient principles of jurisprudence and had been the sworn guardians of property must look upon with horror. Even the clergy are to receive their miserable allowance out of the depreciated paper, which is stamped with the indelible character of sacrilege and with the symbols of their own ruin, or they must starve. So violent an outrage upon credit, property, and liberty as this compulsory paper currency has seldom been exhibited by the alliance of bankruptcy and tyranny, at any time or in any nation.

In the course of all these operations, at length comes out the grand *arcanum*—that in reality, and in a fair sense, the lands of the church (so far as anything certain can be gathered from their proceedings) are not to be sold at all. By the late resolutions of the National Assembly, they are, indeed, to be delivered to the highest bidder. But it is to be observed that *a certain portion only of the purchase money is to be laid down*. A period of twelve years is to be given for the payment of the rest. The philosophic purchasers are therefore, on payment of a sort of fine, to be put instantly into possession of the estate. It becomes in some respects a sort of gift to them—to be held on the feudal tenure of zeal to the new establishment. This project is evidently to let in a body of purchasers without money. The consequence will be that these purchasers, or rather grantees, will pay, not only from the rents as they accrue, which might as well be received by the state, but from the spoil of the materials of buildings, from waste in woods, and from whatever money, by hands habituated to the gripings of usury, they can wring from the miserable peasant. He is to be delivered over to the mercenary and arbitrary discretion of men who will be stimulated to every species of extortion by the growing demands on the growing profits of an estate held under the precarious settlement of a new political system.

When all the frauds, impostures, violences, rapines, burnings, murders, confiscations, compulsory paper currencies, and every description of tyranny and cruelty employed to bring about and to uphold this Revolution have their natural effect, that is, to shock the moral sentiments of all virtuous and sober minds, the abettors of this philosophic system immediately strain their throats in a declamation against the old monarchical government of France. When they have rendered that deposed power sufficiently black, they then proceed in argument as if all those who disapprove of their new abuses must of course be partisans of the old, that those who reprobate their crude and violent schemes of liberty ought to be treated as advocates for servitude. I admit that their necessities do compel them to this base and contemptible fraud. Nothing can reconcile men to their proceedings and projects but the supposition that there is no third option between them and some tyranny as odious as can be furnished by the records of history, or by the invention of poets. This prattling of theirs hardly deserves the name of sophistry. It is nothing but plain impudence. Have these gentlemen never heard, in the whole circle of the worlds of theory and practice, of anything between the despotism of the monarch and the despotism of the multitude? Have they never heard of a monarchy directed by laws, controlled and balanced by the great hereditary wealth and hereditary dignity of a nation, and both again controlled by a judicious check from the reason and feeling of the people at large acting by a suitable and permanent organ? Is it then impossible that a man may be found who, without criminal ill intention or pitiable absurdity, shall prefer such a mixed and tempered government to either of the extremes, and who may repute that nation to be destitute of all wisdom and of all virtue which, having in its choice to obtain such a government with ease, *or rather to confirm it when actually possessed,* thought proper to commit a thousand crimes and to subject their country to a thousand evils in order to avoid it? Is it then a truth so universally acknowledged that a pure democracy is the only tolerable form into which human society can be thrown, that a man is not permitted to hesitate about its merits without the suspicion of being a friend to tyranny, that is, of being a foe to mankind?

I do not know under what description to class the present ruling authority in France. It affects to be a pure democracy, though I think it in a direct train of becoming shortly a mischievous and ignoble oligarchy. But for the present I admit it to be a contrivance of the nature and effect of what it pretends to. I reprobate no form of government merely upon abstract principles. There may be situations in which the purely democratic form will become necessary. There may be some (very few, and very particularly circumstanced) where it would be clearly desirable. This I do not take to be the case of France or of any other great country. Until now, we have seen no examples of considerable democracies. The ancients were better acquainted with them. Not being wholly unread in the authors who had seen the most of those constitutions, and who best understood them, I cannot help concurring with their opinion that an absolute democracy, no more than absolute monarchy, is to be reckoned among the legitimate forms of government. They think it rather the corruption and degeneracy than the sound constitution of a republic. If I recollect rightly, Aristotle observes that a democracy has many striking points of resemblance with a tyranny.[29] Of this I am certain, that in a

---

[29] When I wrote this I quoted from memory, after many years had elapsed from my reading the passage. A learned friend has found it, and it is as follows:

democracy the majority of the citizens is capable of exercising the most cruel oppressions upon the minority whenever strong divisions prevail in that kind of polity, as they often must; and that oppression of the minority will extend to far greater numbers and will be carried on with much greater fury than can almost ever be apprehended from the dominion of a single scepter. In such a popular persecution, individual sufferers are in a much more deplorable condition than in any other. Under a cruel prince they have the balmy compassion of mankind to assuage the smart of their wounds; they have the plaudits of the people to animate their generous constancy under their sufferings; but those who are subjected to wrong under multitudes are deprived of all external consolation. They seem deserted by mankind, overpowered by a conspiracy of their whole species.

BUT ADMITTING DEMOCRACY not to have that inevitable tendency to party tyranny, which I suppose it to have, and admitting it to possess as much good in it when unmixed as I am sure it possesses when compounded with other forms, does monarchy, on its part, contain nothing at all to recommend it? I do not often quote Bolingbroke, nor have his works in general left any permanent impression on my mind. He is a presumptuous and a superficial writer. But he has one observation which, in my opinion, is not without depth and solidity. He says that he prefers a monarchy to other governments because you can better ingraft any description of republic on a monarchy than anything of monarchy upon the republican forms. I think him perfectly in the right. The fact is so historically, and it agrees well with the speculation.

Τὸ ἦθos τὸ αὐτὸ, καὶ ἄμφω δεσποτικὰ τῶν βελτιόνων, καὶ τὰ ψηφίσματα, ὥσπερ ἐκεῖ τὰ ἐπιτάγματα· καὶ ὁ δημαγωγὸς καὶ ὁ κόλαξ, οἱ αὐτοὶ καὶ ἀνάλογοι· καὶ μάλιστα ἑκάτεροι παρ' ἑκατέροις ἰσχύουσιν, οἱ μὲν κόλακες παρὰ τυράννοις, οἱ δὲ δημαγωγοὶ παρὰ τοῖς δήμοις τοῖς τοιούτοις.—

"The ethical character is the same; both exercise despotism over the better class of citizens; and decrees are in the one, what ordinances and arréts are in the other: the demagogue, too, and the court favorite are not unfrequently the same identical men, and always bear a close analogy; and these have the principal power, each in their respective forms of government, favorites with the absolute monarch, and demagogues with a people such as I have described". Arist. *Politic.* lib. iv. cap. 4.

I know how easy a topic it is to dwell on the faults of departed greatness. By a revolution in the state, the fawning sycophant of yesterday is converted into the austere critic of the present hour. But steady, independent minds, when they have an object of so serious a concern to mankind as government under their contemplation, will disdain to assume the part of satirists and declaimers. They will judge of human institutions as they do of human characters. They will sort out the good from the evil, which is mixed in mortal institutions, as it is in mortal men.

YOUR government in France, though usually, and I think justly, reputed the best of the unqualified or ill-qualified monarchies, was still full of abuses. These abuses accumulated in a length of time, as they must accumulate in every monarchy not under the constant inspection of a popular representative. I am no stranger to the faults and defects of the subverted government of France, and I think I am not inclined by nature or policy to make a panegyric upon anything which is a just and natural object of censure. But the question is not now of the vices of that monarchy, but of its existence. Is it, then, true that the French government was such as to be incapable or undeserving of reform, so that it was of absolute necessity that the whole fabric should be at once pulled down and the area cleared for the erection of a theoretic, experimental edifice in its place? All France was of a different opinion in the beginning of the year 1789. The instructions to the representatives to the States-General, from every district in that kingdom, were filled with projects for the reformation of that government without the remotest suggestion of a design to destroy it. Had such a design been even insinuated, I believe there would have been but one voice, and that voice for rejecting it with scorn and horror. Men have been sometimes led by degrees, sometimes hurried, into things of which, if they could have seen the whole together, they never would have permitted the most remote approach. When those instructions were given, there was no question but that abuses existed, and that they demanded a reform; nor is there now. In the interval between the instructions and the revolution things changed their shape; and in consequence of that change, the true question at present is, Whether those who would have reformed or those who have destroyed are in the right?

To hear some men speak of the late monarchy of France, you would imagine that they were talking of Persia bleeding under the ferocious sword of Tahmas Kouli Khân, or at least describing the barbarous anarchic despotism of Turkey, where the finest countries in the most genial climates in the world are wasted by peace more than any countries have been worried by war, where arts are unknown, where manufactures languish, where science is extinguished, where agriculture decays, where the human race itself melts away and perishes under the eye of the observer. Was this the case of France? I have no way of determining the question but by reference to facts. Facts do not support this resemblance. Along with much evil there is some good in monarchy itself, and some corrective to its evil from religion, from laws, from manners, from opinions the French monarchy must have received, which rendered it (though by no means a free, and therefore by no means a good, constitution) a despotism rather in appearance than in reality.

AMONG the standards upon which the effects of government on any country are to be estimated, I must consider the state of its population as not the least certain. No country in which population flourishes and is in progressive improvement can be under a *very* mischievous government. About sixty years ago, the Intendants of the generalities of France made, with other matters, a report of the population of their several districts. I have not the books, which are very voluminous, by me, nor do I know where to procure them (I am obliged to speak by memory, and therefore the less positively), but I think the population of France was by them, even at that period, estimated at twenty-two millions of souls. At the end of the last century it had been generally calculated at eighteen. On either of these estimations, France was not ill peopled. M. Necker, who is an authority for his own time, at least equal to the Intendants for theirs, reckons, and upon apparently sure principles, the people of France in the year 1780 at twenty-four millions six hundred and seventy thousand. But was this the probable ultimate term under the old establishment? Dr. Price is of opinion that the growth of population in France was by no means at its *acmé* in that year. I certainly defer to Dr. Price's authority a good deal more in these speculations than I do in his general politics. This gentleman, taking ground on M. Necker's data, is very confident that since the period of that minister's calculation the French population has increased rapidly—so rapidly that in the year 1789 he will not consent to rate the people of that kingdom at a lower number than thirty millions. After abating much (and much I think ought to be abated) from the sanguine calculation of Dr. Price, I have no doubt that the population of France did increase considerably during this later period; but supposing that it increased to nothing more than will be sufficient to complete the twenty-four millions six hundred and seventy thousand to twenty-five millions, still a population of twenty-five millions, and that in an increasing progress, on a space of about twenty-seven thousand square leagues is immense. It is, for instance, a good deal more than the proportionable population of this island, or even than that of England, the best peopled part of the United Kingdom.

It is not universally true that France is a fertile country. Considerable tracts of it are barren and labor under other natural disadvantages. In the portions of that territory where things are more favorable, as far as I am able to discover, the numbers of the people correspond to the indulgence of nature.[30] The Generality of Lisle (this I admit is the strongest example) upon an extent of four hundred and four leagues and a half, about ten years ago, contained seven hundred and thirty-four thousand six hundred souls, which is one thousand seven hundred and seventy-two inhabitants to each square league. The middle term for the rest of France is about nine hundred inhabitants to the same admeasurement.

I do not attribute this population to the deposed government, because I do not like to compliment the contrivances of men with what is due in a great degree to the bounty of Providence. But that decried government could not have obstructed, most probably it favored, the operation of those causes (whatever they were), whether of nature in the soil or habits of industry among the people, which has produced so large a number of the species throughout that whole kingdom and exhibited in some particular places such prodigies of population. I never will suppose that fabric of a state to be the worst of all political institutions which, by experience, is found to contain a principle favorable (however latent it may be) to the increase of mankind.

The wealth of a country is another, and no contemptible, standard by which we may judge whether, on the whole, a government be protecting or destructive. France far exceeds England in the multitude of her people, but I apprehend that her comparative wealth is much inferior to ours, that it is not so equal in the distribution, nor so ready in the

---

[30] *De l'Administration des Finances de la France,* par Mons. Necker, vol. I, p. 288.

circulation. I believe the difference in the form of the two governments to be amongst the causes of this advantage on the side of
England. I speak of England, not of the whole British dominions,
which, if compared with those of France, will, in some degree, weak-
en the comparative rate of wealth upon our side. But that wealth,
which will not endure a comparison with the riches of England, may
constitute a very respectable degree of opulence. M. Necker's book,
published in 1785,[31] contains an accurate and interesting collection of
facts relative to public economy and to political arithmetic; and his
speculations on the subject are in general wise and liberal. In that
work he gives an idea of the state of France very remote from the
portrait of a country whose government was a perfect grievance, an
absolute evil, admitting no cure but through the violent and uncertain remedy of a total revolution. He affirms that from the year 1726
to the year 1784 there was coined at the mint of France, in the species
of gold and silver, to the amount of about one hundred millions of
pounds sterling.[32]

It is impossible that M. Necker should be mistaken in the amount
of the bullion which has been coined in the mint. It is a matter of
official record. The reasonings of this able financier, concerning the
quantity of gold and silver which remained for circulation, when he
wrote in 1785, that is, about four years before the deposition and
imprisonment of the French king, are not of equal certainty, but they
are laid on grounds so apparently solid that it is not easy to refuse a
considerable degree of assent to his calculation. He calculates the
numeraire, or what we call "specie", then actually existing in France
at about eighty-eight millions of the same English money. A great
accumulation of wealth for one country, large as that country is!
M. Necker was so far from considering this influx of wealth as likely
to cease, when he wrote in 1785, that he presumes upon a future
annual increase of two per cent upon the money brought into France
during the periods from which he computed.

Some adequate cause must have originally introduced all the money
coined at its mint into that kingdom, and some cause as operative
must have kept at home, or returned into its bosom, such a vast
flood of treasure as M. Necker calculates to remain for domestic
circulation. Suppose any reasonable deductions from M. Necker's

[31] *De l'administration des Finances de la France,* par M. Necker.
[32] Ibid., Vol. III. chap. 8 and chap. 9.

computation, the remainder must still amount to an immense sum. Causes thus powerful to acquire, and to retain, cannot be found in discouraged industry, insecure property, and a positively destructive government. Indeed, when I consider the face of the kingdom of France, the multitude and opulence of her cities, the useful magnificence of her spacious high roads and bridges, the opportunity of her artificial canals and navigations opening the conveniences of maritime communication through a solid continent of so immense an extent; when I turn my eyes to the stupendous works of her ports and harbors, and to her whole naval apparatus, whether for war or trade; when I bring before my view the number of her fortifications, constructed with so bold and masterly a skill and made and maintained at so prodigious a charge, presenting an armed front and impenetrable barrier to her enemies upon every side; when I recollect how very small a part of that extensive region is without cultivation, and to what complete perfection the culture of many of the best productions of the earth have been brought in France; when I reflect on the excellence of her manufactures and fabrics, second to none but ours, and in some particulars not second; when I contemplate the grand foundations of charity, public and private; when I survey the state of all the arts that beautify and polish life; when I reckon the men she has bred for extending her fame in war, her able statesmen, the multitude of her profound lawyers and theologians, her philosophers, her critics, her historians and antiquaries, her poets and her orators, sacred and profane—I behold in all this something which awes and commands the imagination, which checks the mind on the brink of precipitate and indiscriminate censure, and which demands that we should very seriously examine what and how great are the latent vices that could authorize us at once to level so spacious a fabric with the ground. I do not recognize in this view of things the despotism of Turkey. Nor do I discern the character of a government that has been, on the whole, so oppressive or so corrupt or so negligent as to be utterly unfit *for all reformation.* I must think such a government well deserved to have its excellence heightened, its faults corrected, and its capacities improved into a British constitution.

Whoever has examined into the proceedings of that deposed government for several years back cannot fail to have observed, amidst the inconstancy and fluctuation natural to courts, an earnest endeavor toward the prosperity and improvement of the country; he must admit that it had long been employed, in some instances wholly to

115

remove, in many considerably to correct, the abusive practices and usages that had prevailed in the state, and that even the unlimited power of the sovereign over the persons of his subjects, inconsistent, as undoubtedly it was, with law and liberty, had yet been every day growing more mitigated in the exercise. So far from refusing itself to reformation, that government was open, with a censurable degree of facility, to all sorts of projects and projectors on the subject. Rather too much countenance was given to the spirit of innovation, which soon was turned against those who fostered it, and ended in their ruin. It is but cold, and no very flattering, justice to that fallen monarchy to say that, for many years, it trespassed more by levity and want of judgment in several of its schemes than from any defect in diligence or in public spirit. To compare the government of France for the last fifteen or sixteen years with wise and well-constituted establishments during that, or during any period, is not to act with fairness. But if in point of prodigality in the expenditure of money, or in point of rigor in the exercise of power, it be compared with any of the former reigns, I believe candid judges will give little credit to the good intentions of those who dwell perpetually on the donations to favorites, or on the expenses of the court, or on the horrors of the Bastille in the reign of Louis the Sixteenth.[33]

WHETHER the system, if it deserves such a name, now built on the ruins of that ancient monarchy will be able to give a better account of the population and wealth of the country which it has taken under its care, is a matter very doubtful. Instead of improving by the change, I apprehend that a long series of years must be told before it can recover in any degree the effects of this philosophic revolution, and before the nation can be replaced on its former footing. If Dr. Price should think fit, a few years hence, to favor us with an estimate of the population of France, he will hardly be able to make up his tale of thirty millions of souls, as computed in 1789, or the Assembly's computation of twenty-six millions of that year, or even M. Necker's twenty-five millions in 1780. I hear that there are considerable emigrations from France, and that many, quitting that voluptuous climate and that seductive *Circean* liberty, have taken refuge in the

---

[33] The world is obliged to M. de Calonne for the pains he has taken to refute the scandalous exaggerations relative to some of the royal expenses, and to detect the fallacious account given of pensions, for the wicked purpose of provoking the populace to all sorts of crimes.

frozen regions, and under the British despotism, of Canada.

In the present disappearance of coin, no person could think it the same country in which the present minister of the finances has been able to discover fourscore millions sterling in specie. From its general aspect one would conclude that it had been for some time past under the special direction of the learned academicians of Laputa and Balnibarbi.[34] Already the population of Paris has so declined that M. Necker stated to the National Assembly the provision to be made for its subsistence at a fifth less than what had formerly been found requisite.[35] It is said (and I have never heard it contradicted) that a hundred thousand people are out of employment in that city, though it is become the seat of the imprisoned court and National Assembly. Nothing, I am credibly informed, can exceed the shocking and disgusting spectacle of mendicancy displayed in that capital. Indeed the votes of the National Assembly leave no doubt of the fact. They have lately appointed a standing committee of mendicancy. They are contriving at once a vigorous police on this subject and, for the first time, the imposition of a tax to maintain the poor, for whose present relief great sums appear on the face of the public accounts of the year.[36] In the meantime the leaders of the legislative clubs and coffeehouses are intoxicated with admiration at their own wisdom and ability. They speak with the most sovereign contempt of the rest of the world. They tell the people, to comfort them in the rags with which they have clothed them, that they are a nation of philosophers; and sometimes by all the arts of quackish parade, by show, tumult, and bustle, sometimes by the alarms of plots and invasions, they attempt to drown the cries of indigence and to divert the eyes of the

---

[34] See *Gulliver's Travels* for the idea of countries governed by philosophers.

[35] M. de Calonne states the falling off of the population of Paris as far more considerable; and it may be so, since the period of M. Necker's calculation.

[36] Travaux de charité pour subvenir au manque de travail à Paris et dans les	*Livres*		£	*s.*	*d.*
provinces	3,866,920	=	161,121	13	4
Destruction de vagabondage et de la mendicité	1,671,417	=	69,642	7	6
Primes pour l'importation de grains	5,671,907	=	236,329	9	2
Dépenses relatives aux subsistances, déduction fait des récouvrements qui ont eu lieu	39,871,790	=	1,661,324	11	8
Total *Liv.*	51,082,034	=	£2,128,418	1	8

observer from the ruin and wretchedness of the state. A brave people will certainly prefer liberty accompanied with a virtuous poverty to a depraved and wealthy servitude. But before the price of comfort and opulence is paid, one ought to be pretty sure it is real liberty which is purchased, and that she is to be purchased at no other price. I shall always, however, consider that liberty as very equivocal in her appearance which has not wisdom and justice for her companions and does not lead prosperity and plenty in her train.

THE advocates for this Revolution, not satisfied with exaggerating the vices of their ancient government, strike at the fame of their country itself by painting almost all that could have attracted the attention of strangers, I mean their nobility and their clergy, as objects of horror. If this were only a libel, there had not been much in it. But it has practical consequences. Had your nobility and gentry, who formed the great body of your landed men and the whole of your military officers, resembled those of Germany at the period when the Hanse-towns were necessitated to confederate against the nobles in defense of their property; had they been like the Orsini and Vitelli in Italy, who used to sally from their fortified dens to rob the trader and traveller; had they been such as the Mamelukes in Egypt or the Nayres[lxxi] on the coast of Malabar, I do admit that too critical an inquiry might not be advisable into the means of freeing the world from such a nuisance. The statues of Equity and Mercy might be veiled for a moment. The tenderest minds, confounded with the dreadful exigency in which morality submits to the suspension of its own rules in favor of its own principles, might turn aside whilst fraud and violence were accomplishing the destruction of a pretended no-

---

When I sent this book to the press, I entertained some doubt concerning the nature and extent of the last article in the above accounts, which is only under a general head, without any detail. Since then I have seen M. de Calonne's work. I must think it a great loss to me that I had not that advantage earlier. M. de Calonne thinks this article to be on account of general subsistence; but as he is not able to comprehend how so great a loss as upwards of £1,661,000 sterling could be sustained on the difference between the price and the sale of grain, he seems to attribute this enormous head of charge to secret expenses of the Revolution. I cannot say anything positively on that subject. The reader is capable of judging, by the aggregate of these immense charges, on the state and condition of France; and the system of public economy adopted in that nation. These articles of account produced no inquiry or discussion in the National Assembly.

bility which disgraced, whilst it persecuted, human nature. The persons most abhorrent from blood, and treason, and arbitrary confiscation might remain silent spectators of this civil war between the vices.

But did the privileged nobility who met under the king's precept at Versailles, in 1789, or their constituents, deserve to be looked on as the Nayres or Mamelukes of this age, or as the Orsini and Vitelli of ancient times? If I had then asked the question I should have passed for a madman. What have they since done that they were to be driven into exile, that their persons should be hunted about, mangled, and tortured, their families dispersed, their houses laid in ashes, and that their order should be abolished and the memory of it, if possible, extinguished by ordaining them to change the very names by which they were usually known? Read their instructions to their representatives. They breathe the spirit of liberty as warmly and they recommend reformation as strongly as any other order. Their privileges relative to contribution were voluntarily surrendered, as the king, from the beginning, surrendered all pretense to a right of taxation. Upon a free constitution there was but one opinion in France. The absolute monarchy was at an end. It breathed its last, without a groan, without struggle, without convulsion. All the struggle, all the dissension arose afterwards upon the preference of a despotic democracy to a government of reciprocal control. The triumph of the victorious party was over the principles of a British constitution.

I have observed the affectation which for many years past has prevailed in Paris, even to a degree perfectly childish, of idolizing the memory of your Henry the Fourth. If anything could put one out of humor with that ornament to the kingly character, it would be this overdone style of insidious panegyric. The persons who have worked this engine the most busily are those who have ended their panegyrics in dethroning his successor and descendant, a man as good-natured, at the least, as Henry the Fourth, altogether as fond of his people, and who has done infinitely more to correct the ancient vices of the state than that great monarch did, or we are sure he ever meant to do. Well it is for his panegyrists that they have not him to deal with. For Henry of Navarre was a resolute, active, and politic prince. He possessed, indeed, great humanity and mildness, but a humanity and mildness that never stood in the way of his interests. He never sought to be loved without putting himself first in a condition to be feared. He used soft language with determined conduct. He asserted and maintained his authority in the gross, and distributed his acts of concession only in the detail. He spent the income of his prerogative nobly, but he took care not to break in upon the capital, never abandoning for a moment any of the claims which he made under the fundamental laws, nor sparing to shed the blood of those who opposed him, often in the field, sometimes upon the scaffold. Because he knew how to make his virtues respected by the ungrateful, he has merited the praises of those whom, if they had lived in his time, he would have shut up in the Bastille and brought to punishment along with the regicides whom he hanged after he had famished Paris into a surrender.

If these panegyrists are in earnest in their admiration of Henry the Fourth, they must remember that they cannot think more highly of him than he did of the noblesse of France, whose virtue, honor, courage, patriotism, and loyalty were his constant theme.

But the nobility of France are degenerated since the days of Henry the Fourth. This is possible. But it is more than I can believe to be true in any great degree. I do not pretend to know France as correctly as some others, but I have endeavored through my whole life to make myself acquainted with human nature, otherwise I should be unfit to take even my humble part in the service of mankind. In that study I could not pass by a vast portion of our nature as it appeared modified in a country but twenty-four miles from the shore of this island. On my best observation, compared with my best inquiries, I found your nobility for the greater part composed of men of high spirit and of a delicate sense of honor, both with regard to themselves individually and with regard to their whole corps, over whom they kept, beyond what is common in other countries, a censorial eye. They were tolerably well bred, very officious, humane, and hospitable; in their conversation frank and open; with a good military tone, and reasonably tinctured with literature, particularly of the authors in their own language. Many had pretensions far above this description. I speak of those who were generally met with.

As to their behavior to the inferior classes, they appeared to me to comport themselves toward them with good nature and with something more nearly approaching to familiarity than is generally practiced with us in the intercourse between the higher and lower ranks of life. To strike any person, even in the most abject condition, was a thing in a manner unknown and would be highly disgraceful. Instances of other ill-treatment of the humble part of the community were rare; and as to attacks made upon the property or the personal liberty of the commons, I never heard of any whatsoever from *them;* nor, whilst the laws were in vigor under the ancient government, would such tyranny in subjects have been permitted. As men of landed estates, I had no fault to find with their conduct, though much to reprehend and much to wish changed in many of the old tenures. Where the letting of their land was by rent, I could not discover that their agreements with their farmers were oppressive; nor when they were in partnership with the farmer, as often was the case, have I heard that they had taken the lion's share. The proportions seemed not inequitable. There might be exceptions, but certainly they were exceptions only. I have no reason to believe that in these respects the landed noblesse of France were worse than the landed gentry of this country, certainly in no respect more vexatious than the landholders, not noble, of their own nation. In cities the nobility had no manner of power, in the country very little. You know, Sir, that much of the civil government, and the police in the most essential parts, was not in the hands of that nobility which presents itself first to our consideration. The revenue, the system and collection of which were the most grievous parts of the French government, was not administered by the men of the sword, nor were they answerable for the vices of its principle or the vexations, where any such existed, in its management.

Denying, as I am well warranted to do, that the nobility had any considerable share in the oppression of the people in cases in which real oppression existed, I am ready to admit that they were not without considerable faults and errors. A foolish imitation of the worst part of the manners of England, which impaired their natural character without substituting in its place what, perhaps, they meant to copy, has certainly rendered them worse than formerly they were. Habitual dissoluteness of manners, continued beyond the pardonable period of life, was more common amongst them than it is with us; and it reigned with the less hope of remedy, though possibly with something of less mischief by being covered with more exterior decorum. They countenanced too much that licentious philosophy which has helped to bring on their ruin. There was another error amongst them more fatal. Those of the commons who approached to or exceeded many of the nobility in point of wealth were not fully admitted to the rank and estimation which wealth, in reason and good policy, ought to bestow in every country, though I think not equally with that of other nobility. The two kinds of aristocracy were too punctiliously kept asunder, less so, however, than in Germany and some other nations.

This separation, as I have already taken the liberty of suggesting to

121

you, I conceive to be one principal cause of the destruction of the old nobility. The military, particularly, was too exclusively reserved for men of family. But, after all, this was an error of opinion, which a conflicting opinion would have rectified. A permanent assembly in which the commons had their share of power would soon abolish whatever was too invidious and insulting in these distinctions, and even the faults in the morals of the nobility would have been probably corrected by the greater varieties of occupation and pursuit to which a constitution by orders would have given rise.

All this violent cry against the nobility I take to be a mere work of art. To be honored and even privileged by the laws, opinions, and inveterate usages of our country, growing out of the prejudice of ages, has nothing to provoke horror and indignation in any man. Even to be too tenacious of those privileges is not absolutely a crime. The strong struggle in every individual to preserve possession of what he has found to belong to him and to distinguish him is one of the securities against injustice and despotism implanted in our nature. It operates as an instinct to secure property and to preserve communities in a settled state. What is there to shock in this? Nobility is a graceful ornament to the civil order. It is the Corinthian capital of polished society. *Omnes boni nobilitati semper favemus,*[lxxii] was the saying of a wise and good man. It is indeed one sign of a liberal and benevolent mind to incline to it with some sort of partial propensity. He feels no ennobling principle in his own heart who wishes to level all the artificial institutions which have been adopted for giving a body to opinion, and permanence to fugitive esteem. It is a sour, malignant, envious disposition, without taste for the reality or for any image or representation of virtue, that sees with joy the unmerited fall of what had long flourished in splendor and in honor. I do not like to see anything destroyed, any void produced in society, any ruin on the face of the land. It was, therefore, with no disappointment or dissatisfaction that my inquiries and observations did not present to me any incorrigible vices in the noblesse of France, or any abuse which could not be removed by a reform very short of abolition. Your noblesse did not deserve punishment; but to degrade is to punish.

IT WAS WITH THE SAME SATISFACTION I found that the result of my inquiry concerning your clergy was not dissimilar. It is no soothing news to my ears that great bodies of men are incurably corrupt. It is not with much credulity I listen to any when they speak evil of those whom they are going to plunder. I rather suspect that vices are feigned or exaggerated when profit is looked for in their punishment. An enemy is a bad witness; a robber is a worse. Vices and abuses there were undoubtedly in that order, and must be. It was an old establishment, and not frequently revised. But I saw no crimes in the individuals that merited confiscation of their substance, nor those cruel insults and degradations, and that unnatural persecution which have been substituted in the place of meliorating regulation.

If there had been any just cause for this new religious persecution, the atheistic libellers, who act as trumpeters to animate the populace to plunder, do not love anybody so much as not to dwell with complacency on the vices of the existing clergy. This they have not done. They find themselves obliged to rake into the histories of former ages (which they have ransacked with a malignant and profligate industry) for every instance of oppression and persecution which has been made by that body or in its favor in order to justify, upon very iniquitous, because very illogical, principles of retaliation, their own persecutions and their own cruelties. After destroying all other genealogies and family distinctions, they invent a sort of pedigree of crimes. It is not very just to chastise men for the offenses of their natural ancestors, but to take the fiction of ancestry in a corporate succession as a ground for punishing men who have no relation to guilty acts, except in names and general descriptions, is a sort of refinement in injustice belonging to the philosophy of this enlightened age. The Assembly punishes men, many, if not most, of whom abhor the violent conduct of ecclesiastics in former times as much as their present persecutors can do, and who would be as loud and as strong in the expression of that sense, if they were not well aware of the purposes for which all this declamation is employed.

Corporate bodies are immortal for the good of the members, but not for their punishment. Nations themselves are such corporations. As well might we in England think of waging inexpiable war upon all Frenchmen for the evils which they have brought upon us in the several periods of our mutual hostilities. You might, on your part, think yourselves justified in falling upon all Englishmen on account of the unparalleled calamities brought on the people of France by the unjust invasions of our Henries and our Edwards. Indeed, we should be mutually justified in this exterminatory war upon each other, full as much as you are in the unprovoked persecution of your present countrymen, on account of the conduct of men of the same name in other times.

We do not draw the moral lessons we might from history. On the contrary, without care it may be used to vitiate our minds and to destroy our happiness. In history a great volume is unrolled for our instruction, drawing the materials of future wisdom from the past errors and infirmities of mankind. It may, in the perversion, serve for a magazine furnishing offensive and defensive weapons for parties in church and state, and supplying the means of keeping alive or reviving dissensions and animosities, and adding fuel to civil fury. History consists for the greater part of the miseries brought upon the world by pride, ambition, avarice, revenge, lust, sedition, hypocrisy, ungoverned zeal, and all the train of disorderly appetites which shake the public with the same

—troublous storms that toss
The private state, and render life unsweet.[lxxiii]

These vices are the *causes* of those storms. Religion, morals, laws, prerogatives, privileges, liberties, rights of men are the *pretexts*. The pretexts are always found in some specious appearance of a real good. You would not secure men from tyranny and sedition by rooting out of the mind the principles to which these fraudulent pretexts apply? If you did, you would root out everything that is valuable in the human breast. As these are the pretexts, so the ordinary actors and instruments in great public evils are kings, priests, magistrates, senates, parliaments, national assemblies, judges, and captains. You would not cure the evil by resolving that there should be no more monarchs, nor ministers of state, nor of the gospel; no interpreters of law; no general officers; no public councils. You might change the names. The things in some shape must remain. A certain *quantum* of power must always exist in the community in some hands and under some appellation. Wise men will apply their remedies to vices, not to names; to the causes of evil which are permanent, not to the occasional organs by which they act, and the transitory modes in which they appear. Otherwise you will be wise historically, a fool in practice. Seldom have two ages the same fashion in their pretexts and the same modes of mischief. Wickedness is a little more inventive. Whilst you are discussing fashion, the fashion is gone by.

The very same vice assumes a new body. The spirit transmigrates, and, far from losing its principle of life by the change of its appearance, it is renovated in its new organs with a fresh vigor of a juvenile activity. It walks abroad, it continues its ravages, whilst you are gibbeting the carcass or demolishing the tomb. You are terrifying yourselves with ghosts and apparitions, whilst your house is the haunt of robbers. It is thus with all those who, attending only to the shell and husk of history, think they are waging war with intolerance, pride, and cruelty, whilst, under color of abhorring the ill principles of antiquated parties, they are authorizing and feeding the same odious vices in different factions, and perhaps in worse.

Your citizens of Paris formerly had lent themselves as the ready instruments to slaughter the followers of Calvin, at the infamous massacre of St. Bartholomew. What should we say to those who could think of retaliating on the Parisians of this day the abominations and horrors of that time? They are indeed brought to abhor *that* massacre. Ferocious as they are, it is not difficult to make them dislike it, because the politicians and fashionable teachers have no interest in giving their passions exactly the same direction. Still, however, they find it their interest to keep the same savage dispositions alive. It was but the other day that they caused this very massacre to be acted on the stage for the diversion of the descendants of those who committed it. In this tragic farce they produced the cardinal of Lorraine in his robes of function, ordering general slaughter. Was this spectacle intended to make the Parisians abhor persecution and loathe the effusion of blood?—No; it was to teach them to persecute their own pastors; it was to excite them, by raising a disgust and horror of their clergy, to an alacrity in hunting down to destruction an order which, if it ought to exist at all, ought to exist not only in safety, but in reverence. It was to stimulate their cannibal appetites (which one would think had been gorged sufficiently) by variety and seasoning; and to quicken them to an alertness in new murders and massacres, if it should suit the purpose of the Guises of the day. An assembly, in which sat a multitude of priests and prelates, was obliged to suffer this indignity at its door. The author was not sent to the galleys, nor the players to the house of correction. Not long after this exhibition, those players came forward to the Assembly to claim the rites of that very religion which they had dared to expose, and to show their prostituted faces in the senate, whilst the archbishop of Paris, whose function was known to his people only by his prayers and benedictions, and his wealth only by his alms, is forced to abandon his house and to fly from his flock (as from ravenous wolves) because, truly, in the sixteenth century, the cardinal of Lorraine was a rebel and a murderer.[37]

Such is the effect of the perversion of history by those who, for the same nefarious purposes, have perverted every other part of learning. But those who will stand upon that elevation of reason which places centuries under our eye and brings things to the true point of comparison, which obscures little names and effaces the colors of little parties, and to which nothing can ascend but the spirit and moral quality of human actions, will say to the teachers of the Palais Royal: The cardinal of Lorraine was the murderer of the sixteenth century, you have the glory of being the murderers in the eighteenth, and this is the only difference between you. But history in the nineteenth century, better understood and better employed, will, I trust, teach a civilized posterity to abhor the misdeeds of both these barbarous ages. It will teach future priests and magistrates not to retaliate upon the speculative and inactive atheists of future times the enormities committed by the present practical zealots and furious fanatics of that wretched error, which, in its quiescent state, is more than punished whenever it is embraced. It will teach posterity not to make war upon either religion or philosophy for the abuse which the hypocrites of both have made of the two most valuable blessings conferred upon us by the bounty of the universal Patron, who in all things eminently favors and protects the race of man.

If your clergy, or any clergy, should show themselves vicious beyond the fair bounds allowed to human infirmity, and to those professional faults which can hardly be separated from professional virtues, though their vices never can countenance the exercise of oppression, I do admit that they would naturally have the effect of abating very much of our indignation against the tyrants who exceed measure and justice in their punishment. I can allow in clergymen, through all their divisions, some tenaciousness of their own opinion, some overflowings of zeal for its propagation, some predilection to their own state and office, some attachment to the interests of their own corps, some preference to those who listen with docility to their doctrines, beyond those who scorn and deride them. I allow all this, because I

---

[37] This is on the supposition of the truth of the story, but he was not in France at the time. One name serves as well as another. [1803]

am a man who has to deal with men, and who would not, through a violence of toleration, run into the greatest of all intolerance. I must bear with infirmities until they fester into crimes.

Undoubtedly, the natural progress of the passions, from frailty to vice, ought to be prevented by a watchful eye and a firm hand. But is it true that the body of your clergy had passed those limits of a just allowance? From the general style of your late publications of all sorts one would be led to believe that your clergy in France were a sort of monsters, a horrible composition of superstition, ignorance, sloth, fraud, avarice, and tyranny. But is this true? Is it true that the lapse of time, the cessation of conflicting interests, the woeful experience of the evils resulting from party rage have had no sort of influence gradually to meliorate their minds? Is it true that they were daily renewing invasions on the civil power, troubling the domestic quiet of their country, and rendering the operations of its government feeble and precarious? Is it true that the clergy of our times have pressed down the laity with an iron hand and were in all places lighting up the fires of a savage persecution? Did they by every fraud endeavor to increase their estates? Did they use to exceed the due demands on estates that were their own? Or, rigidly screwing up right into wrong, did they convert a legal claim into a vexatious extortion? When not possessed of power, were they filled with the vices of those who envy it? Were they inflamed with a violent, litigious spirit of controversy? Goaded on with the ambition of intellectual sovereignty, were they ready to fly in the face of all magistracy, to fire churches, to massacre the priests of other descriptions, to pull down altars, and to make their way over the ruins of subverted governments to an empire of doctrine, sometimes flattering, sometimes forcing the consciences of men from the jurisdiction of public institutions into a submission of their personal authority, beginning with a claim of liberty and ending with an abuse of power?

These, or some of these, were the vices objected, and not wholly without foundation, to several of the churchmen of former times who belonged to the two great parties which then divided and distracted Europe.

If there was in France, as in other countries there visibly is, a great abatement rather than any increase of these vices, instead of loading the present clergy with the crimes of other men and the odious character of other times, in common equity they ought to be praised, encouraged, and supported in their departure from a spirit which disgraced their predecessors, and for having assumed a temper of mind and manners more suitable to their sacred function.

When my occasions took me into France, toward the close of the late reign, the clergy, under all their forms, engaged a considerable part of my curiosity. So far from finding (except from one set of men, not then very numerous, though very active) the complaints and discontents against that body, which some publications had given me reason to expect, I perceived little or no public or private uneasiness on their account. On further examination, I found the clergy, in general, persons of moderate minds and decorous manners; I include the seculars and the regulars of both sexes. I had not the good fortune to know a great many of the parochial clergy, but in general I received a perfectly good account of their morals and of their attention to their duties. With some of the higher clergy I had a personal acquaintance, and of the rest in that class a very good means of information. They were, almost all of them, persons of noble birth. They resembled others of their own rank; and where there was any difference, it was in their favor. They were more fully educated than the military noblesse, so as by no means to disgrace their profession by ignorance or by want of fitness for the exercise of their authority. They seemed to me, beyond the clerical character, liberal and open, with the hearts of gentlemen and men of honor, neither insolent nor servile in their manners and conduct. They seemed to me rather a superior class, a set of men amongst whom you would not be surprised to find a Fénelon. I saw among the clergy in Paris (many of the description are not to be met with anywhere) men of great learning and candor; and I had reason to believe that this description was not confined to Paris. What I found in other places I know was accidental, and therefore to be presumed a fair example. I spent a few days in a provincial town where, in the absence of the bishop, I passed my evenings with three clergymen, his vicars-general, persons who would have done honor to any church. They were all well informed; two of them of deep, general, and extensive erudition, ancient and modern, oriental and western, particularly in their own profession. They had a more extensive knowledge of our English divines than I expected, and they entered into the genius of those writers with a critical accuracy. One of these gentlemen is since dead, the Abbé Morangis. I pay this tribute, without reluctance, to the memory of that noble, reverend, learned, and excellent person; and I should do the same with equal cheerfulness to the merits of the others who, I believe, are still living, if I did not fear to hurt those whom I am unable to serve.

Some of these ecclesiastics of rank are by all titles persons deserving of general respect. They are deserving of gratitude from me and from many English. If this letter should ever come into their hands, I hope they will believe there are those of our nation who feel for their unmerited fall and for the cruel confiscation of their fortunes with no common sensibility. What I say of them is a testimony, as far as one feeble voice can go, which I owe to truth. Whenever the question of this unnatural persecution is concerned, I will pay it. No one shall prevent me from being just and grateful. The time is fitted for the duty, and it is particularly becoming to show our justice and gratitude when those who have deserved well of us and of mankind are laboring under popular obloquy and the persecutions of oppressive power.

YOU had before your Revolution about a hundred and twenty bishops. A few of them were men of eminent sanctity, and charity without limit. When we talk of the heroic, of course we talk of rare virtue. I believe the instances of eminent depravity may be as rare amongst them as those of transcendent goodness. Examples of avarice and of licentiousness may be picked out, I do not question it, by those who delight in the investigation which leads to such discoveries. A man as old as I am will not be astonished that several, in every description, do not lead that perfect life of self-denial, with regard to wealth or to pleasure, which is wished for by all, by some expected, but by none exacted with more rigor than by those who are the most attentive to their own interests, or the most indulgent to their own passions. When I was in France, I am certain that the number of vicious prelates was not great. Certain individuals among them, not distinguishable for the regularity of their lives, made some amends for their want of the severe virtues in their possession of the liberal, and were endowed with qualities which made them useful in the church and state. I am told that, with few exceptions, Louis the Sixteenth had been more attentive to character, in his promotions to that rank, than his immediate predecessor; and I believe (as some spirit of reform has prevailed through the whole reign) that it may be true. But the present ruling power has shown a disposition only to plunder the church. It has punished *all* prelates, which is to favor the vicious, at least in point of reputation. It has made a degrading pensionary establishment to which no man of liberal ideas or liberal condition will destine his children. It must settle into the lowest classes of the people. As with you the inferior clergy are not numerous enough for their duties; as these duties are, beyond measure, minute and toilsome; as you have left no middle classes of clergy at their ease, in future nothing of science or erudition can exist in the Gallican church. To complete the project without the least attention to the rights of patrons, the Assembly has provided in future an elective clergy, an arrangement which will drive out of the clerical profession all men of sobriety, all who can pretend to independence in their function or their conduct, and which will throw the whole direction of the public mind into the hands of a set of licentious, bold, crafty, factious, flattering wretches, of such condition and such habits of life as will make their contemptible pensions (in comparison of which the stipend of an exciseman is lucrative and honorable) an object of low and illiberal intrigue. Those officers whom they still call bishops are to be elected to a provision comparatively mean, through the same arts (that is, electioneering arts), by men of all religious tenets that are known or can be invented. The new lawgivers have not ascertained anything whatsoever concerning their qualifications relative either to doctrine or to morals, no more than they have done with regard to the subordinate clergy; nor does it appear but that both the higher and the lower may, at their discretion, practice or preach any mode of religion or irreligion that they please. I do not yet see what the jurisdiction of bishops over their subordinates is to be, or whether they are to have any jurisdiction at all.

In short, Sir, it seems to me that this new ecclesiastical establishment is intended only to be temporary and preparatory to the utter abolition, under any of its forms, of the Christian religion, whenever the minds of men are prepared for this last stroke against it, by the accomplishment of the plan for bringing its ministers into universal contempt. They who will not believe that the philosophical fanatics who guide in these matters have long entertained such a design are utterly ignorant of their character and proceedings. These enthusiasts do not scruple to avow their opinion that a state can subsist without any religion better than with one, and that they are able to supply the place of any good which may be in it by a project of their own—namely, by a sort of eduction they have imagined, founded in a knowledge of the physical wants of men, progressively carried to an enlightened self-interest which, when well understood, they tell us, will identify with an interest more enlarged and public. The scheme of this education has been long known. Of late they distinguish it (as they have got an entirely new nomenclature of technical terms) by the name of a *Civic Education.*

I hope their partisans in England (to whom I rather attribute very inconsiderate conduct than the ultimate object in this detestable design) will succeed neither in the pillage of the ecclesiastics, nor in the introduction of a principle of popular election to our bishoprics and parochial cures. This, in the present condition of the world, would be the last corruption of the church, the utter ruin of the clerical character, the most dangerous shock that the state ever received through a misunderstood arrangement of religion. I know well enough that the bishoprics and cures under kingly and seignioral patronage, as now they are in England, and as they have been lately in France, are sometimes acquired by unworthy methods; but the other mode of ecclesiastical canvass subjects them infinitely more surely and more generally to all the evil arts of low ambition, which, operating on and through greater numbers, will produce mischief in proportion.

Those of you who have robbed the clergy think that they shall easily reconcile their conduct to all Protestant nations, because the clergy, whom they have thus plundered, degraded, and given over to mockery and scorn, are of the Roman Catholic, that is, of *their own* pretended persuasion. I have no doubt that some miserable bigots will be found here, as well as elsewhere, who hate sects and parties different from their own more than they love the substance of religion, and who are more angry with those who differ from them in their particular plans and systems than displeased with those who attack the foundation of our common hope. These men will write and speak on the subject in the manner that is to be expected from their temper and character. Burnet says that when he was in France, in the year 1683, "the method which carried over the men of the finest parts to Popery was this—they brought themselves to doubt of the whole Christian religion. When that was once done, it seemed a more indifferent thing of what side or form they continued outwardly."[lxxiv] If this was then the ecclesiastical policy of France, it is what they have since but too much reason to repent of. They preferred atheism to a form of religion not agreeable to their ideas. They succeeded in destroying that form; and atheism has succeeded in destroying them. I can readily give credit to Burnet's story, because I have observed too much of a similar spirit (for a little of it is "much too much") amongst ourselves. The humor, however, is not general.

THE teachers who reformed our religion in England bore no sort of resemblance to your present reforming doctors in Paris. Perhaps they were (like those whom they opposed) rather more than could be wished under the influence of a party spirit, but they were more

131

sincere believers, men of the most fervent and exalted piety, ready to die (as some of them did die) like true heroes in defense of their particular ideas of Christianity, as they would with equal fortitude, and more cheerfully, for that stock of general truth for the branches of which they contended with their blood. These men would have disavowed with horror those wretches who claimed a fellowship with them upon no other titles than those of their having pillaged the persons with whom they maintained controversies, and their having despised the common religion for the purity of which they exerted themselves with a zeal which unequivocally bespoke their highest reverence for the substance of that system which they wished to reform. Many of their descendants have retained the same zeal, but (as less engaged in conflict) with more moderation. They do not forget that justice and mercy are substantial parts of religion. Impious men do not recommend themselves to their communion by iniquity and cruelty toward any description of their fellow creatures.

We hear these new teachers continually boasting of their spirit of toleration. That those persons should tolerate all opinions, who think none to be of estimation, is a matter of small merit. Equal neglect is not impartial kindness. The species of benevolence which arises from contempt is no true charity. There are in England abundance of men who tolerate in the true spirit of toleration. They think the dogmas of religion, though in different degrees, are all of moment, and that amongst them there is, as amongst all things of value, a just ground of preference. They favor, therefore, and they tolerate. They tolerate, not because they despise opinions, but because they respect justice. They would reverently and affectionately protect all religions because they love and venerate the great principle upon which they all agree, and the great object to which they are all directed. They begin more and more plainly to discern that we have all a common cause, as against a common enemy. They will not be so misled by the spirit of faction as not to distinguish what is done in favor of their subdivision from those acts of hostility which, through some particular description, are aimed at the whole corps, in which they themselves, under another denomination, are included. It is impossible for me to say what may be the character of every description of men amongst us. But I speak for the greater part; and for them, I must tell you that sacrilege is no part of their doctrine of good works; that, so far from calling you into their fellowship on such title, if your professors are admitted to their communion, they must carefully conceal their doctrine of the lawfulness of the prescription of innocent men; and that they must make restitution of all stolen goods whatsoever. Till then they are none of ours.

YOU may suppose that we do not approve your confiscation of the revenues of bishops, and deans, and chapters, and parochial clergy possessing independent estates arising from land, because we have the same sort of establishment in England. That objection, you will say, cannot hold as to the confiscation of the goods of monks and nuns and the abolition of their order. It is true that this particular part of your general confiscation does not affect England, as a precedent in point; but the reason implies, and it goes a great way. The Long Parliament confiscated the lands of deans and chapters in England on the same ideas upon which your Assembly set to sale the lands of the monastic orders. But it is in the principle of injustice that the danger lies, and not in the description of persons on whom it is first exercised. I see, in a country very near us, a course of policy pursued which sets justice, the common concern of mankind, at defiance. With the National Assembly of France possession is nothing, law and usage are nothing. I see the National Assembly openly reprobate the doctrine of prescription, which[38] one of the greatest of their own lawyers[lxxv] tells us, with great truth, is a part of the law of nature. He tells us that the positive ascertainment of its limits, and its security from invasion, were among the causes for which civil society itself has been instituted. If prescription be once shaken, no species of property is secure when it once becomes an object large enough to tempt the cupidity of indigent power. I see a practice perfectly correspondent to their contempt of this great fundamental part of natural law. I see the confiscators begin with bishops and chapters, and monasteries, but I do not see them end there. I see the princes of the blood, who by the oldest usages of that kingdom held large landed estates, (hardly with the compliment of a debate) deprived of their possessions and, in lieu of their stable, independent property, reduced to the hope of some precarious, charitable pension at the pleasure of an assembly which of course will pay little regard to the rights of pensioners at pleasure when it despises those of legal proprietors. Flushed with the insolence of their first inglorious victories, and pressed by the distresses caused by their lust of unhallowed lucre, disappointed but not discouraged, they have at length ventured com-

[38] Domat.

pletely to subvert all property of all descriptions throughout the extent of a great kingdom. They have compelled all men, in all transactions of commerce, in the disposal of lands, in civil dealing, and through the whole communion of life, to accept as perfect payment and good and lawful tender the symbols of their speculations on a projected sale of their plunder. What vestiges of liberty or property have they left? The tenant right of a cabbage garden, a year's interest in a hovel, the goodwill of an alehouse or a baker's shop, the very shadow of a constructive property, are more ceremoniously treated in our parliament than with you the oldest and most valuable landed possessions, in the hands of the most respectable personages, or than the whole body of the monied and commercial interest of your country. We entertain a high opinion of the legislative authority, but we have never dreamt that parliaments had any right whatever to violate property, to overrule prescription, or to force a currency of their own fiction in the place of that which is real and recognized by the law of nations. But you, who began with refusing to submit to the most moderate restraints, have ended by establishing an unheard-of despotism. I find the ground upon which your confiscators go is this: that, indeed, their proceedings could not be supported in a court of justice, but that the rules of prescription cannot bind a legislative assembly.[39] So that this legislative assembly of a free nation sits, not for the security, but for the destruction, of property, and not of property only, but of every rule and maxim which can give it stability, and of those instruments which can alone give it circulation.

When the Anabaptists of Münster, in the sixteenth century, had filled Germany with confusion by their system of leveling and their wild opinions concerning property, to what country in Europe did not the progress of their fury furnish just cause of alarm? Of all things, wisdom is the most terrified with epidemical fanaticism, because of all enemies it is that against which she is the least able to furnish any kind of resource. We cannot be ignorant of the spirit of atheistical fanaticism that is inspired by a multitude of writings dispersed with incredible assiduity and expense, and by sermons delivered in all the streets and places of public resort in Paris. These writings and sermons have filled the populace with a black and savage atrocity of mind, which supersedes in them the common feelings of nature as well as all sentiments of morality and religion, insomuch that these

[39] Speech of Mr. Camus, published by order of the National Assembly.

wretches are induced to bear with a sullen patience the intolerable distresses brought upon them by the violent convulsions and permutations that have been made in property.[40] The spirit of proselytism attends this spirit of fanaticism. They have societies to cabal and correspond at home and abroad for the propagation of their tenets. The republic of Berne, one of the happiest, the most prosperous, and the best governed countries upon earth, is one of the great objects at the destruction of which they aim. I am told they have in some measure succeeded in sowing there the seeds of discontent. They are busy throughout Germany. Spain and Italy have not been untried. England is not left out of the comprehensive scheme of their malignant charity; and in England we find those who stretch out their arms to them, who recommend their example from more than one pulpit, and who choose in more than one periodical meeting publicly to correspond with them, to applaud them, and to hold them up as objects for imitation; who receive from them tokens of confraternity, and standards consecrated amidst their rites and mysteries;[41] who suggest to them leagues of perpetual amity, at the very time when the power to which our constitution has exclusively delegated the federative capacity of this kingdom may find it expedient to make war upon them.

[40] Whether the following description is strictly true, I know not; but it is what the publishers would have pass for true in order to animate others. In a letter from Toul, given in one of their papers, is the following passage concerning the people of that district: "Dans la Révolution actuelle, ils ont résisté à toutes les *séductions du bigotisme, aux persécutions, et aux tracasseries* des ennemis de la Révolution. *Oubliant leurs plus grands intérêts* pour rendre hommage aux vues d'ordre général qui ont déterminé l'Assemblée Nationale, ils voient, *sans se plaindre,* supprimer cette foule détablissemens [*sic!*] ecclésiastiques par lesquels *ils subsistoient;* et même, en perdant leur siège épiscopal, la seule de toutes ces ressources qui pouvoit, ou plutôt *qui devoit, en toute équité,* leur être conservée; condamnés *à la plus effrayante misère,* sans avoir *été ni pu être entendus, ils ne murmurent point,* ils restent fidèles aux principes du plus pur patriotisme; ils sont encore prêts à *verser leur sang* pour le maintien de la Constitution, qui va réduire leur ville *à la plus déplorable nullité".* These people are not supposed to have endured those sufferings and injustices in a struggle for liberty, for the same account states truly that they had been always free; their patience in beggary and ruin, and their suffering, without remonstrance, the most flagrant and confessed injustice, if strictly true, can be nothing but the effect of this dire fanaticism. A great multitude all over France is in the same condition and the same temper.[lxxvi]

[41] See the proceedings of the confederation at Nantz.

It is not the confiscation of our church property from this example in France that I dread, though I think this would be no trifling evil. The great source of my solicitude is, lest it should ever be considered in England as the policy of a state to seek a resource in confiscations of any kind, or that any one description of citizens should be brought to regard any of the others as their proper prey.[42] Nations are wading deeper and deeper into an ocean of boundless debt. Public debts, which at first were a security to governments by interesting many in the public tranquillity, are likely in their excess to become the means of their subversion. If governments provide for these debts by heavy impositions, they perish by becoming odious to the people. If they do not provide for them, they will be undone by the efforts of the most dangerous of all parties—I mean an extensive, discontented monied interest, injured and not destroyed. The men who compose this interest look for their security, in the first instance, to the fidelity of government; in the second, to its power. If they find the old governments effete, worn out, and with their springs relaxed, so as not to be of sufficient vigor for their purposes, they may seek new ones that shall be possessed of more energy; and this energy will be derived, not from an acquisition of resources, but from a contempt of justice. Revolutions are favorable to confiscation; and it is impossible to know under what obnoxious names the next confiscations will be authorized. I am sure that the principles predominant in France extend to very many persons and descriptions of persons, in all countries, who think their innoxious indolence their security. This

---

[42] "Si plures sunt ii quibus improbe datum est, quam illi quibus injuste ademptum est, idcirco plus etiam valent? Non enim numero haec judicantur sed pondere. Quam autem habet aequitatem, ut agrum multis annis, aut etiam saeculis ante possessum, qui nullum habuit habeat; qui autem habuit amittat? Ac, propter hoc injuriae genus, Lacedaemonii Lysandrum Ephorum expulerunt: Agin regem (quod nunquam antea apud eos acciderat) necaverunt: exque eo tempore tantae discordiae secutae sunt, ut et tyranni existerint, et optimates exterminarentur, et preclarissime constituta respublica dilaberetur. Nec vero solum ipsa cecidit, sed etiam reliquam Graeciam evertit contagionibus malorum, quae a Lacedaemoniis profectae manarunt latius".—After speaking of the conduct of the model of true patriots, Aratus of Sicyon, which was in a very different spirit, he says, "Sic par est agere cum civibus; non ut bis jam vidimus, hastam in foro ponere et bona civium voci subjicere praeconis. At ille Graecus (id quod fuit sapientis et praestantis viri) omnibus consulendum esse putavit: eaque est summa ratio et sapientia boni civis, commoda civium non divellere, sed omnes eadem aequitate continere."[lxxvii] Cic. *Off.* 1. 2.

kind of innocence in proprietors may be argued into inutility; and inutility into an unfitness for their estates. Many parts of Europe are in open disorder. In many others there is a hollow murmuring under ground; a confused movement is felt that threatens a general earth-quake in the political world. Already confederacies and correspon-dencies of the most extraordinary nature are forming in several coun-tries.[43] In such a state of things we ought to hold ourselves upon our guard. In all mutations (if mutations must be) the circumstance which will serve most to blunt the edge of their mischief and to promote what good may be in them is that they should find us with our minds tenacious of justice and tender of property.

But it will be argued that this confiscation in France ought not to alarm other nations. They say it is not made from wanton rapacity, that it is a great measure of national policy adopted to remove an extensive, inveterate, superstitious mischief. It is with the greatest difficulty that I am able to separate policy from justice. Justice itself is the great standing policy of civil society, and any eminent departure from it, under any circumstances, lies under the suspicion of being no policy at all.

When men are encouraged to go into a certain mode of life by the existing laws, and protected in that mode as in a lawful occupation; when they have accommodated all their ideas and all their habits to it; when the law had long made their adherence to its rules a ground of reputation, and their departure from them a ground of disgrace and even of penalty—I am sure it is unjust in legislature, by an arbitrary act, to offer a sudden violence to their minds and their feelings, forcibly to degrade them from their state and condition and to stigmatize with shame and infamy that character and those cus-toms which before had been made the measure of their happiness and honor. If to this be added an expulsion from their habitations and a confiscation of all their goods, I am not sagacious enough to discover how this despotic sport, made of the feelings, consciences, prejudices, and properties of men, can be discriminated from the rankest tyranny.

If the injustice of the course pursued in France be clear, the policy of the measure, that is, the public benefit to be expected from it, ought to be at least as evident and at least as important. To a man who acts under the influence of no passion, who has nothing in view

---

[43] See two books entitled, *Einige Originalschriften des Illuminatenordens.—System und Folgen des Illuminatenordens.* München, 1787.

in his projects but the public good, a great difference will immediately strike him between what policy would dictate on the original introduction of such institutions and on a question of their total abolition, where they have cast their roots wide and deep, and where, by long habit, things more valuable than themselves are so adapted to them, and in a manner interwoven with them, that the one cannot be destroyed without notably impairing the other. He might be embarrassed if the case were really such as sophisters represent it in their paltry style of debating. But in this, as in most questions of state, there is a middle. There is something else than the mere alternative of absolute destruction or unreformed existence. *Spartam nactus es; hanc exorna.*[lxxviii] This is, in my opinion, a rule of profound sense and ought never to depart from the mind of an honest reformer. I cannot conceive how any man can have brought himself to that pitch of presumption to consider his country as nothing but *carte blanche*— upon which he may scribble whatever he pleases. A man full of warm, speculative benevolence may wish his society otherwise constituted than he finds it, but a good patriot and a true politician always considers how he shall make the most of the existing materials of his country. A disposition to preserve and an ability to improve, taken together, would be my standard of a statesman. Everything else is vulgar in the conception, perilous in the execution.

There are moments in the fortune of states when particular men are called to make improvements by great mental exertion. In those moments, even when they seem to enjoy the confidence of their prince and country, and to be invested with full authority, they have not always apt instruments. A politician, to do great things, looks for a *power,* what our workmen call a *purchase;* and if he finds that power, in politics as in mechanics, he cannot be at a loss to apply it. In the monastic institutions, in my opinion, was found a great *power* for the mechanism of politic benevolence. There were revenues with a public direction; there were men wholly set apart and dedicated to public purposes, without any other than public ties and public principles; men without the possibility of converting the estate of the community into a private fortune; men denied to self-interests, whose avarice is for some community; men to whom personal poverty is honor, and implicit obedience stands in the place of freedom. In vain shall a man look to the possibility of making such things when he wants them. The winds blow as they list. These institutions are the products of enthusiasm; they are the instruments of wisdom. Wisdom cannot create materials; they are the gifts of nature or of chance;

her pride is in the use. The perennial existence of bodies corporate and their fortunes are things particularly suited to a man who has long views; who meditates designs that require time in fashioning, and which propose duration when they are accomplished. He is not deserving to rank high, or even to be mentioned in the order of great statesmen, who, having obtained the command and direction of such a power as existed in the wealth, the discipline, and the habits of such corporations, as those which you have rashly destroyed, cannot find any way of converting it to the great and lasting benefit of his country[lxxix]. On the view of this subject, a thousand uses suggest themselves to a contriving mind. To destroy any power growing wild from the rank productive force of the human mind is almost tantamount, in the moral world, to the destruction of the apparently active properties of bodies in the material. It would be like the attempt to destroy (if it were in our competence to destroy) the expansive force of fixed air in nitre, or the power of steam, or of electricity, or of magnetism. These energies always existed in nature, and they were always discernible. They seemed, some of them unserviceable, some noxious, some no better than a sport to children, until contemplative ability, combining with practic skill, tamed their wild nature, subdued them to use, and rendered them at once the most powerful and the most tractable agents in subservience to the great views and designs of men. Did fifty thousand persons whose mental and whose bodily labor you might direct, and so many hundred thousand a year of a revenue which was neither lazy nor superstitious, appear too big for your abilities to wield? Had you no way of using them but by converting monks into pensioners? Had you no way of turning the revenue to account but through the improvident resource of a spendthrift sale? If you were thus destitute of mental funds, the proceeding is in its natural course. Your politicians do not understand their trade; and therefore they sell their tools.

But the institutions savor of superstition in their very principle, and they nourish it by a permanent and standing influence. This I do not mean to dispute, but this ought not to hinder you from deriving from superstition itself any resources which may thence be furnished for the public advantage. You derive benefits from many dispositions and many passions of the human mind which are of as doubtful a color, in the moral eye, as superstition itself. It was your business to correct and mitigate everything which was noxious in this passion, as in all the passions. But is superstition the greatest of all possible vices?

139

In its possible excess I think it becomes a very great evil. It is, however, a moral subject and, of course, admits of all degrees and all modifications. Superstition is the religion of feeble minds; and they must be tolerated in an intermixture of it, in some trifling or some enthusiastic shape or other, else you will deprive weak minds of a resource found necessary to the strongest. The body of all true religion consists, to be sure, in obedience to the will of the Sovereign of the world, in a confidence in his declarations, and in imitation of his perfections. The rest is our own. It may be prejudicial to the great end; it may be auxiliary. Wise men, who as such are not *admirers* (not admirers at least of the *Munera Terrae*[xxx]), are not violently attached to these things, nor do they violently hate them. Wisdom is not the most severe corrector of folly. They are the rival follies which mutually wage so unrelenting a war, and which make so cruel a use of their advantages as they can happen to engage the immoderate vulgar, on the one side or the other, in their quarrels. Prudence would be neuter, but if, in the contention between fond attachment and fierce antipathy concerning things in their nature not made to produce such heats, a prudent man were obliged to make a choice of what errors and excesses of enthusiasm he would condemn or bear, perhaps he would think the superstition which builds to be more tolerable than that which demolishes; that which adorns a country, than that which deforms it; that which endows, than that which plunders; that which disposes to mistaken beneficence, than that which stimulates to real injustice; that which leads a man to refuse to himself lawful pleasures, than that which snatches from others the scanty subsistence of their self-denial. Such, I think, is very nearly the state of the question between the ancient founders of monkish superstition and the superstition of the pretended philosophers of the hour.

For the present I postpone all consideration of the supposed public profit of the sale, which however I conceive to be perfectly delusive. I shall here only consider it as a transfer of property. On the policy of that transfer I shall trouble you with a few thoughts.

In every prosperous community something more is produced than goes to the immediate support of the producer. This surplus forms the income of the landed capitalist. It will be spent by a proprietor who does not labor. But this idleness is itself the spring of labor; this repose the spur to industry. The only concern of the state is that the capital taken in rent from the land should be returned again to the

140

industry from whence it came, and that its expenditure should be with the least possible detriment to the morals of those who expend it, and to those of the people to whom it is returned.

In all the views of receipt, expenditure, and personal employment, a sober legislator would carefully compare the possessor whom he was recommended to expel with the stranger who was proposed to fill his place. Before the inconveniences are incurred which *must* attend all violent revolutions in property through extensive confiscation, we ought to have some rational assurance that the purchasers of the confiscated property will be in a considerable degree more laborious, more virtuous, more sober, less disposed to extort an unreasonable proportion of the gains of the laborer, or to consume on themselves a larger share than is fit for the measure of an individual; or that they should be qualified to dispense the surplus in a more steady and equal mode, so as to answer the purposes of a politic expenditure, than the old possessors, call those possessors bishops, or canons, or commendatory abbots, or monks, or what you please. The monks are lazy. Be it so. Suppose them no otherwise employed than by singing in the choir. They are as usefully employed as those who neither sing nor say; as usefully even as those who sing upon the stage. They are as usefully employed as if they worked from dawn to dark in the innumerable servile, degrading, unseemly, unmanly, and often most unwholesome and pestiferous occupations to which by the social economy so many wretches are inevitably doomed. If it were not generally pernicious to disturb the natural course of things and to impede in any degree the great wheel of circulation which is turned by the strangely-directed labor of these unhappy people, I should be infinitely more inclined forcibly to rescue them from their miserable industry than violently to disturb the tranquil repose of monastic quietude. Humanity, and perhaps policy, might better justify me in the one than in the other. It is a subject on which I have often reflected, and never reflected without feeling from it. I am sure that no consideration, except the necessity of submitting to the yoke of luxury and the despotism of fancy, who in their own imperious way will distribute the surplus product of the soil, can justify the toleration of such trades and employments in a well-regulated state. But for this purpose of distribution, it seems to me that the idle expenses of monks are quite as well directed as the idle expenses of us lay-loiterers.

When the advantages of the possession and of the project are on a

141

par, there is no motive for a change. But in the present case, perhaps, they are not upon a par, and the difference is in favor of the possession. It does not appear to me that the expenses of those whom you are going to expel do in fact take a course so directly and so generally leading to vitiate and degrade and render miserable those through whom they pass as the expenses of those favorites whom you are intruding into their houses. Why should the expenditure of a great landed property, which is a dispersion of the surplus product of the soil, appear intolerable to you or to me when it takes its course through the accumulation of vast libraries, which are the history of the force and weakness of the human mind; through great collections of ancient records, medals, and coins, which attest and explain laws and customs; through paintings and statues that, by imitating nature, seem to extend the limits of creation; through grand monuments of the dead, which continue the regards and connections of life beyond the grave; through collections of the specimens of nature which become a representative assembly of all the classes and families of the world that by disposition facilitate and, by exciting curiosity, open the avenues to science? If by great permanent establishments all these objects of expense are better secured from the inconstant sport of personal caprice and personal extravagance, are they worse than if the same tastes prevailed in scattered individuals? Does not the sweat of the mason and carpenter, who toil in order to partake of the sweat of the peasant, flow as pleasantly and as salubriously in the construction and repair of the majestic edifices of religion as in the painted booths and sordid sties of vice and luxury; as honorably and as profitably in repairing those sacred works which grow hoary with innumerable years as on the momentary receptacles of transient voluptuousness; in opera houses, and brothels, and gaming houses, and clubhouses, and obelisks in the Champ de Mars? Is the surplus product of the olive and the vine worse employed in the frugal sustenance of persons whom the fictions of a pious imagination raise to dignity by construing in the service of God, than in pampering the innumerable multitude of those who are degraded by being made useless domestics, subservient to the pride of man? Are the decorations of temples an expenditure less worthy a wise man than ribbons, and laces, and national cockades, and *petit maisons,* and *petit soupers,* and all the innumerable fopperies and follies in which opulence sports away the burden of its superfluity?

We tolerate even these, not from love of them, but for fear of worse. We tolerate them because property and liberty, to a degree, require that toleration. But why proscribe the other, and surely, in every point of view, the more laudable, use of estates? Why, through the violation of all property, through an outrage upon every principle of liberty, forcibly carry them from the better to the worse?

This comparison between the new individuals and the old corps is made upon a supposition that no reform could be made in the latter. But in a question of reformation I always consider corporate bodies, whether sole or consisting of many, to be much more susceptible of a public direction by the power of the state, in the use of their property and in the regulation of modes and habits of life in their members, than private citizens ever can be or, perhaps, ought to be; and this seems to me a very material consideration for those who undertake anything which merits the name of a politic enterprise.—So far as to the estates of monasteries.

With regard to the estates possessed by bishops and canons and commendatory abbots, I cannot find out for what reason some land-ed estates may not be held otherwise than by inheritance. Can any philosophic spoiler undertake to demonstrate the positive or the comparative evil of having a certain, and that too a large, portion of landed property passing in succession through persons whose title to it is, always in theory and often in fact, an eminent degree of piety, morals, and learning—a property which, by its destination, in their turn, and on the score of merit, gives to the noblest families renovation and support, to the lowest the means of dignity and elevation; a property the tenure of which is the performance of some duty (whatever value you may choose to set upon that duty), and the character of whose proprietors demands, at least, an exterior decorum and gravity of manners; who are to exercise a generous but temperate hospitality; part of whose income they are to consider as a trust for charity; and who, even when they fail in their trust, when they slide from their character and degenerate into a mere common secular nobleman or gentleman, are in no respect worse than those who may succeed them in their forfeited possessions? Is it better that estates should be held by those who have no duty than by those who have one?—by those whose character and destination point to virtues than by those who have no rule and direction in the expenditure of their estates but their own will and appetite? Nor are these estates held together in the character or with the evils supposed inherent in mortmain. They pass from hand to hand with a more rapid circulation than any other. No excess is good; and, therefore, too great a proportion of landed property may be held officially for life; but it does not seem to me of material injury to any commonwealth that there should exist some estates that have a chance of being acquired by other means than the previous acquisition of money.

THIS LETTER HAS GROWN to a great length, though it is, indeed, short with regard to the infinite extent of the subject. Various avocations have from time to time called my mind from the subject[lxxxi]. I was not sorry to give myself leisure to observe whether, in the proceedings of the National Assembly, I might not find reasons to change or to qualify some of my first sentiments. Everything has confirmed me more strongly in my first opinions. It was my original purpose to take a view of the principles of the National Assembly with regard to the great and fundamental establishments, and to compare the whole of what you have substituted in the place of what you have destroyed with the several members of our British constitution. But this plan is of a greater extent than at first I computed, and I find that you have little desire to take the advantage of any examples. At present I must content myself with some remarks upon your establishments, reserving for another time what I proposed to say concerning the spirit of our British monarchy, aristocracy, and democracy, as practically they exist.[lxxxii]

I have taken a view of what has been done by the governing power in France. I have certainly spoken of it with freedom. Those whose principle it is to despise the ancient, permanent sense of mankind and to set up a scheme of society on new principles must naturally expect that such of us who think better of the judgment of the human race than of theirs should consider both them and their devices as men and schemes upon their trial. They must take it for granted that we attend much to their reason, but not at all to their authority. They have not one of the great influencing prejudices of mankind in their favor. They avow their hostility to opinion. Of course, they must expect no support from that influence which, with every other authority, they have deposed from the seat of its jurisdiction.[lxxxiii]

I can never consider this Assembly as anything else than a voluntary association of men who have availed themselves of circumstances to seize upon the power of the state. They have not the sanction and authority of the character under which they first met. They have assumed another of a very different nature and have completely altered and inverted all the relations in which they originally stood. They do not hold the authority they exercise under any constitutional law of the state. They have departed from the instructions of the people by whom they were sent, which instructions, as the Assembly did not act in virtue of any ancient usage or settled law, were the sole source of their authority. The most considerable of their acts have not been done by great majorities; and in this sort of near divisions, which carry only the constructive authority of the whole, strangers will consider reasons as well as resolutions.

If they had set up this new experimental government as a necessary substitute for an expelled tyranny, mankind would anticipate the time of prescription which, through long usage, mellows into legality governments that were violent in their commencement. All those who have affections which lead them to the conservation of civil order would recognize, even in its cradle, the child as legitimate which has been produced from those principles of cogent expediency to which all just governments owe their birth, and on which they justify their continuance. But they will be late and reluctant in giving any sort of countenance to the operations of a power which has derived its birth from no law and no necessity, but which, on the contrary, has had its origin in those vices and sinister practices by which the social union is often disturbed and sometimes destroyed. This Assembly has hardly a year's prescription. We have their own word for it that they have made a revolution. To make a revolution is a measure which, *prima fronte,* requires an apology. To make a revolution is to subvert the ancient state of our country; and no common reasons are called for to justify so violent a proceeding. The sense of mankind authorizes us to examine into the mode of acquiring new power, and to criticize on the use that is made of it, with less awe and reverence than that which is usually conceded to a settled and recognized authority.

In obtaining and securing their power the Assembly proceeds upon principles the most opposite to those which appear to direct them in . the use of it. An observation on this difference will let us into the true spirit of their conduct. Everything which they have done, or continue to do, in order to obtain and keep their power is by the most common arts. They proceed exactly as their ancestors of ambition have done before them.—Trace them through all their artifices, frauds, and violences, you can find nothing at all that is new. They follow precedents and examples with the punctilious exactness of a pleader. They never depart an iota from the authentic formulas of tyranny and usurpation. But in all the regulations relative to the public good, the spirit has been the very reverse of this. There they commit the whole to the mercy of untried speculations; they abandon the dearest interests of the public to those loose theories to which none of them would choose to trust the slightest of his private concerns. They make this difference, because in their desire of obtaining and securing power they are thoroughly in earnest; there they travel in the beaten road. The public interests, because about them they have no real solicitude, they abandon wholly to chance; I say to chance, because their schemes have nothing in experience to prove their tendency beneficial.

We must always see with a pity not unmixed with respect the errors of those who are timid and doubtful of themselves with regard to points wherein the happiness of mankind is concerned. But in these gentlemen there is nothing of the tender, parental solicitude which fears to cut up the infant for the sake of an experiment. In the vastness of their promises and the confidence of their predictions, they far outdo all the boasting of empirics. The arrogance of their pretensions in a manner provokes and challenges us to an inquiry into their foundation.

I AM convinced that there are men of considerable parts among the popular leaders in the National Assembly. Some of them display eloquence in their speeches and their writings. This cannot be without powerful and cultivated talents. But eloquence may exist without a proportionable degree of wisdom. When I speak of ability, I am obliged to distinguish. What they have done toward the support of their system bespeaks no ordinary men. In the system itself, taken as the scheme of a republic constructed for procuring the prosperity and security of the citizen, and for promoting the strength and grandeur of the state, I confess myself unable to find out anything which displays in a single instance the work of a comprehensive and disposing mind or even the provisions of a vulgar prudence. Their purpose everywhere seems to have been to evade and slip aside from *difficulty.* This it has been the glory of the great masters in all the arts to confront, and to overcome; and when they had overcome the first difficulty, to turn it into an instrument for new conquests over new difficulties, thus to enable them to extend the empire of their science and even to push forward, beyond the reach of their original thoughts, the landmarks of the human understanding itself. Difficulty is a severe instructor, set over us by the supreme ordinance of a parental Guardian and Legislator, who knows us better than we know ourselves, as he loves us better, too. *Pater ipse colendi haud facilem*

146

esse viam voluit.[lxxxiv] He that wrestles with us strengthens our nerves and sharpens our skill. Our antagonist is our helper. This amicable conflict with difficulty obliges us to an intimate acquaintance with our object and compels us to consider it in all its relations. It will not suffer us to be superficial. It is the want of nerves of understanding for such a task, it is the degenerate fondness for tricking shortcuts and little fallacious facilities that has in so many parts of the world created governments with arbitrary powers. They have created the late arbitrary monarchy of France. They have created the arbitrary republic of Paris. With them defects in wisdom are to be supplied by the plenitude of force. They get nothing by it. Commencing their labors on a principle of sloth, they have the common fortune of slothful men. The difficulties, which they rather had eluded than escaped, meet them again in their course; they multiply and thicken on them; they are involved, through a labyrinth of confused detail, in an industry without limit and without direction; and, in conclusion, the whole of their work becomes feeble, vicious, and insecure.

It is this inability to wrestle with difficulty which has obliged the arbitrary Assembly of France to commence their schemes of reform with abolition and total destruction.[44] But is it in destroying and pulling down that skill is displayed? Your mob can do this as well at least as your assemblies. The shallowest understanding, the rudest hand is more than equal to that task. Rage and frenzy will pull down more in half an hour than prudence, deliberation, and foresight can build up in a hundred years. The errors and defects of old establishments are visible and palpable. It calls for little ability to point them out; and where absolute power is given, it requires but a word wholly to abolish the vice and the establishment together. The same lazy but

---

[44] A leading member of the Assembly, M. Rabaud de St. Etienne, has expressed the principle of all their proceedings as clearly as possible—Nothing can be more simple: *"Tous les établissemens en France couronnent le malheur du peuple: pour le rendre heureux il faut le rénouveler; changer ses idées; changer ses loix; changer ses moeurs; . . . changer les hommes; changer les choses; changer les mots . . . tout détruire; oui, tout détruire; puisque tout est à recréer".* This gentleman was chosen president in an assembly not sitting at the *Quinze-vingt,* or the *Petits Maisons;* and composed of persons giving themselves out to be rational beings; but neither his ideas, language, or conduct, differ in the smallest degree from the discourses, opinions, and actions of those within and without the Assembly, who direct the operations of the machine now at work in France.[lxxxv]

restless disposition which loves sloth and hates quiet directs the politicians when they come to work for supplying the place of what they have destroyed. To make everything the reverse of what they have seen is quite as easy as to destroy. No difficulties occur in what has never been tried. Criticism is almost baffled in discovering the defects of what has not existed; and eager enthusiasm and cheating hope have all the wide field of imagination in which they may expatiate with little or no opposition.

At once to preserve and to reform is quite another thing. When the useful parts of an old establishment are kept, and what is superadded is to be fitted to what is retained, a vigorous mind, steady, persevering attention, various powers of comparison and combination, and the resources of an understanding fruitful in expedients are to be exercised; they are to be exercised in a continued conflict with the combined force of opposite vices, with the obstinacy that rejects all improvement and the levity that is fatigued and disgusted with everything of which it is in possession. But you may object—"A process of this kind is slow. It is not fit for an assembly which glories in performing in a few months the work of ages. Such a mode of reforming, possibly, might take up many years". Without question it might; and it ought. It is one of the excellences of a method in which time is amongst the assistants, that its operation is slow and in some cases almost imperceptible. If circumspection and caution are a part of wisdom when we work only upon inanimate matter, surely they become a part of duty, too, when the subject of our demolition and construction is not brick and timber but sentient beings, by the sudden alteration of whose state, condition, and habits multitudes may be rendered miserable. But it seems as if it were the prevalent opinion in Paris that an unfeeling heart and an undoubting confidence are the sole qualifications for a perfect legislator. Far different are my ideas of that high office. The true lawgiver ought to have a heart full of sensibility. He ought to love and respect his kind, and to fear himself. It may be allowed to his temperament to catch his ultimate object with an intuitive glance, but his movements toward it ought to be deliberate. Political arrangement, as it is a work for social ends, is to be only wrought by social means. There mind must conspire with mind. Time is required to produce that union of minds which alone can produce all the good we aim at. Our patience will achieve more than our force. If I might venture to appeal to what is so much out of fashion in Paris, I mean to experience, I should tell you that in my course I have known and, according to my measure, have co-operated with great men; and I have never yet seen any plan which has not been mended by the observation of those who were much inferior in understanding to the person who took the lead in the business. By a slow but well-sustained progress the effect of each step is watched; the good or ill success of the first gives light to us in the second; and so, from light to light, we are conducted with safety through the whole series. We see that the parts of the system do not clash. The evils latent in the most promising contrivances are provided for as they arise. One advantage is as little as possible sacrificed to another. We compensate, we reconcile, we balance. We are enabled to unite into a consistent whole the various anomalies and contending principles that are found in the minds and affairs of men. From hence arises, not an excellence in simplicity, but one far superior, an excellence in composition. Where the great interests of mankind are concerned through a long succession of generations, that succession ought to be admitted into some share in the councils which are so deeply to affect them. If justice requires this, the work itself requires the aid of more minds than one age can furnish. It is from this view of things that the best legislators have been often satisfied with the establishment of some sure, solid, and ruling principle in government—a power like that which some of the philosophers have called a plastic nature; and having fixed the principle, they have left it afterwards to its own operation.

To proceed in this manner, that is, to proceed with a presiding principle and a prolific energy is with me the criterion of profound wisdom. What your politicians think the marks of a bold, hardy genius are only proofs of a deplorable want of ability. By their violent haste and their defiance of the process of nature, they are delivered over blindly to every projector and adventurer, to every alchemist and empiric. They despair of turning to account anything that is common. Diet is nothing in their system of remedy. The worst of it is that this their despair of curing common distempers by regular methods arises not only from defect of comprehension but, I fear, from some malignity of disposition. Your legislators seem to have taken their opinions of all professions, ranks, and offices from the declamations and buffooneries of satirists; who would themselves be astonished if they were held to the letter of their own descriptions. By listening only to these, your leaders regard all things only on the side of their vices and faults, and view those vices and faults under every color of exaggeration. It is undoubtedly true, though it may seem paradoxical; but in general, those who are habitually employed in finding and displaying faults are unqualified for the work of reformation, because their minds are not only unfurnished with patterns of the fair and good, but by habit they come to take no delight in the contemplation of those things. By hating vices too much, they come to love men too little. It is, therefore, not wonderful that they should be indisposed and unable to serve them. From hence arises the complexional disposition of some of your guides to pull everything in pieces. At this malicious game they display the whole of their *quadrimanous*[lxxxvi] activity. As to the rest, the paradoxes of eloquent writers, brought forth purely as a sport of fancy to try their talents, to rouse attention and excite surprise, are taken up by these gentlemen, not in the spirit of the original authors, as means of cultivating their taste and improving their style. These paradoxes become with them serious grounds of action upon which they proceed in regulating the most important concerns of the state. Cicero ludicrously describes Cato as endeavoring to act, in the commonwealth, upon the school paradoxes which exercised the wits of the junior students in the Stoic philosophy. If this was true of Cato, these gentlemen copy after him in the manner of some persons who lived about his time—*pede nudo Catonem.*[lxxxvii] Mr. Hume told me that he had from Rousseau himself the secret of his principles of composition. That acute though eccentric observer had perceived that to strike and interest the public the marvelous must be produced; that the marvelous of the heathen mythology had long since lost its effect; that the giants, magicians, fairies, and heroes of romance which succeeded had exhausted the portion of credulity which belonged to their age; that now nothing was left to the writer but that species of the marvelous which might still be produced, and with as great an effect as ever, though in another way; that is, the marvelous in life, in manners, in characters, and in extraordinary situations, giving rise to new and unlooked-for strokes in politics and morals. I believe that were Rousseau alive and in one of his lucid intervals, he would be shocked at the practical frenzy of his scholars, who in their paradoxes are servile imitators, and even in their incredulity discover an implicit faith.

Men who undertake considerable things, even in a regular way, ought to give us ground to presume ability. But the physician of the state who, not satisfied with the cure of distempers, undertakes to regenerate constitutions ought to show uncommon powers. Some very unusual appearances of wisdom ought to display themselves on the face of the designs of those who appeal to no practice, and who copy after no model. Has any such been manifested? I shall take a view (it shall for the subject be a very short one) of what the Assembly has done with regard, first, to the constitution of the legislature; in the next place, to that of the executive power; then to that of the judicature; afterwards to the model of the army; and conclude with the system of finance; to see whether we can discover in any part of their schemes the portentous ability which may justify these bold undertakers in the superiority which they assume over mankind.

IT IS IN THE MODEL of the sovereign and presiding part of this new republic that we should expect their grand display. Here they were to prove their title to their proud demands. For the plan itself at large, and for the reasons on which it is grounded, I refer to the journals of the Assembly of the 29th of September, 1789, and to the subsequent proceedings which have made any alterations in the plan. So far as in a matter somewhat confused I can see light, the system remains substantially as it has been originally framed. My few remarks will be such as regard its spirit, its tendency, and its fitness for framing a popular commonwealth, which they profess theirs to be, suited to the ends for which any commonwealth, and particularly such a commonwealth, is made. At the same time I mean to consider its consistency with itself and its own principles.

Old establishments are tried by their effects. If the people are happy, united, wealthy, and powerful, we presume the rest. We conclude that to be good from whence good is derived. In old establishments various correctives have been found for their aberrations from theory. Indeed, they are the results of various necessities and expediencies. They are not often constructed after any theory; theories are rather drawn from them. In them we often see the end best obtained where the means seem not perfectly reconcilable to what we may fancy was the original scheme. The means taught by experience may be better suited to political ends than those contrived in the original project. They again react upon the primitive constitution, and sometimes improve the design itself, from which they seem to have departed. I think all this might be curiously exemplified in the British constitution. At worst, the errors and deviations of every kind in reckoning are found and computed, and the ship proceeds in her course. This is the case of old establishments; but in a new and merely theoretic system, it is expected that every contrivance shall

151

appear, on the face of it, to answer its ends, especially where the projectors are no way embarrassed with an endeavor to accommodate the new building to an old one, either in the walls or on the foundations.

The French builders, clearing away as mere rubbish whatever they found and, like their ornamental gardeners, forming everything into an exact level, propose to rest the whole local and general legislature on three bases of three different kinds: one geometrical, one arithmetical, and the third financial; the first of which they call the *basis of territory;* the second, the *basis of population;* and the third, the *basis of contribution.* For the accomplishment of the first of these purposes they divide the area of their country into eighty-three pieces, regularly square, of eighteen leagues by eighteen.[lxxxviii] These large divisions are called *Departments.* These they portion, proceeding by square measurement, into seventeen hundred and twenty districts called *Communes.* These again they subdivide, still proceeding by square measurement, into smaller districts called *Cantons,* making in all 6400.

At first view this geometrical basis of theirs presents not much to admire or to blame. It calls for no great legislative talents. Nothing more than an accurate land surveyor, with his chain, sight, and theodolite, is requisite for such a plan as this. In the old divisions of the country, various accidents at various times and the ebb and flow of various properties and jurisdictions settled their bounds. These bounds were not made upon any fixed system, undoubtedly. They were subject to some inconveniences, but they were inconveniences for which use had found remedies, and habit had supplied accommodation and patience. In this new pavement of square within square, and this organization and semi-organization, made on the system of Empedocles and Buffon, and not upon any politic principle, it is impossible that innumerable local inconveniences, to which men are not habituated, must not arise. But these I pass over, because it requires an accurate knowledge of the country, which I do not possess, to specify them.

When these state surveyors came to take a view of their work of measurement, they soon found that in politics the most fallacious of all things was geometrical demonstration. They had then recourse to another basis (or rather buttress) to support the building, which tottered on that false foundation. It was evident that the goodness of the soil, the number of the people, their wealth, and the largeness of their contribution made such infinite variations between square and square as to render mensuration a ridiculous standard of power in the commonwealth, and equality in geometry the most unequal of all measures in the distribution of men. However, they could not give it up. But dividing their political and civil representation into three parts, they allotted one of those parts to the square measurement, without a single fact or calculation to ascertain whether this territorial proportion of representation was fairly assigned, and ought upon any principle really to be a third. Having, however, given to geometry this portion (of a third for her dower) out of compliment, I suppose, to that sublime science, they left the other two to be scuffled for between the other parts, population and contribution.

When they came to provide for population, they were not able to proceed quite so smoothly as they had done in the field of their geometry. Here their arithmetic came to bear upon their juridical metaphysics. Had they stuck to their metaphysic principles, the arithmetical process would be simple indeed. Men, with them, are strictly equal and are entitled to equal rights in their own government. Each head, on this system, would have its vote, and every man would vote directly for the person who was to represent him in the legislature. "But soft—by regular degrees, not yet".[lxxxix] This metaphysic principle to which law, custom, usage, policy, reason were to yield is to yield itself to their pleasure. There must be many degrees, and some stages, before the representative can come in contact with his constituent. Indeed, as we shall soon see, these two persons are to have no sort of communion with each other. First, the voters in the *Canton,* who compose what they call "primary assemblies", are to have a *qualification.* What! a qualification on the indefeasible rights of men? Yes; but it shall be a very small qualification. Our injustice shall be very little oppressive: only the local valuation of three days' labor paid to the public. Why, this is not much, I readily admit, for anything but the utter subversion of your equalizing principle. As a qualification it might as well be let alone, for it answers no one purpose for which qualifications are established; and, on your ideas, it excludes from a vote the man of all others whose natural equality stands the most in need of protection and defense—I mean the man who has nothing else but his natural equality to guard him. You order him to buy the right which you before told him nature had given to him gratuitously at his birth, and of which no authority on earth could lawfully deprive him. With regard to the person who

153

cannot come up to your market, a tyrannous aristocracy, as against him, is established at the very outset by you who pretend to be its sworn foe.

The gradation proceeds. These primary assemblies of the *Canton* elect deputies to the *Commune;* one for every two hundred qualified inhabitants. Here is the first medium put between the primary elector and the representative legislator; and here a new turnpike is fixed for taxing the rights of men with a second qualification; for none can be elected into the *Commune* who does not pay the amount of ten days' labor. Nor have we yet done. There is still to be another gradation.[45] These *Communes,* chosen by the *Canton,* choose to the *Department;* and the deputies of the *Department* choose their deputies to the *National Assembly.* Here is a third barrier of a senseless qualification. Every deputy to the National Assembly must pay, in direct contribution, to the value of a *mark of silver.* Of all these qualifying barriers we must think alike—that they are impotent to secure independence, strong only to destroy the rights of men.

In all this process, which in its fundamental elements affects to consider only *population* upon a principle of natural right, there is a manifest attention to *property,* which, however just and reasonable on other schemes, is on theirs perfectly unsupportable.

When they come to their third basis, that of *contribution,* we find that they have more completely lost sight of their rights of men. This last basis rests *entirely* on property. A principle totally different from the equality of men, and utterly irreconcilable to it, is thereby admitted; but no sooner is this principle admitted than (as usual) it is subverted; and it is not subverted (as we shall presently see) to approximate the inequality of riches to the level of nature. The additional share in the third portion of representation (a portion reserved exclusively for the higher contribution) is made to regard the *district* only, and not the individuals in it who pay. It is easy to perceive, by the course of their reasonings, how much they were

---

[45] The Assembly, in executing the plan of their committee, made some alterations. They have struck out one stage in these gradations; this removes a part of the objection; but the main objection, namely, that in their scheme the first constituent voter has no connection with the representative legislator, remains in all its force. There are other alterations, some possibly for the better, some certainly for the worse; but to the author the merit or demerit of these smaller alterations appears to be of no moment where the scheme itself is fundamentally vicious and absurd.

embarrassed by their contradictory ideas of the rights of men and the privileges of riches. The committee of constitution do as good as admit that they are wholly irreconcilable. "The relation with regard to the contributions is without doubt *null* (say they) when the question is on the balance of the political rights as between individual and individual, without which *personal equality would be destroyed* and *an aristocracy of the rich* would be established. But this inconvenience entirely disappears when the proportional relation of the contribution is only considered in the *great masses,* and is solely between province and province; it serves in that case only to form a just reciprocal proportion between the cities without affecting the personal rights of the citizens".

Here the principle of *contribution,* as taken between man and man, is reprobated as *null* and destructive to equality, and as pernicious, too, because it leads to the establishment of an *aristocracy of the rich.* However, it must not be abandoned. And the way of getting rid of the difficulty is to establish the inequality as between department and department, leaving all the individuals in each department upon an exact par. Observe that this parity between individuals had been before destroyed when the qualifications within the departments were settled; nor does it seem a matter of great importance whether the equality of men be injured by masses or individually. An individual is not of the same importance in a mass represented by a few as in a mass represented by many. It would be too much to tell a man jealous of his equality that the elector has the same franchise who votes for three members as he who votes for ten.

Now take it in the outer point of view and let us suppose their principle of representation according to contribution, that is, according to riches, to be well imagined and to be a necessary basis for their republic. In this their third basis they assume that riches ought to be respected, and that justice and policy require that they should entitle men, in some mode or other, to a larger share in the administration of public affairs; it is now to be seen how the Assembly provides for the preeminence, or even for the security, of the rich by conferring, in virtue of their opulence, that larger measure of power to their district which is denied to them personally. I readily admit (indeed I should lay it down as a fundamental principle) that in a republican government which has a democratic basis the rich do require an additional security above what is necessary to them in monarchies. They are subject to envy, and through envy to oppression. On the present scheme it is impossible to divine what advantage they derive from the aristocratic preference upon which the unequal representation of the masses is founded. The rich cannot feel it, either as a support to dignity or as security to fortune, for the aristocratic mass is generated from purely democratic principles, and the preference given to it in the general representation has no sort of reference to, or connection with, the persons upon account of whose property this superiority of the mass is established. If the contrivers of this scheme meant any sort of favor to the rich, in consequence of their contribution, they ought to have conferred the privilege either on the individual rich or on some class formed of rich persons (as historians represent Servius Tullius to have done in the early constitution of Rome), because the contest between the rich and the poor is not a struggle between corporation and corporation, but a contest between men and men—a competition not between districts, but between descriptions. It would answer its purpose better if the scheme were inverted: that the vote of the masses were rendered equal, and that the votes within each mass were proportioned to property.

Let us suppose one man in a district (it is an easy supposition) to contribute as much as a hundred of his neighbors. Against these he has but one vote. If there were but one representative for the mass, his poor neighbors would outvote him by a hundred to one for that single representative. Bad enough. But amends are to be made him. How? The district, in virtue of his wealth, is to choose, say, ten members instead of one; that is to say, by paying a very large contribution he has the happiness of being outvoted a hundred to one by the poor for ten representatives, instead of being outvoted exactly in the same proportion for a single member. In truth, instead of benefiting by this superior quantity of representation, the rich man is subjected to an additional hardship. The increase of representation within his province sets up nine persons more, and as many more than nine as there may be democratic candidates, to cabal and intrigue, and to flatter the people at his expense and to his oppression. An interest is by this means held out to multitudes of the inferior sort, in obtaining a salary of eighteen livres a day (to them a vast object) besides the pleasure of a residence in Paris and their share in the government of the kingdom. The more the objects of ambition are multiplied and become democratic, just in that proportion the rich are endangered.

Thus it must fare between the poor and the rich in the province deemed aristocratic, which in its internal relation is the very reverse of that character. In its external relation, that is, its relation to the other provinces, I cannot see how the unequal representation which is given to masses on account of wealth becomes the means of preserving the equipoise and the tranquillity of the commonwealth. For if it be one of the objects to secure the weak from being crushed by the strong (as in all society undoubtedly it is), how are the smaller and poorer of these masses to be saved from the tyranny of the more wealthy? Is it by adding to the wealthy further and more systematical means of oppressing them? When we come to a balance of representation between corporate bodies, provincial interests, emulations, and jealousies are full as likely to arise among them as among individuals; and their divisions are likely to produce a much hotter spirit of dissension, and something leading much more nearly to a war.

I see that these aristocratic masses are made upon what is called the principle of direct contribution. Nothing can be a more unequal standard than this. The indirect contribution, that which arises from duties on consumption, is in truth a better standard and follows and discovers wealth more naturally than this of direct contribution. It is difficult, indeed, to fix a standard of local preference on account of the one, or of the other, or of both, because some provinces may pay the more of either or of both on account of causes not intrinsic, but originating from those very districts over whom they have obtained a preference in consequence of their ostensible contribution. If the masses were independent, sovereign bodies who were to provide for a federative treasury by distinct contingents, and that the revenue had not (as it has) many impositions running through the whole, which affect men individually, and not corporately, and which, by their nature, confound all territorial limits, something might be said for the basis of contribution as founded on masses. But of all things, this representation, to be measured by contribution, is the most difficult to settle upon principles of equity in a country which considers its districts as members of a whole. For a great city, such as Bordeaux or Paris, appears to pay a vast body of duties, almost out of all assignable proportion to other places, and its mass is considered accordingly. But are these cities the true contributors in that proportion? No. The consumers of the commodities imported into Bordeaux, who are scattered through all France, pay the import duties of Bordeaux. The produce of the vintage in Guienne and Languedoc give to that city the means of its contribution growing out of an export commerce. The landholders who spend their estates in Paris, and are thereby the creators of that city, contribute for Paris from the provinces out of which their revenues arise. Very nearly the same arguments will apply to the representative share given on account of *direct* contributions, because the direct contribution must be assessed on wealth, real or presumed; and that local wealth will itself arise from causes not local, and which therefore in equity ought not to produce a local preference.

It is very remarkable that in this fundamental regulation which settles the representation of the mass upon the direct contribution, they have not yet settled how that direct contribution shall be laid, and how apportioned. Perhaps there is some latent policy toward the continuance of the present Assembly in this strange procedure. However, until they do this, they can have no certain constitution. It must depend at last upon the system of taxation, and must vary with every variation in that system. As they have contrived matters, their taxation does not so much depend on their constitution as their constitution on their taxation. This must introduce great confusion among the masses, as the variable qualification for votes within the district must, if ever real contested elections take place, cause infinite internal controversies.

TO compare together the three bases, not on their political reason, but on the ideas on which the Assembly works, and to try its consistency with itself, we cannot avoid observing that the principle which the committee call the basis of *population* does not begin to operate from the same point with the two other principles called the bases of *territory* and of *contribution,* which are both of an aristocratic nature. The consequence is that, where all three begin to operate together, there is the most absurd inequality produced by the operation of the former on the two latter principles. Every canton contains four square leagues, and is estimated to contain, on the average, 4000 inhabitants or 680 voters in the *primary assemblies,* which vary in numbers with the population of the canton, and send *one deputy* to the *commune* for every 200 voters. *Nine cantons* make a *commune.*

Now let us take *a canton* containing *a seaport town of trade,* or *a great manufacturing town.* Let us suppose the population of this canton to be 12,700 inhabitants, or 2193 voters, forming *three primary assemblies,* and sending *ten deputies* to the *commune.*

Oppose to this *one* canton *two* others of the remaining eight in the same commune. These we may suppose to have their fair population of 4000 inhabitants and 680 voters each, or 8000 inhabitants and 1360 voters, both together. These will form only *two primary assem-*

blies and send only *six* deputies to the *commune.*

When the assembly of the *commune* comes to vote on the *basis of territory,* which principle is first admitted to operate in that assembly, the *single canton* which has *half* the territory of the *other two* will have *ten* voices to *six* in the election of *three deputies* to the assembly of the department chosen on the express ground of a representation of territory.

This inequality, striking as it is, will be yet highly aggravated if we suppose, as we fairly may, the *several* other cantons of the *commune* to fall proportionably short of the average population, as much as the *principal canton* exceeds it. Now as to *the basis of contribution,* which also is a principle admitted first to operate in the assembly of the *commune.* Let us again take *one* canton, such as is stated above. If the whole of the direct contributions paid by a great trading or manufacturing town be divided equally among the inhabitants, each individual will be found to pay much more than an individual living in the country according to the same average. The whole paid by the inhabitants of the former will be more than the whole paid by the inhabitants of the latter—we may fairly assume one-third more. Then the 12,700 inhabitants, or 2193 voters of the canton, will pay as much as 19,050 inhabitants, or 3289 voters of the *other cantons,* which are nearly the estimated proportion of inhabitants and voters of *five* other cantons. Now the 2193 voters will, as I before said, send only *ten* deputies to the assembly; the 3289 voters will send *sixteen.* Thus, for an *equal* share in the contribution of the whole *commune,* there will be a difference of *sixteen* voices to *ten* in voting for deputies to be chosen on the principle of representing the general contribution of the whole *commune.*

By the same mode of computation we shall find 15,875 inhabitants, or 2741 voters of the *other* cantons, who pay *one-sixth* LESS to the contribution of the whole *commune,* will have *three* VOICES MORE than the 12,700 inhabitants, or 2193 voters of the *one* canton.

Such is the fantastical and unjust inequality between mass and mass in this curious repartition of the rights of representation arising out of *territory* and *contribution.* The qualifications which these confer are in truth negative qualifications, that give a right in an inverse proportion to the possession of them.

In this whole contrivance of the three bases, consider it in any light you please, I do not see a variety of objects reconciled in one consistent whole, but several contradictory principles reluctantly and irreconcilably brought and held together by your philosophers, like wild beasts shut up in a cage to claw and bite each other to their mutual destruction.

I am afraid I have gone too far into their way of considering the formation of a constitution. They have much, but bad, metaphysics; much, but bad, geometry; much, but false, proportionate arithmetic; but if it were all as exact as metaphysics, geometry, and arithmetic ought to be, and if their schemes were perfectly consistent in all their parts, it would make only a more fair and sightly vision. It is remarkable that, in a great arrangement of mankind, not one reference whatsoever is to be found to anything moral or anything politic, nothing that relates to the concerns, the actions, the passions, the interests of men. *Hominem non sapiunt.*[xc]

You see I only consider this constitution as electoral, and leading by steps to the National Assembly. I do not enter into the internal government of the departments and their genealogy through the communes and cantons. These local governments are, in the original plan, to be as nearly as possible composed in the same manner and on the same principles with the elective assemblies. They are each of them bodies perfectly compact and rounded in themselves.

You cannot but perceive in this scheme that it has a direct and immediate tendency to sever France into a variety of republics, and to render them totally independent of each other without any direct constitutional means of coherence, connection, or subordination, except what may be derived from their acquiescence in the determinations of the general congress of the ambassadors from each independent republic. Such in reality is the National Assembly, and such governments I admit do exist in the world, though in forms infinitely more suitable to the local and habitual circumstances of their people. But such associations, rather than bodies politic, have generally been the effect of necessity, not choice; and I believe the present French power is the very first body of citizens who, having obtained full authority to do with their country what they pleased, have chosen to dissever it in this barbarous manner.

It is impossible not to observe that, in the spirit of this geometrical distribution and arithmetical arrangement, these pretended citizens treat France exactly like a country of conquest. Acting as conquerors, they have imitated the policy of the harshest of that harsh race. The policy of such barbarous victors, who contemn a subdued people and insult their feelings, has ever been, as much as in them lay, to destroy all vestiges of the ancient country, in religion, in polity, in laws, and in manners; to confound all territorial limits; to produce a general poverty; to put up their properties to auction; to crush their princes, nobles, and pontiffs; to lay low everything which had lifted its head above the level, or which could serve to combine or rally, in their distresses, the disbanded people under the standard of old opinion. They have made France free in the manner in which those sincere friends to the rights of mankind, the Romans, freed Greece, Macedon, and other nations. They destroyed the bonds of their union under color of providing for the independence of each of their cities.

When the members who compose these new bodies of cantons, communes, and departments—arrangements purposely produced through the medium of confusion—begin to act, they will find themselves in a great measure strangers to one another. The electors and elected throughout, especially in the rural *cantons,* will be frequently without any civil habitudes or connections, or any of that natural discipline which is the soul of a true republic. Magistrates and collectors of revenue are now no longer acquainted with their districts, bishops with their dioceses, or curates with their parishes. These new colonies of the rights of men bear a strong resemblance to that sort of military colonies which Tacitus has observed upon in the declining policy of Rome. In better and wiser days (whatever course they took with foreign nations) they were careful to make the elements of methodical subordination and settlement to be coeval, and even to lay the foundations of civil discipline in the military.[46] But when all the good arts had fallen into ruin, they proceeded, as your Assembly does, upon the equality of men, and with as little judgment and as little care for those things which make a republic tolerable or durable. But in this, as well as almost every instance, your new commonwealth is born and bred and fed in those corruptions which mark degenerated and worn-out republics. Your child comes into the world with the symptoms of death: the *facies Hippocratica*[xcii] forms the character of its physiognomy, and the prognostic of its fate.

[46] Non, ut olim, universae legiones deducebantur cum tribunis, et centurionibus, et sui cujusque ordinis militibus, ut consensu et caritate rempublicam ·afficerent; sed ignoti inter se, diversis manipulis, sine rectore, sine affectibus mutuis, quasi ex alio genere mortalium, repente in unum collecti, numerus magis quam colonia.[xci] Tac. *Annal.* 1. 14, sect. 27. All this will be still more applicable to the unconnected, rotatory, biennial national assemblies, in this absurd and senseless constitution.

The legislators who framed the ancient republics knew that their business was too arduous to be accomplished with no better apparatus than the metaphysics of an undergraduate, and the mathematics and arithmetic of an exciseman. They had to do with men, and they were obliged to study human nature. They had to do with citizens, and they were obliged to study the effects of those habits which are communicated by the circumstances of civil life. They were sensible that the operation of this second nature on the first produced a new combination; and thence arose many diversities amongst men, according to their birth, their education, their professions, the periods of their lives, their residence in towns or in the country, their several ways of acquiring and of fixing property, and according to the quality of the property itself—all which rendered them as it were so many different species of animals. From hence they thought themselves obliged to dispose their citizens into such classes, and to place them in such situations in the state, as their peculiar habits might qualify them to fill, and to allot to them such appropriated privileges as might secure to them what their specific occasions required, and which might furnish to each description such force as might protect it in the conflict caused by the diversity of interests that must exist and must contend in all complex society; for the legislator would have been ashamed that the coarse husbandman should well know how to assort and to use his sheep, horses, and oxen, and should have enough of common sense not to abstract and equalize them all into animals without providing for each kind an appropriate food, care, and employment, whilst he, the economist, disposer, and shepherd of his own kindred, subliming himself into an airy metaphysician, was resolved to know nothing of his flocks but as men in general. It is for this reason that Montesquieu observed very justly that in their classification of the citizens the great legislators of antiquity made the greatest display of their powers, and even soared above themselves. It is here that your modern legislators have gone deep into the negative series, and sunk even below their own nothing. As the first sort of legislators attended to the different kinds of citizens and combined them into one commonwealth, the others, the metaphysical and alchemistical legislators, have taken the direct contrary course. They have attempted to confound all sorts of citizens, as well as they could, into one homogeneous mass; and then they divided this their amalgama into a number of incoherent republics. They reduce men to loose counters, merely for the sake of simple telling, and not to figures whose power is to arise from their place in the table. The elements of their own metaphysics might have taught them better lessons. The troll of their categorical table might have informed them that there was something else in the intellectual world besides *substance* and *quantity.* They might learn from the catechism of metaphysics that there were eight heads more[47] in every complex deliberation which they have never thought of, though these, of all the ten, are the subjects on which the skill of man can operate anything at all.

So far from this able disposition of some of the old republican legislators, which follows with a solicitous accuracy the moral conditions and propensities of men, they have leveled and crushed together all the orders which they found, even under the coarse unartificial arrangement of the monarchy, in which mode of government the classing of the citizens is not of so much importance as in a republic. It is true, however, that every such classification, if properly ordered, is good in all forms of government, and composes a strong barrier against the excesses of despotism, as well as it is the necessary means of giving effect and permanence to a republic. For want of something of this kind, if the present project of a republic should fail, all securities to a moderated freedom fail along with it; all the indirect restraints which mitigate despotism are removed, insomuch that if monarchy should ever again obtain an entire ascendancy in France, under this or under any other dynasty, it will probably be, if not voluntarily tempered at setting out by the wise and virtuous counsels of the prince, the most completely arbitrary power that has ever appeared on earth. This is to play a most desperate game.

The confusion which attends on all such proceedings they even declare to be one of their objects, and they hope to secure their constitution by a terror of a return of those evils which attended their making it. "By this," say they, "its destruction will become difficult to authority, which cannot break it up without the entire disorganization of the whole state." They presume that, if this authority should ever come to the same degree of power that they have acquired, it would make a more moderate and chastised use of it, and would piously tremble entirely to disorganize the state in the savage manner that they have done. They expect, from the virtues of returning despotism, the security which is to be enjoyed by the offspring of their popular vices.

---

[47] *Qualitas, relatio, actio, passio, ubi, quando, situs, habitus.*[xciii]

I WISH, Sir, that you and my readers would give an attentive perusal to the work of M. de Calonne on this subject. It is, indeed, not only an eloquent, but an able and instructive, performance. I confine myself to what he says relative to the constitution of the new state and to the condition of the revenue. As to the disputes of this minister with his rivals, I do not wish to pronounce upon them. As little do I mean to hazard any opinion concerning his ways and means, financial or political, for taking his country out of its present disgraceful and deplorable situation of servitude, anarchy, bankruptcy, and beggary. I cannot speculate quite so sanguinely as he does; but he is a Frenchman, and has a closer duty relative to those objects, and better means of judging of them, than I can have. I wish that the formal avowal which he refers to, made by one of the principal leaders in the Assembly concerning the tendency of their scheme to bring France not only from a monarchy to a republic, but from a republic to a mere confederacy, may be very particularly attended to. It adds new force to my observations, and indeed M. de Calonne's work supplies my deficiencies by many new and striking arguments on most of the subjects of this letter.[48]

It is this resolution, to break their country into separate republics, which has driven them into the greatest number of their difficulties and contradictions. If it were not for this, all the questions of exact equality and these balances, never to be settled, of individual rights, population, and contribution would be wholly useless. The representation, though derived from parts, would be a duty which equally regarded the whole. Each deputy to the Assembly would be the representative of France, and of all its descriptions, of the many and of the few, of the rich and of the poor, of the great districts and of the small. All these districts would themselves be subordinate to some standing authority, existing independently of them, an authority in which their representation, and everything that belongs to it, originated, and to which it was pointed. This standing, unalterable, fundamental government would make, and it is the only thing which could make, that territory truly and properly a whole. With us, when we elect popular representatives, we send them to a council in which each man individually is a subject and submitted to a government complete in all its ordinary functions. With you the elective Assembly is the sovereign, and the sole sovereign; all the members are therefore integral parts of this sole sovereignty. But with us it is totally

[48] See *l'Etat de la France,* p. 363.

different. With us the representative, separated from the other parts, can have no action and no existence. The government is the point of reference of the several members and districts of our representation. This is the center of our unity. This government of reference is a trustee for the *whole,* and not for the parts. So is the other branch of our public council, I mean the House of Lords. With us the king and the lords are several and joint securities for the equality of each district, each province, each city. When did you hear in Great Britain of any province suffering from the inequality of its representation, what district from having no representation at all? Not only our monarchy and our peerage secure the equality on which our unity depends, but it is the spirit of the House of Commons itself. The very inequality of representation, which is so foolishly complained of, is perhaps the very thing which prevents us from thinking or acting as members for districts. Cornwall elects as many members as all Scotland. But is Cornwall better taken care of than Scotland? Few trouble their heads about any of your bases, out of some giddy clubs. Most of those who wish for any change, upon any plausible grounds, desire it on different ideas.

Your new constitution is the very reverse of ours in its principle; and I am astonished how any persons could dream of holding out anything done in it as an example for Great Britain. With you there is little, or rather no, connection between the last representative and the first constituent. The member who goes to the National Assembly is not chosen by the people, nor accountable to them. There are three elections before he is chosen; two sets of magistracy intervene between him and the primary assembly, so as to render him, as I have said, an ambassador of a state, and not the representative of the people within a state. By this the whole spirit of the election is changed, nor can any corrective which your constitution-mongers have devised render him anything else than what he is. The very attempt to do it would inevitably introduce a confusion, if possible, more horrid than the present. There is no way to make a connection between the original constituent and the representative, but by the circuitous means which may lead the candidate to apply in the first instance to the primary electors, in order that by their authoritative instructions (and something more perhaps) these primary electors may force the two succeeding bodies of electors to make a choice agreeable to their wishes. But this would plainly subvert the whole scheme. It would be to plunge them back into that tumult and

165

confusion of popular election which, by their interposed gradation of elections, they mean to avoid, and at length to risk the whole fortune of the state with those who have the least knowledge of it and the least interest in it. This is a perpetual dilemma into which they are thrown by the vicious, weak, and contradictory principles they have chosen. Unless the people break up and level this gradation, it is plain that they do not at all substantially elect to the Assembly; indeed, they elect as little in appearance as reality.

What is it we all seek for in an election? To answer its real purposes, you must first possess the means of knowing the fitness of your man; and then you must retain some hold upon him by personal obligation or dependence. For what end are these primary electors complimented, or rather mocked, with a choice? They can never know anything of the qualities of him that is to serve them, nor has he any obligation whatsoever to them. Of all the powers unfit to be delegated by those who have any real means of judging, that most peculiarly unfit is what relates to a *personal* choice. In case of abuse, that body of primary electors never can call the representative to an account for his conduct. He is too far removed from them in the chain of representation. If he acts improperly at the end of his two years' lease, it does not concern him for two years more. By the new French constitution the best and the wisest representatives go equally with the worst into this *Limbus Patrum*.[xciv] Their bottoms are supposed foul, and they must go into dock to be refitted. Every man who has served in an assembly is ineligible for two years after. Just as these magistrates begin to learn their trade, like chimney sweepers, they are disqualified for exercising it. Superficial, new, petulant acquisition, and interrupted, dronish, broken, ill recollection is to be the destined character of all your future governors. Your constitution has too much of jealousy to have much of sense in it. You consider the breach of trust in the representative so principally that you do not at all regard the question of his fitness to execute it.

This purgatory interval is not unfavorable to a faithless representative, who may be as good a canvasser as he was a bad governor. In this time he may cabal himself into a superiority over the wisest and most virtuous. As in the end all the members of this elective constitution are equally fugitive and exist only for the election, they may be no longer the same persons who had chosen him, to whom he is to be responsible when he solicits for a renewal of his trust. To call all the secondary electors of the *Commune* to account is ridiculous, impracticable, and unjust; they may themselves have been deceived in their choice, as the third set of electors, those of the *Department,* may be in theirs. In your elections responsibility cannot exist.

FINDING NO SORT OF PRINCIPLE of coherence with each other in the nature and constitution of the several new republics of France, I considered what cement the legislators had provided for them from any extraneous materials. Their confederations, their *spectacles,* their civic feasts, and their enthusiasm I take no notice of; they are nothing but mere tricks; but tracing their policy through their actions, I think I can distinguish the arrangements by which they propose to hold these republics together. The first is the *confiscation,* with the compulsory paper currency annexed to it; the second is the supreme power of the city of Paris; the third is the general army of the state. Of this last I shall reserve what I have to say until I come to consider the army as a head by itself.

AS to the operation of the first (the confiscation and paper currency) merely as a cement, I cannot deny that these, the one depending on the other, may for some time compose some sort of cement if their madness and folly in the management, and in the tempering of the parts together, does not produce a repulsion in the very outset. But allowing to the scheme some coherence and some duration, it appears to me that if, after a while, the confiscation should not be found sufficient to support the paper coinage (as I am morally certain it will not), then, instead of cementing, it will add infinitely to the dissociation, distraction, and confusion of these confederate republics, both with relation to each other and to the several parts within themselves. But if the confiscation should so far succeed as to sink the paper currency, the cement is gone with the circulation. In the meantime its binding force will be very uncertain, and it will straiten or relax with every variation in the credit of the paper.

One thing only is certain in this scheme, which is an effect seemingly collateral, but direct, I have no doubt, in the minds of those who conduct this business, that is, its effect in producing an *oligarchy* in every one of the republics. A paper circulation, not founded on any real money deposited or engaged for, amounting already to forty-four millions of English money, and this currency by force substituted in the place of the coin of the kingdom, becoming thereby the substance of its revenue as well as the medium of all its commercial and civil intercourse, must put the whole of what power, authority, and influence is left, in any form whatsoever it may assume, into the hands of the managers and conductors of this circulation.

In England, we feel the influence of the Bank, though it is only the center of a voluntary dealing. He knows little indeed of the influence of money upon mankind who does not see the force of the management of a monied concern which is so much more extensive and in its nature so much more depending on the managers than any of ours. But this is not merely a money concern. There is another member in the system inseparably connected with this money management. It consists in the means of drawing out at discretion portions of the confiscated lands for sale, and carrying on a process of continual transmutation of paper into land, and land into paper. When we follow this process in its effects, we may conceive something of the intensity of the force with which this system must operate. By this means the spirit of money-jobbing and speculation goes into the mass of land itself and incorporates with it. By this kind of operation that species of property becomes (as it were) volatilized; it assumes an unnatural and monstrous activity, and thereby throws into the hands of the several managers, principal and subordinate, Parisian and provincial, all the representative of money and perhaps a full tenth part of all the land in France, which has now acquired the worst and most pernicious part of the evil of a paper circulation, the greatest possible uncertainty in its value. They have reversed the Latonian kindness to the landed property of Delos.[xcv] They have sent theirs to be blown about, like the light fragments of a wreck, *oras et littora circum.*

The new dealers, being all habitually adventurers and without any fixed habits of local predilections, will purchase to job out again, as the market of paper or of money or of land shall present an advantage. For though a holy bishop thinks that agriculture will derive great advantages from the "enlightened" usurers who are to purchase the church confiscations, I, who am not a good but an old farmer, with great humility beg leave to tell his late lordship that usury is not a tutor of agriculture; and if the word "enlightened" be understood according to the new dictionary, as it always is in your new schools, I cannot conceive how a man's not believing in God can teach him to cultivate the earth with the least of any additional skill or encouragement. *"Diis immortalibus sero",*[xcvi] said an old Roman, when he held one handle of the plough, whilst Death held the other. Though you were to join in the commission all the directors of the two academies to the directors of the *Caisse d'Escompte,* one old, experienced peasant is worth them all. I have got more information upon a curious and interesting branch of husbandry, in one short conversation with an old Carthusian monk, than I have derived from all the Bank directors that I have ever conversed with. However, there is no cause for apprehension from the meddling of money dealers with rural economy. These gentlemen are too wise in their generation. At first, perhaps, their tender and susceptible imaginations may be captivated with the innocent and unprofitable delights of a pastoral life; but in a little time they will find that agriculture is a trade much more laborious, and much less lucrative, than that which they had left. After making its panegyric, they will turn their backs on it like their great precursor and prototype. They may, like him, begin by singing *"Beatus ille"* but what will be the end?

> *Haec ubi locutus foenerator Alphius,*
> *Jam jam futurus rusticus*
> *Omnem redegit idibus pecuniam;*
> *Quaerit calendis ponere.*[xcvii]

They will cultivate the *Caisse d'Eglise,* under the sacred auspices of this prelate, with much more profit than its vineyards and its cornfields. They will employ their talents according to their habits and their interests. They will not follow the plough whilst they can direct treasuries and govern provinces.

Your legislators, in everything new, are the very first who have founded a commonwealth upon gaming, and infused this spirit into it as its vital breath. The great object in these politics is to metamorphose France from a great kingdom into one great playtable; to turn its inhabitants into a nation of gamesters; to make speculation as extensive as life; to mix it with all its concerns and to divert the whole of the hopes and fears of the people from their usual channels into the impulses, passions, and superstitions of those who live on chances. They loudly proclaim their opinion that this their present system of a republic cannot possibly exist without this kind of gaming fund, and that the very thread of its life is spun out of the staple of these speculations. The old gaming in funds was mischievous enough, undoubtedly, but it was so only to individuals. Even when it had its greatest extent, in the Mississippi and South Sea,[xcviii] it affected but few, comparatively; where it extends further, as in lotteries, the spirit has but a single object. But where the law, which in most circumstances forbids, and in none countenances, gaming, is itself debauched so as to reverse its nature and policy and expressly to force the subject to this destructive table by bringing the spirit and symbols of gaming into the minutest matters and engaging everybody in it, and in everything, a more dreadful epidemic distemper of that kind is spread than yet has appeared in the world. With you a man can neither earn nor buy his dinner without a speculation. What he receives in the morning will not have the same value at night. What he is compelled to take as pay for an old debt will not be received as the same when he comes to pay a debt contracted by himself, nor will it be the same when by prompt payment he would avoid contracting any debt at all. Industry must wither away. Economy must be driven from your country. Careful provision will have no existence. Who will labor without knowing the amount of his pay? Who will study to increase what none can estimate? Who will accumulate, when he does not know the value of what he saves? If you abstract it from its uses in gaming, to accumulate your paper wealth would be not the providence of a man, but the distempered instinct of a jackdaw.

The truly melancholy part of the policy of systematically making a nation of gamesters is this, that though all are forced to play, few can understand the game; and fewer still are in a condition to avail themselves of the knowledge. The many must be the dupes of the few who conduct the machine of these speculations. What effect it must have on the country people is visible. The townsman can calculate from day to day, not so the inhabitant of the country. When the peasant first brings his corn to market, the magistrate in the towns obliges him to take the assignat at par; when he goes to the shop with his money, he finds it seven per cent the worse for crossing the way. This market he will not readily resort to again. The townspeople will be inflamed; they will force the country people to bring their corn. Resistance will begin, and the murders of Paris and St. Denis may be renewed through all France.

What signifies the empty compliment paid to the country by giving it, perhaps, more than its share in the theory of your representation? Where have you placed the real power over monied and landed circulation? Where have you placed the means of raising and falling the value of every man's freehold? Those whose operations can take form, or add ten per cent to, the possessions of every man in France must be the masters of every man in France. The whole of the power obtained by this revolution will settle in the towns among the burghers and the monied directors who lead them. The landed gentleman, the yeoman, and the peasant have, none of them, habits or inclinations or experience which can lead them to any share in this the sole source of power and influence now left in France. The very nature of a country life, the very nature of landed property, in all the occupations, and all the pleasures they afford, render combination and arrangement (the sole way of procuring and exerting influence) in a manner impossible amongst country people.[xcix] Combine them by all the art you can, and all the industry, they are always dissolving into individuality. Anything in the nature of incorporation is almost impracticable amongst them. Hope, fear, alarm, jealousy, the ephemerous tale that does its business and dies in a day—all these things which are the reins and spurs by which leaders check or urge the minds of followers are not easily employed, or hardly at all, amongst scattered people. They assemble, they arm, they act with the utmost difficulty and at the greatest charge. Their efforts, if ever they can be commenced, cannot be sustained. They cannot proceed systematically. If the country gentlemen attempt an influence through the mere income of their property, what is it to that of those who have ten times their income to sell, and who can ruin their property by bringing their plunder to meet it at market? If the landed man wishes to mortgage, he falls the value of his land and raises the value of assignats. He augments the power of his enemy by the very means he must take to contend with him. The country gentleman, therefore, the officer by sea and land, the man of liberal views and habits, attached to no profession, will be as completely excluded from the government of his country as if he were legislatively proscribed. It is obvious that in the towns all things which conspire against the country gentleman combine in favor of the money manager and director. In towns combination is natural. The habits of burghers, their occupations, their diversion, their business, their idleness continually bring them into mutual contact. Their virtues and their vices are sociable; they are always in garrison; and they come embodied and half disciplined into the hands of those who mean to form them for civil or military action.

All these considerations leave no doubt on my mind that, if this monster of a constitution can continue, France will be wholly governed by the agitators in corporations, by societies in the towns formed of directors of assignats, and trustees for the sale of church lands, attorneys, agents, money jobbers, speculators, and adventurers, composing an ignoble oligarchy founded on the destruction of the crown, the church, the nobility, and the people. Here end all the deceitful dreams and visions of the equality and rights of men. In the Serbonian bog of this base oligarchy they are all absorbed, sunk, and lost forever.

Though human eyes cannot trace them, one would be tempted to think some great offenses in France must cry to heaven, which has thought fit to punish it with a subjection to a vile and inglorious domination in which no comfort or compensation is to be found in any, even of those false, splendors which, playing about other tyrannies, prevent mankind from feeling themselves dishonored even whilst they are oppressed. I must confess I am touched with a sorrow, mixed with some indignation, at the conduct of a few men, once of great rank and still of great character, who, deluded with specious names, have engaged in a business too deep for the line of their understanding to fathom; who have lent their fair reputation and the authority of their high-sounding names to the designs of men with whom they could not be acquainted, and have thereby made their very virtues operate to the ruin of their country.

So far as to the first cementing principle.

THE second material of cement for their new republic is the superiority of the city of Paris; and this I admit is strongly connected with the other cementing principle of paper circulation and confiscation. It is in this part of the project we must look for the cause of the destruction of all the old bounds of provinces and jurisdictions, ecclesiastical and secular, and the dissolution of all ancient combinations of things, as well as the formation of so many small unconnected republics. The power of the city of Paris is evidently one great spring of all their politics. It is through the power of Paris, now become the center and focus of jobbing, that the leaders of this faction direct, or rather command, the whole legislative and the whole executive government. Everything, therefore, must be done which can confirm the authority of that city over the other republics. Paris is compact; she has an enormous strength, wholly disproportioned to the force of any of the square republics; and this strength is collected and condensed within a narrow compass. Paris has a natural and easy connection of its parts, which will not be affected by any scheme of a geometrical constitution, nor does it much signify whether its proportion of representation be more or less, since it has the whole draft of fishes in its dragnet. The other divisions of the kingdom, being hackled and torn to pieces, and separated from all their habitual means and even principles of union, cannot, for some time at least, confederate against her. Nothing was to be left in all the subordinate members but weakness, disconnection, and confusion. To confirm this part of the plan, the Assembly has lately come to a resolution that no two of their republics shall have the same commander-in-chief.

To a person who takes a view of the whole, the strength of Paris, thus formed, will appear a system of general weakness. It is boasted that the geometrical policy has been adopted, that all local ideas should be sunk, and that the people should no longer be Gascons, Picards, Bretons, Normans, but Frenchmen, with one country, one heart, and one Assembly. But instead of being all Frenchmen, the greater likelihood is that the inhabitants of that region will shortly have no country. No man ever was attached by a sense of pride, partiality, or real affection to a description of square measurement. He never will glory in belonging to the Chequer No. 71, or to any other badge-ticket. We begin our public affections in our families. No cold relation is a zealous citizen. We pass on to our neighborhoods and our habitual provincial connections. These are inns and resting places. Such divisions of our country as have been formed by habit, and not by a sudden jerk of authority, were so many little images of the great country in which the heart found something which it could fill. The love to the whole is not extinguished by this subordinate partiality. Perhaps it is a sort of elemental training to those higher and more large regards by which alone men come to be affected, as with their own concern, in the prosperity of a kingdom so extensive as that of France. In that general territory itself, as in the old name of provinces, the citizens are interested from old prejudices and unreasoned habits, and not on account of the geometric properties of its figure. The power and pre-eminence of Paris does certainly press down and hold these republics together as long as it lasts. But, for the reasons I have already given you, I think it cannot last very long.

Passing from the civil creating and the civil cementing principles of this constitution to the National Assembly, which is to appear and act as sovereign, we see a body in its constitution with every possible power, and no possible external control. We see a body without fundamental laws, without established maxims, without respected rules of proceeding, which nothing can keep firm to any system whatsoever. Their idea of their powers is always taken at the utmost

173

stretch of legislative competence, and their examples for common cases from the exceptions of the most urgent necessity. The future is to be in most respects like the present Assembly; but, by the mode of the new elections and the tendency of the new circulations, it will be purged of the small degree of internal control existing in a minority chosen originally from various interests, and preserving something of their spirit. If possible, the next Assembly must be worse than the present. The present, by destroying and altering everything, will leave to their successors apparently nothing popular to do. They will be roused by emulation and example to enterprises the boldest and the most absurd. To suppose such an Assembly sitting in perfect quietude is ridiculous.

Your all-sufficient legislators, in their hurry to do everything at once, have forgotten one thing that seems essential, and which I believe never has been before, in the theory or the practice, omitted by any projector of a republic. They have forgotten to constitute a *senate* or something of that nature and character. Never before this time was heard of a body politic composed of one legislative and active assembly, and its executive officers, without such a council, without something to which foreign states might connect themselves; something to which, in the ordinary detail of government, the people could look up; something which might give a bias and steadiness and preserve something like consistency in the proceedings of state. Such a body kings generally have as a council. A monarchy may exist without it, but it seems to be in the very essence of a republican government. It holds a sort of middle place between the supreme power exercised by the people, or immediately delegated from them, and the mere executive. Of this there are no traces in your constitution, and in providing nothing of this kind your Solons and Numas have, as much as in anything else, discovered a sovereign incapacity.

LET US NOW TURN OUR EYES to what they have done toward the formation of an executive power. For this they have chosen a degraded king. This their first executive officer is to be a machine without any sort of deliberative discretion in any one act of his function. At best he is but a channel to convey to the National Assembly such matter as it may import that body to know. If he had been made the exclusive channel, the power would not have been without its importance, though infinitely perilous to those who would choose to exercise it. But public intelligence and statement of facts may pass to the

174

Assembly with equal authenticity through any other conveyance. As to the means, therefore, of giving a direction to measures by the statement of an authorized reporter, this office of intelligence is as nothing.

To consider the French scheme of an executive officer, in its two natural divisions of civil and political.—In the first, it must be observed that, according to the new constitution, the higher parts of judicature, in either of its lines, are not in the king. The king of France is not the fountain of justice. The judges, neither the original nor the appellate, are of his nomination. He neither proposes the candidates, nor has a negative on the choice. He is not even the public prosecutor. He serves only as a notary to authenticate the choice made of the judges in the several districts. By his officers he is to execute their sentence. When we look into the true nature of his authority, he appears to be nothing more than a chief of bum bailiffs, sergeants at mace, catchpoles,ᶜ jailers, and hangmen. It is impossible to place anything called royalty in a more degrading point of view. A thousand times better had it been for the dignity of this unhappy prince that he had nothing at all to do with the administration of justice, deprived as he is of all that is venerable and all that is consolatory in that function, without power of originating any process, without a power of suspension, mitigation, or pardon. Everything in justice that is vile and odious is thrown upon him. It was not for nothing that the Assembly has been at such pains to remove the stigma from certain offices when they are resolved to place the person who had lately been their king in a situation but one degree above the executioner, and in an office nearly of the same quality. It is not in nature that, situated as the king of the French now is, he can respect himself or can be respected by others.

View this new executive officer on the side of his political capacity, as he acts under the orders of the National Assembly. To execute laws is a royal office; to execute orders is not to be a king. However, a political executive magistracy, though merely such, is a great trust. It is a trust indeed that has much depending upon its faithful and diligent performance, both in the person presiding in it and in all its subordinates. Means of performing this duty ought to be given by regulation; and dispositions toward it ought to be infused by the circumstances attendant on the trust. It ought to be environed with dignity, authority, and consideration, and it ought to lead to glory. The office of execution is an office of exertion. It is not from impotence we are to expect the tasks of power. What sort of person is a king to command executory service, who has no means whatsoever to reward it? Not in a permanent office; not in a grant of land; no, not in a pension of fifty pounds a year; not in the vainest and most trivial title. In France, the king is no more the fountain of honor than he is the fountain of justice. All rewards, all distinctions are in other hands. Those who serve the king can be actuated by no natural motive but fear—by a fear of everything except their master. His functions of internal coercion are as odious as those which he exercises in the department of justice. If relief is to be given to any municipality, the Assembly gives it. If troops are to be sent to reduce them to obedience to the Assembly, the king is to execute the order; and upon every occasion he is to be spattered over with the blood of his people. He has no negative; yet his name and authority is used to enforce every harsh decree. Nay, he must concur in the butchery of those who shall attempt to free him from his imprisonment or show the slightest attachment to his person or to his ancient authority.

Executive magistracy ought to be constituted in such a manner that those who compose it should be disposed to love and to venerate those whom they are bound to obey. A purposed neglect or, what is worse, a literal but perverse and malignant obedience must be the ruin of the wisest counsels. In vain will the law attempt to anticipate or to follow such studied neglects and fraudulent attentions. To make them act zealously is not in the competence of law. Kings, even such as are truly kings, may and ought to bear the freedom of subjects that are obnoxious to them. They may, too, without derogating from themselves, bear even the authority of such persons if it promotes their service. Louis the Thirteenth mortally hated the Cardinal de Richelieu, but his support of that minister against his rivals was the source of all the glory of his reign and the solid foundation of his throne itself. Louis the Fourteenth, when come to the throne, did not love the Cardinal Mazarin, but for his interests he preserved him in power. When old, he detested Louvois, but for years, whilst he faithfully served his greatness, he endured his person. When George the Second took Mr. Pitt, who certainly was not agreeable to him, into his councils, he did nothing which could humble a wise sovereign. But these ministers, who were chosen by affairs, not by affections, acted in the name of, and in trust for, kings, and not as their avowed, constitutional, and ostensible masters. I think it impossible that any king, when he has recovered his first terrors, can cordially infuse vivacity and vigor into measures which he knows to be dictated by those who, he must be persuaded, are in the highest degree ill affected to his person. Will any ministers who serve such a king (or whatever he may be called) with but a decent appearance of respect cordially obey the orders of those whom but the other day in his name they had committed to the Bastille? Will they obey the orders of those whom, whilst they were exercising despotic justice upon them, they conceived they were treating with lenity, and from whom, in a prison, they thought they had provided an asylum? If you expect such obedience amongst your other innovations and regenerations, you ought to make a revolution in nature and provide a new constitution for the human mind. Otherwise, your supreme government cannot harmonize with its executory system. There are cases in which we cannot take up with names and abstractions. You may call half a dozen leading individuals, whom we have reason to fear and hate, the nation. It makes no other difference than to make us fear and hate them the more. If it had been thought justifiable and expedient to make such a revolution by such means, and through such persons, as you have made yours, it would have been more wise to have completed the business of the fifth and sixth of October. The new executive officer would then owe his situation to those who are his creators as well as his masters; and he might be bound in interest, in the society of crime, and (if in crimes there could be virtues) in gratitude to serve those who had promoted him to a place of great lucre and great sensual indulgence, and of something more; for more he must have received from those who certainly would not have limited an aggrandized creature, as they have done a submitting antagonist.

A king circumstanced as the present, if he is totally stupefied by his misfortunes so as to think it not the necessity but the premium and privilege of life to eat and sleep, without any regard to glory, can never be fit for the office. If he feels as men commonly feel, he must be sensible that an office so circumstanced is one in which he can obtain no fame or reputation. He has no generous interest that can excite him to action. At best, his conduct will be passive and defensive. To inferior people such an office might be matter of honor. But to be raised to it, and to descend to it, are different things and suggest different sentiments. Does he *really* name the ministers? They will have a sympathy with him. Are they forced upon him? The whole business between them and the nominal king will be mutual counteraction. In all other countries, the office of ministers of state is of the highest dignity. In France it is full of peril, and incapable of glory. Rivals, however, they will have in their nothingness, whilst shallow ambition exists in the world, or the desire of a miserable salary is an incentive to short-sighted avarice. Those competitors of the ministers are enabled by your constitution to attack them in their vital parts, whilst they have not the means of repelling their charges in any other than the degrading character of culprits. The ministers of state in France are the only persons in that country who are incapable of a share in the national councils. What ministers! What councils! What a nation!—But they are responsible. It is a poor service that is to be had from responsibility. The elevation of mind to be derived from fear will never make a nation glorious. Responsibility prevents crimes. It makes all attempts against the laws dangerous. But for a principle of active and zealous service, none but idiots could think of it. Is the conduct of a war to be trusted to a man who may abhor its principle, who, in every step he may take to render it successful, confirms the power of those by whom he is oppressed? Will foreign states seriously treat with him who has no prerogative of peace or war? No, not so much as in a single vote by himself or his ministers, or by any one whom he can possibly influence. A state of contempt is not a state for a prince; better get rid of him at once.

I know it will be said that these humors in the court and executive government will continue only through this generation, and that the king has been brought to declare the dauphin[ci] shall be educated in a conformity to his situation. If he is made to conform to his situation, he will have no education at all. His training must be worse, even, than that of an arbitrary monarch. If he reads—whether he reads or not—some good or evil genius will tell him his ancestors were kings. Thenceforward his object must be to assert himself and to avenge his parents. This you will say is not his duty. That may be; but it is nature; and whilst you pique nature against you, you do unwisely to trust to duty. In this futile scheme of polity, the state nurses in its bosom, for the present, a source of weakness, perplexity, counteraction, inefficiency, and decay; and it prepares the means of its final ruin. In short, I see nothing in the executive force (I cannot call it authority) that has even an appearance of vigor, or that has the smallest degree of just correspondence or symmetry, or amicable relation with the supreme power, either as it now exists or as it is planned for the future government.

You have settled, by an economy as perverted as the policy, two[49] establishments of government—one real, one fictitious. Both maintained at a vast expense, but the fictitious at, I think, the greatest. Such a machine as the latter is not worth the grease of its wheels. The expense is exorbitant, and neither the show nor the use deserve the tenth part of the charge. Oh! but I don't do justice to the talents of the legislators: I don't allow, as I ought to do, for necessity. Their scheme of executive force was not their choice. This pageant must be kept. The people would not consent to part with it. Right; I understand you. You do, in spite of your grand theories, to which you would have heaven and earth to bend—you do know how to conform yourselves to the nature and circumstances of things. But when you were obliged to conform thus far to circumstances, you ought to have carried your submission further, and to have made, what you were obliged to take, a proper instrument, and useful to its end. That was in your power. For instance, among many others, it was in your power to leave to your king the right of peace and war. What! to leave to the executive magistrate the most dangerous of all prerogatives? I know none more dangerous, nor any one more necessary to be so trusted. I do not say that this prerogative ought to be trusted to your king unless he enjoyed other auxiliary trusts along with it, which he does not now hold. But if he did possess them, hazardous as they are undoubtedly, advantages would arise from such a constitution, more than compensating the risk. There is no other way of keeping the several potentates of Europe from intriguing distinctly and personally with the members of your Assembly, from intermeddling in all your concerns, and fomenting, in the heart of your country, the most pernicious of all factions—factions in the interest and under the direction of foreign powers. From that worst of evils, thank God, we are still free. Your skill, if you had any, would be well employed to find out indirect correctives and controls upon this perilous trust. If you did not like those which in England we have chosen, your leaders might have exerted their abilities in contriving better. If it were necessary to exemplify the consequences of such an executive government as yours, in the management of great affairs, I should refer you to the late reports of M. de Montmorin to the National Assembly, and all the other proceedings relative to the differences between Great Britain and Spain. It would be treating your understanding with disrespect to point them out to you.

[49] In reality three, to reckon the provincial republican establishments.

I hear that the persons who are called ministers have signified an intention of resigning their places. I am rather astonished that they have not resigned long since. For the universe I would not have stood in the situation in which they have been for this last twelvemonth. They wished well, I take it for granted, to the revolution. Let this fact be as it may, they could not, placed as they were upon an eminence, though an eminence of humiliation, but be the first to see collectively, and to feel each in his own department, the evils which have been produced by that revolution. In every step which they took, or forbore to take, they must have felt the degraded situation of their country and their utter incapacity of serving it. They are in a species of subordinate servitude, in which no men before them were ever seen. Without confidence from their sovereign, on whom they were forced, or from the Assembly, who forced them upon him, all the noble functions of their office are executed by committees of the Assembly without any regard whatsoever to their personal or their official authority. They are to execute, without power; they are to be responsible, without discretion; they are to deliberate, without choice. In their puzzled situations, under two sovereigns, over neither of whom they have any influence, they must act in such a manner as (in effect, whatever they may intend) sometimes to betray the one, sometimes the other, and always to betray themselves. Such has been their situation, such must be the situation of those who succeed them. I have much respect and many good wishes for M. Necker. I am obliged to him for attentions. I thought, when his enemies had driven him from Versailles, that his exile was a subject of most serious congratulations—*sed multae urbes et publica vota vicerunt.*[cii] He is now sitting on the ruins of the finances and of the monarchy of France.

A great deal more might be observed on the strange constitution of the executory part of the new government, but fatigue must give bounds to the discussion of subjects which in themselves have hardly any limits.

AS little genius and talent am I able to perceive in the plan of judicature formed by the National Assembly. According to their invariable course, the framers of your constitution have begun with the utter abolition of the parliaments. These venerable bodies, like the rest of the old government, stood in need of reform, even though there should be no change made in the monarchy. They required several more alterations to adapt them to the system of a free constitution.

But they had particulars in their constitution, and those not a few, which deserved approbation from the wise. They possessed one fundamental excellence: they were independent. The most doubtful circumstance attendant on their office, that of its being vendible, contributed however to this independence of character. They held for life. Indeed, they may be said to have held by inheritance. Appointed by the monarch, they were considered as nearly out of his power. The most determined exertions of that authority against them only showed their radical independence. They composed permanent bodies politic, constituted to resist arbitrary innovation; and from that corporate constitution, and from most of their forms, they were well calculated to afford both certainty and stability to the laws. They had been a safe asylum to secure these laws in all the revolutions of humor and opinion. They had saved that sacred deposit of the country during the reigns of arbitrary princes and the struggles of arbitrary factions. They kept alive the memory and record of the constitution. They were the great security to private property which might be said (when personal liberty had no existence) to be, in fact, as well guarded in France as in any other country. Whatever is supreme in a state ought to have, as much as possible, its judicial authority so constituted as not only not to depend upon it, but in some sort to balance it. It ought to give a security to its justice against its power. It ought to make its judicature, as it were, something exterior to the state.

These parliaments had furnished, not the best certainly, but some considerable corrective to the excesses and vices of the monarchy. Such an independent judicature was ten times more necessary when a democracy became the absolute power of the country. In that constitution, elective temporary, local judges, such as you have contrived, exercising their dependent functions in a narrow society, must be the worst of all tribunals. In them it will be vain to look for any appearance of justice toward strangers, toward the obnoxious rich, toward the minority of routed parties, toward all those who in the election have supported unsuccessful candidates. It will be impossible to keep the new tribunals clear of the worst spirit of faction. All contrivances by ballot we know experimentally to be vain and childish to prevent a discovery of inclinations. Where they may the best answer the purposes of concealment, they answer to produce suspicion, and this is a still more mischievous cause of partiality.

If the parliaments had been preserved, instead of being dissolved at so ruinous a charge to the nation, they might have served in this new commonwealth, perhaps not precisely the same (I do not mean an

181

exact parallel), but nearly the same, purposes as the court and senate of Areopagus did in Athens; that is, as one of the balances and correctives to the evils of a light and unjust democracy. Every one knows that this tribunal was the great stay of that state; every one knows with what care it was upheld, and with what a religious awe it was consecrated. The parliaments were not wholly free from faction, I admit; but this evil was exterior and accidental, and not so much the vice of their constitution itself, as it must be in your new contrivance of sexennial elective judicatories. Several English commend the abolition of the old tribunals, as supposing that they determined everything by bribery and corruption. But they have stood the test of monarchic and republican scrutiny. The court was well disposed to prove corruption on those bodies when they were dissolved in 1771. Those who have again dissolved them would have done the same if they could, but both inquisitions having failed, I conclude that gross pecuniary corruption must have been rather rare amongst them.

It would have been prudent, along with the parliaments, to preserve their ancient power of registering, and of remonstrating at least upon, all the decrees of the National Assembly, as they did upon those which passed in the time of the monarchy. It would be a means of squaring the occasional decrees of a democracy to some principles of general jurisprudence. The vice of the ancient democracies, and one cause of their ruin, was that they ruled, as you do, by occasional decrees, *psephismata*.^{ciii} This practice soon broke in upon the tenor and consistency of the laws; it abated the respect of the people toward them, and totally destroyed them in the end.

Your vesting the power of remonstrance, which, in the time of the monarchy, existed in the parliament of Paris, in your principal executive officer, whom, in spite of common sense, you persevere in calling king, is the height of absurdity. You ought never to suffer remonstrance from him who is to execute. This is to understand neither council nor execution, neither authority nor obedience. The person whom you call king ought not to have this power, or he ought to have more.

Your present arrangement is strictly judicial. Instead of imitating your monarchy and seating your judges on a bench of independence, your object is to reduce them to the most blind obedience. As you have changed all things, you have invented new principles of order. You first appoint judges, who, I suppose, are to determine according to law, and then you let them know that, at some time or other, you intend to give them some law by which they are to determine. Any studies which they have made (if any they have made) are to be useless to them. But to supply these studies, they are to be sworn to obey all the rules, orders, and instructions which from time to time they are to receive from the National Assembly. These if they submit to, they leave no ground of law to the subject. They become complete and most dangerous instruments in the hands of the governing power which, in the midst of a cause or on the prospect of it, may wholly change the rule of decision. If these orders of the National Assembly come to be contrary to the will of the people, who locally choose judges, such confusion must happen as is terrible to think of. For the judges owe their places to the local authority, and the commands they are sworn to obey come from those who have no share in their appointment. In the meantime they have the example of the court of Chatelet to encourage and guide them in the exercise of their functions. That court is to try criminals sent to it by the National Assembly, or brought before it by other courses of delation. They sit under a guard to save their own lives. They know not by what law they judge, nor under what authority they act, nor by what tenure they hold. It is thought that they are sometimes obliged to condemn at peril of their lives. This is not perhaps certain, nor can it be ascertained; but when they acquit, we know they have seen the persons whom they discharge, with perfect impunity to the actors, hanged at the door of their court.

The Assembly indeed promises that they will form a body of law, which shall be short, simple, clear, and so forth. That is, by their short laws they will leave much to the discretion of the judge, whilst they have exploded the authority of all the learning which could make judicial discretion (a thing perilous at best) deserving the appellation of a *sound* discretion.

It is curious to observe that the administrative bodies are carefully exempted from the jurisdiction of these new tribunals. That is, those persons are exempted from the power of the laws who ought to be the most entirely submitted to them. Those who execute public pecuniary trusts ought of all men to be the most strictly held to their duty. One would have thought that it must have been among your earliest cares, if you did not mean that those administrative bodies should be real, sovereign, independent states, to form an awful tribunal, like your late parliaments, or like our king's bench, where all corporate officers might obtain protection in the legal exercise of their functions, and would find coercion if they trespassed against their legal duty. But the cause of the exemption is plain. These administrative bodies are the great instruments of the present leaders in their progress through democracy to oligarchy. They must, therefore, be put above the law. It will be said that the legal tribunals which you have made are unfit to coerce them. They are, undoubtedly. They are unfit for any rational purpose. It will be said, too, that the administrative bodies will be accountable to the General Assembly. This I fear is talking without much consideration of the nature of that Assembly, or of these corporations. However, to be subject to the pleasure of that Assembly is not to be subject to law either for protection or for constraint.

This establishment of judges as yet wants something to its completion. It is to be crowned by a new tribunal. This is to be a grand state judicature, and it is to judge of crimes committed against the nation, that is, against the power of the Assembly. It seems as if they had something in their view of the nature of the high court of justice erected in England during the time of the great usurpation. As they have not yet finished this part of the scheme, it is impossible to form a right judgment upon it. However, if great care is not taken to form it in a spirit very different from that which has guided them in their proceedings relative to state offenses, this tribunal, subservient to their inquisition, the Committee of Research, will extinguish the last sparks of liberty in France and settle the most dreadful and arbitrary tyranny ever known in any nation. If they wish to give to this tribunal any appearance of liberty and justice, they must not evoke from or send to it the causes relative to their own members, at their pleasure. They must also remove the seat of that tribunal out of the republic of Paris.[50]

HAS more wisdom been displayed in the constitution of your army than what is discoverable in your plan of judicature? The able arrangement of this part is the more difficult, and requires the greatest skill and attention, not only as the great concern in itself, but as it is the third cementing principle in the new body of republics which you call the French nation. Truly it is not easy to divine what that army

---

[50] For further elucidations upon the subject of all these judicatures, and of the committee of research, see M. de Calonne's work.

may become at last. You have voted a very large one, and on good appointments, at least fully equal to your apparent means of payment. But what is the principle of its discipline, or whom is it to obey? You have got the wolf by the ears, and I wish you joy of the happy position in which you have chosen to place yourselves, and in which you are well circumstanced for a free deliberation relatively to that army or to anything else.

The minister and secretary of state for the war department is M. de la Tour du Pin. This gentleman, like his colleagues in administration, is a most zealous assertor of the revolution, and a sanguine admirer of the new constitution which originated in that event. His statement of facts, relative to the military of France, is important, not only from his official and personal authority, but because it displays very clearly the actual condition of the army in France, and because it throws light on the principles upon which the Assembly proceeds in the administration of this critical object. It may enable us to form some judgment how far it may be expedient in this country to imitate the martial policy of France.

M. de la Tour du Pin, on the fourth of last June, comes to give an account of the state of his department as it exists under the auspices of the National Assembly. No man knows it so well; no man can express it better. Addressing himself to the National Assembly, he says—

His Majesty has *this day* sent me to apprise you of the multiplied disorders of which *every day* he receives the most distressing intelligence. The army *(le corps militaire)* threatens to fall into the most turbulent anarchy. Entire regiments have dared to violate at once the respect due to the laws, to the king, to the order established by your decrees, and to the oaths which they have taken with the most awful solemnity. Compelled by my duty to give you information of these excesses, my heart bleeds when I consider who they are that have committed them. Those against whom it is not in my power to withhold the most grievous complaints are a part of that very soldiery which to this day have been so full of honor and loyalty, and with whom, for fifty years, I have lived the comrade and the friend.

What incomprehensible spirit of delirium and delusion has all at once led them astray? Whilst you are indefatigable in establishing uniformity in the empire, and molding the whole into one coherent and consistent body; whilst the French are taught by you at once the

185

respect which the laws owe to the rights of man, and that which the citizens owe to the laws, the administration of the army presents nothing but disturbance and confusion. I see in more than one corps the bonds of discipline relaxed or broken; the most unheard-of pretensions avowed directly and without any disguise; the ordinances without force; the chiefs without authority; the military chest and the colors carried off; the authority of the king himself *(risum teneatis?*[civ]*)* proudly defied; the officers despised, degraded, threatened, driven away, and some of them prisoners in the midst of their corps, dragging on a precarious life in the bosom of disgust and humiliation. To fill up the measure of all these horrors, the commandants of places have had their throats cut, under the eyes and almost in the arms of their own soldiers.

These evils are great; but they are not the worst consequences which may be produced by such military insurrections. Sooner or later they may menace the nation itself. *The nature of things requires* that the army should never act but as *an instrument.* The moment that, erecting itself into a deliberative body, it shall act according to its own resolutions, the *government, be it what it may, will immediately degenerate into a military democracy*—a species of political monster which has always ended by devouring those who have produced it.

After all this, who must not be alarmed at the irregular consultations and turbulent committees formed in some regiments by the common soldiers and non-commissioned officers without the knowledge, or even in contempt of the authority, of their superiors, although the presence and concurrence of those superiors could give no authority to such monstrous democratic assemblies *(comices).*[cv]

It is not necessary to add much to this finished picture—finished as far as its canvas admits, but, as I apprehend, not taking in the whole of the nature and complexity of the disorders of this military democracy which, the minister at war truly and wisely observes, wherever it exists must be the true constitution of the state, by whatever formal appellation it may pass. For though he informs the Assembly that the more considerable part of the army have not cast off their obedience, but are still attached to their duty, yet those travelers who have seen the corps whose conduct is the best rather observe in them the absence of mutiny than the existence of discipline.

I cannot help pausing here for a moment to reflect upon the expressions of surprise which this minister has let fall, relative to the excesses he relates. To him the departure of the troops from their ancient principles of loyalty and honor seems quite inconceivable. Surely those to whom he addresses himself know the causes of it but too well. They know the doctrines which they have preached, the decrees which they have passed, the practices which they have countenanced. The soldiers remember the 6th of October. They recollect the French guards. They have not forgotten the taking of the king's castles in Paris and Marseilles. That the governors in both places were murdered with impunity is a fact that has not passed out of their minds. They do not abandon the principles laid down so ostentatiously and laboriously of the equality of men. They cannot shut their eyes to the degradation of the whole noblesse of France and the suppression of the very idea of a gentleman. The total abolition of titles and distinctions is not lost upon them. But M. de la Tour du Pin is astonished at their disloyalty, when the doctors of the Assembly have taught them at the same time the respect due to laws. It is easy to judge which of the two sorts of lessons men with arms in their hands are likely to learn. As to the authority of the king, we may collect from the minister himself (if any argument on that head were not quite superfluous) that it is not of more consideration with these troops than it is with everybody else. "The king", says he, "has over and over again repeated his orders to put a stop to these excesses; but in so terrible a crisis *your* (the Assembly's) concurrence is become indispensably necessary to prevent the evils which menace the state. *You* unite to the force of the legislative power *that of opinion* still more important". To be sure the army can have no opinion of the power or authority of the king. Perhaps the soldier has by this time learned that the Assembly itself does not enjoy a much greater degree of liberty than that royal figure.

It is now to be seen what has been proposed in this exigency, one of the greatest that can happen in a state. The minister requests the Assembly to array itself in all its terrors, and to call forth all its majesty. He desires that the grave and severe principles announced by them may give vigor to the king's proclamation. After this we should have looked for courts, civil and martial, breaking of some corps, decimating of others, and all the terrible means which necessity has employed in such cases to arrest the progress of the most terrible of all evils; particularly, one might expect that a serious inquiry would be made into the murder of commandants in the view of their soldiers. Not one word of all this or of anything like it. After they had been told that the soldiery trampled upon the decrees of the Assembly promulgated by the king, the Assembly pass new decrees, and they authorize the king to make new proclamations. After the secretary at war had stated that the regiments had paid no regard to oaths *prêtés avec la plus imposante solemnité,*[cvi] they propose—what? More oaths. They renew decrees and proclamations as they experience their insufficiency, and they multiply oaths in proportion as they weaken, in the minds of men, the sanctions of religion. I hope that handy abridgments of the excellent sermons of Voltaire, d'Alembert, Diderot, and Helvetius, on the Immortality of the Soul, on a particular superintending Providence, and on a Future State of Rewards and Punishments are sent down to the soldiers along with their civic oaths. Of this I have no doubt; as I understand that a certain description of reading makes no inconsiderable part of their military exercises, and that they are full as well supplied with the ammunition of pamphlets as of cartridges.

To prevent the mischiefs arising from conspiracies, irregular consultations, seditious committees, and monstrous democratic assemblies *(comitia, comices)* of the soldiers, and all the disorders arising from idleness, luxury, dissipation, and insubordination, I believe the most astonishing means have been used that ever occurred to men, even in all the inventions of this prolific age. It is no less than this: the king has promulgated in circular letters to all the regiments his direct authority and encouragement that the several corps should join themselves with the clubs and confederations in the several municipalities, and mix with them in their feasts and civic entertainments! This jolly discipline, it seems, is to soften the ferocity of their minds, to reconcile them to their bottle companions of other descriptions, and to merge particular conspiracies in more general associations.[51] That this remedy would be pleasing to the soldiers, as they are

---

[51] Comme sa Majesté y a reconnu, non une système d'associations particulières, mais une réunion de volontés de tous les François pour la liberté et la prosperité communes, ainsi pour la maintien de l'ordre publique; il a pensé qu'il convenoit que chaque régiment prît part à ces fêtes civiques pour multiplier les rapports et reserrer les liens d'union entre les citoyens et les troupes.[cvii]—Lest I should not be credited, I insert the words, authorizing the troops to feast with the popular confederacies.

described by M. de la Tour du Pin, I can readily believe; and that, however mutinous otherwise, they will dutifully submit themselves to *these* royal proclamations. But I should question whether all this civic swearing, clubbing, and feasting would dispose them, more than at present they are disposed, to an obedience to their officers, or teach them better to submit to the austere rules of military discipline. It will make them admirable citizens after the French mode, but not quite so good soldiers after any mode. A doubt might well arise whether the conversations at these good tables would fit them a great deal the better for the character of *mere instruments,* which this veteran officer and statesman justly observes the nature of things always requires an army to be.

Concerning the likelihood of this improvement in discipline by the free conversation of the soldiers with municipal festive societies, which is thus officially encouraged by royal authority and sanction, we may judge by the state of the municipalities themselves, furnished to us by the war minister in this very speech. He conceives good hopes of the success of his endeavors toward restoring order *for the present* from the good disposition of certain regiments, but he finds something cloudy with regard to the future. As to preventing the return of confusion, for this the administration (says he) cannot be answerable to you as long as they see the municipalities arrogate to themselves an authority over the troops which your institutions have reserved wholly to the monarch. You have fixed the limits of the military authority and the municipal authority. You have bounded the action which you have permitted to the latter over the former to the right of requisition, but never did the letter or the spirit of your decrees authorize the commons in these municipalities to break the officers, to try them, to give orders to the soldiers, to drive them from the posts committed to their guard, to stop them in their marches ordered by the king, or, in a word, to enslave the troops to the caprice of each of the cities or even market towns through which they are to pass.

Such is the character and disposition of the municipal society which is to reclaim the soldiery, to bring them back to the true principles of military subordination, and to render them machines in the hands of the supreme power of the country! Such are the distempers of the French troops! Such is their cure! As the army is, so is the navy. The municipalities supersede the orders of the Assembly, and the seamen in their turn supersede the orders of the municipalities. From my heart I pity the condition of a respectable servant of

189

the public like this war minister, obliged in his old age to pledge the Assembly in their civic cups, and to enter with a hoary head into all the fantastic vagaries of these juvenile politicians. Such schemes are not like propositions coming from a man of fifty years' wear and tear amongst mankind. They seem rather such as ought to be expected from those grand compounders in politics who shorten the road to their degrees in the state and have a certain inward fanatical assurance and illumination upon all subjects, upon the credit of which one of their doctors has thought fit, with great applause, and greater success, to caution the Assembly not to attend to old men or to any persons who valued themselves upon their experience. I suppose all the ministers of state must qualify and take this test—wholly abjuring the errors and heresies of experience and observation. Every man has his own relish. But I think if I could not attain to the wisdom, I would at least preserve something of the stiff and peremptory dignity of age. These gentlemen deal in regeneration; but at any price I should hardly yield my rigid fibers to be regenerated by them, nor begin, in my grand climacteric, to squall in their new accents or to stammer, in my second cradle, the elemental sounds of their barbarous metaphysics.[52] *Si isti mihi largiantur ut repuerascam, et in eorum cunis vagiam, valde recusem!*[cviii]

The imbecility of any part of the puerile and pedantic system, which they call a constitution, cannot be laid open without discovering the utter insufficiency and mischief of every other part with which it comes in contact, or that bears any the remotest relation to it. You cannot propose a remedy for the incompetence of the crown without displaying the debility of the Assembly. You cannot deliberate on the confusion of the army of the state without disclosing the worse disorders of the armed municipalities. The military lays open the civil, and the civil betrays the military, anarchy. I wish everybody carefully to peruse the eloquent speech (such it is) of M. de la Tour du Pin. He attributes the salvation of the municipalities to the good behavior of some of the troops. These troops are to preserve the well-disposed part of those municipalities, which is confessed to be the weakest, from the pillage of the worst-disposed, which is the strongest. But the municipalities affect a sovereignty and will command those troops which are necessary for their protection. Indeed they must command them or court them. The municipalities, by the necessity of their situation, and by the republican powers they have

---

[52] This war minister has since quitted the school and resigned his office.

obtained, must, with relation to the military, be the masters, or the servants, or the confederates, or each successively; or they must make a jumble of all together, according to circumstances. What government is there to coerce the army but the municipality, or the municipality but the army? To preserve concord where authority is extinguished, at the hazard of all consequences, the Assembly attempts to cure the distempers by the distempers themselves; and they hope to preserve themselves from a purely military democracy by giving it a debauched interest in the municipal.

If the soldiers once come to mix for any time in the municipal clubs, cabals, and confederacies, an elective attraction will draw them to the lowest and most desperate part. With them will be their habits, affections, and sympathies. The military conspiracies, which are to be remedied by civic confederacies; the rebellious municipalities, which are to be rendered obedient by furnishing them with the means of seducing the very armies of the state that are to keep them in order; all these chimeras of a monstrous and portentous policy must aggravate the confusion from which they have arisen. There must be blood. The want of common judgment manifested in the construction of all their descriptions of forces and in all their kinds of civil and judicial authorities will make it flow. Disorders may be quieted in one time and in one part. They will break out in others, because the evil is radical and intrinsic. All these schemes of mixing mutinous soldiers with seditious citizens must weaken still more and more the military connection of soldiers with their officers, as well as add military and mutinous audacity to turbulent artificers and peasants. To secure a real army, the officer should be first and last in the eye of the soldier; first and last in his attention, observance, and esteem. Officers it seems there are to be, whose chief qualification must be temper and patience. They are to manage their troops by electioneering arts. They must bear themselves as candidates, not as commanders. But as by such means power may be occasionally in their hands, the authority by which they are to be nominated becomes of high importance.

What you may do finally does not appear, nor is it of much moment whilst the strange and contradictory relation between your army and all the parts of your republic, as well as the puzzled relation of those parts to each other and to the whole, remain as they are. You seem to have given the provisional nomination of the officers in the first instance to the king, with a reserve of approbation by the National

Assembly. Men who have an interest to pursue are extremely sagacious in discovering the true seat of power. They must soon perceive that those who can negative indefinitely in reality appoint. The officers must, therefore, look to their intrigues in that Assembly as the sole certain road to promotion. Still, however, by your new constitution they must begin their solicitation at court. This double negotiation for military rank seems to me a contrivance as well adapted, as if it were studied for no other end, to promote faction in the Assembly itself, relative to this vast military patronage, and then to poison the corps of officers with factions of a nature still more dangerous to the safety of government, upon any bottom on which it can be placed, and destructive in the end to the efficiency of the army itself. Those officers who lose the promotions intended for them by the crown must become of a faction opposite to that of the Assembly, which has rejected their claims, and must nourish discontents in the heart of the army against the ruling powers. Those officers, on the other hand, who, by carrying their point through an interest in the Assembly, feel themselves to be at best only second in the good will of the crown, though first in that of the Assembly, must slight an authority which would not advance and could not retard their promotion. If to avoid these evils you will have no other rule for command or promotion than seniority, you will have an army of formality; at the same time it will become more independent and more of a military republic. Not they, but the king is the machine. A king is not to be deposed by halves. If he is not everything in the command of an army, he is nothing. What is the effect of a power placed nominally at the head of the army who to that army is no object of gratitude or of fear? Such a cipher is not fit for the administration of an object, of all things the most delicate, the supreme command of military men. They must be constrained (and their inclinations lead them to what their necessities require) by a real, vigorous, effective, decided, personal authority. The authority of the Assembly itself suffers by passing through such a debilitating channel as they have chosen. The army will not long look to an assembly acting through the organ of false show and palpable imposition. They will not seriously yield obedience to a prisoner. They will either despise a pageant, or they will pity a captive king. This relation of your army to the crown will, if I am not greatly mistaken, become a serious dilemma in your politics.

It is, besides, to be considered whether an assembly like yours, even supposing that it was in possession of another sort of organ through which its orders were to pass, is fit for promoting the obedience and discipline of an army. It is known that armies have hitherto yielded a very precarious and uncertain obedience to any senate or popular authority; and they will least of all yield it to an assembly which is only to have a continuance of two years. The officers must totally lose the characteristic disposition of military men if they see with perfect submission and due admiration the dominion of pleaders; especially when they find that they have a new court to pay to an endless succession of those pleaders, whose military policy, and the genius of whose command (if they should have any), must be as uncertain as their duration is transient. In the weakness of one kind of authority, and in the fluctuation of all, the officers of an army will remain for some time mutinous and full of faction until some popular general, who understands the art of conciliating the soldiery, and who possesses the true spirit of command, shall draw the eyes of all men upon himself. Armies will obey him on his personal account. There is no other way of securing military obedience in this state of things. But the moment in which that event shall happen, the person who really commands the army is your master—the master (that is little) of your king, the master of your Assembly, the master of your whole republic.

How came the Assembly by their present power over the army? Chiefly, to be sure, by debauching the soldiers from their officers. They have begun by a most terrible operation. They have touched the central point about which the particles that compose armies are at repose. They have destroyed the principle of obedience in the great, essential, critical link between the officer and the soldier, just where the chain of military subordination commences and on which the whole of that system depends. The soldier is told he is a citizen and has the rights of man and citizen. The right of a man, he is told, is to be his own governor and to be ruled only by those to whom he delegates that self-government. It is very natural he should think that he ought most of all to have his choice where he is to yield the greatest degree of obedience. He will therefore, in all probability, systematically do what he does at present occasionally; that is, he will exercise at least a negative in the choice of his officers. At present the officers are known at best to be only permissive, and on their good behavior. In fact, there have been many instances in which they have been cashiered by their corps. Here is a second negative on the choice of the king—a negative as effectual at least as the other of the Assembly. The soldiers know already that it has been a question, not ill received in the National Assembly, whether they ought not to have the direct choice of their officers, or some proportion of them? When such matters are in deliberation it is no extravagant supposition that they will incline to the opinion most favorable to their pretensions. They will not bear to be deemed the army of an imprisoned king whilst another army in the same country, with whom, too, they are to feast and confederate, is to be considered as the free army of a free constitution. They will cast their eyes on the other and more permanent army; I mean the municipal. That corps, they well know, does actually elect its own officers. They may not be able to discern the grounds of distinction on which they are not to elect a Marquis de la Fayette (or what is his new name?) of their own. If this election of a commander-in-chief be a part of the rights of men, why not of theirs? They see elective justices of peace, elective judges, elective curates, elective bishops, elective municipalities, and elective commanders of the Parisian army—why should they alone be excluded? Are the brave troops of France the only men in that nation who are not the fit judges of military merit and of the qualifications necessary for a commander-in-chief? Are they paid by the state and do they, therefore, lose the rights of men? They are a part of that nation themselves and contribute to that pay. And is not the king, is not the National Assembly, and are not all who elect the National Assembly, likewise paid? Instead of seeing all these forfeit their rights by their receiving a salary, they perceive that in all these cases a salary is given for the exercise of those rights. All your resolutions, all your proceedings, all your debates, all the works of your doctors in religion and politics have industriously been put into their hands, and you expect that they will apply to their own case just as much of your doctrines and examples as suits your pleasure.

EVERYTHING depends upon the army in such a government as yours, for you have industriously destroyed all the opinions and prejudices and, as far as in you lay, all the instincts which support government. Therefore, the moment any difference arises between your National Assembly and any part of the nation, you must have recourse to force. Nothing else is left to you, or rather you have left nothing else to yourselves. You see, by the report of your war minister, that the distribution of the army is in a great measure made with a view of internal coercion.[53] You must rule by an army; and you have infused into that army by which you rule, as well as into the whole body of the nation, principles which after a time must disable you in the use you resolve to make of it. The king is to call out troops to act against his people, when the world has been told, and the assertion is still ringing in our ears, that troops ought not to fire on citizens. The colonies assert to themselves an independent constitution and a free trade. They must be constrained by troops. In what chapter of your code of the rights of men are they able to read that it is a part of the rights of men to have their commerce monopolized and restrained for the benefit of others? As the colonists rise on you, the Negroes rise on them. Troops again—massacre, torture, hanging! These are your rights of men! These are the fruits of metaphysic declarations wantonly made, and shamefully retracted! It was but the other day that the farmers of land in one of your provinces refused to pay some sort of rents to the lord of the soil. In consequence of this, you decree that the country people shall pay all rents and dues, except those which as grievances you have abolished; and if they refuse, then you order the king to march troops against them. You lay down metaphysic propositions which infer universal consequences, and then you attempt to limit logic by despotism. The leaders of the present system tell them of their rights, as men, to take fortresses, to murder guards, to seize on kings without the least appearance of authority even from the Assembly, whilst, as the sovereign legislative body, that Assembly was sitting in the name of the nation—and yet these leaders presume to order out the troops which have acted in these very disorders, to coerce those who shall judge on the principles, and follow the examples, which have been guaranteed by their own approbation.

The leaders teach the people to abhor and reject all feudality as the barbarism of tyranny, and they tell them afterwards how much of that barbarous tyranny they are to bear with patience. As they are prodigal of light with regard to grievances, so the people find them sparing in the extreme with regard to redress. They know that not only certain quitrents and personal duties, which you have permitted them to redeem (but have furnished no money for the redemption), are as nothing to those burdens for which you have made no provi-

[53] Courier François, 30th July, 1790. Assemblée Nationale, Numéro 210.

sion at all. They know that almost the whole system of landed property in its origin is feudal; that it is the distribution of the possessions of the original proprietors, made by a barbarous conqueror to his barbarous instruments; and that the most grievous effects of the conquest are the land rents of every kind, as without question they are.[cix]

The peasants, in all probability, are the descendants of these ancient proprietors, Romans or Gauls. But if they fail, in any degree, in the titles which they make on the principles of antiquaries and lawyers, they retreat into the citadel of the rights of men. There they find that men are equal; and the earth, the kind and equal mother of all, ought not to be monopolized to foster the pride and luxury of any men, who by nature are no better than themselves, and who, if they do not labor for their bread, are worse. They find that by the laws of nature the occupant and subduer of the soil is the true proprietor; that there is no prescription against nature; and that the agreements (where any there are) which have been made with the landlords, during the time of slavery, are only the effect of duress and force; and that when the people reentered into the rights of men, those agreements were made as void as everything else which had been settled under the prevalence of the old feudal and aristocratic tyranny. They will tell you that they see no difference between an idler with a hat and a national cockade and an idler in a cowl or in a rochet. If you ground the title to rents on succession and prescription, they tell you from the speech of M. Camus, published by the National Assembly for their information, that things ill begun cannot avail themselves of prescription; that the title of these lords was vicious in its origin; and that force is at least as bad as fraud. As to the title by succession, they will tell you that the succession of those who have cultivated the soil is the true pedigree of property, and not rotten parchments and silly substitutions; that the lords have enjoyed their usurpation too long; and that if they allow to these lay monks any charitable pension, they ought to be thankful to the bounty of the true proprietor, who is so generous toward a false claimant to his goods.

When the peasants give you back that coin of sophistic reason on which you have set your image and superscription, you cry it down as base money and tell them you will pay for the future with French guards, and dragoons, and hussars. You hold up, to chastise them, the second-hand authority of a king, who is only the instrument of destroying, without any power of protecting either the people or his own person. Through him it seems you will make yourselves obeyed.

They answer: You have taught us that there are no gentlemen, and which of your principles teach us to bow to kings whom we have not elected? We know without your teaching that lands were given for the support of feudal dignities, feudal titles, and feudal offices. When you took down the cause as a grievance, why should the more grievous effect remain? As there are now no hereditary honors, and no distinguished families, why are we taxed to maintain what you tell us ought not to exist? You have sent down our old aristocratic landlords in no other character, and with no other title, but that of exactors under your authority. Have you endeavored to make these your rent-gatherers respectable to us? No. You have sent them to us with their arms reversed, their shields broken, their impresses defaced; and so displumed, degraded, and metamorphosed, such unfeathered two-legged things, that we no longer know them. They are strangers to us. They do not even go by the names of our ancient lords. Physically they may be the same men, though we are not quite sure of that, on your new philosophic doctrines of personal identity. In all other respects they are totally changed. We do not see why we have not as good a right to refuse them their rents as you have to abrogate all their honors, titles, and distinctions. This we have never commissioned you to do; and it is one instance, among many indeed, of your assumption of undelegated power. We see the burghers of Paris, through their clubs, their mobs, and their national guards, directing you at their pleasure and giving that as law to you which, under your authority, is transmitted as law to us. Through you these burghers dispose of the lives and fortunes of us all. Why should not you attend as much to the desires of the laborious husbandman with regard to our rent, by which we are affected in the most serious manner, as you do to the demands of these insolent burghers, relative to distinctions and titles of honor, by which neither they nor we are affected at all? But we find you pay more regard to their fancies than to our necessities. Is it among the rights of man to pay tribute to his equals? Before this measure of yours, we might have thought we were not perfectly equal. We might have entertained some old, habitual, unmeaning prepossession in favor of those landlords; but we cannot conceive with what other view than that of destroying all respect to them, you could have made the law that degrades them. You have forbidden us to treat them with any of the old formalities of respect, and now you send troops to saber and to bayonet us into a submission to fear and force, which you did not suffer us to yield to the mild authority of opinion.

The ground of some of these arguments is horrid and ridiculous to all rational ears, but to the politicians of metaphysics who have opened schools for sophistry and made establishments for anarchy, it is solid and conclusive. It is obvious that, on a mere consideration of the right, the leaders in the Assembly would not in the least have scrupled to abrogate the rents along with the title and family ensigns. It would be only to follow up the principle of their reasonings and to complete the analogy of their conduct. But they had newly possessed themselves of a great body of landed property by confiscation. They had this commodity at market; and the market would have been wholly destroyed if they were to permit the husbandmen to riot in the speculations with which they so freely intoxicated themselves. The only security which property enjoys in any one of its descriptions is from the interests of their rapacity with regard to some other. They have left nothing but their own arbitrary pleasure to determine what property is to be protected and what subverted.

Neither have they left any principle by which any of their municipalities can be bound to obedience, or even conscientiously obliged not to separate from the whole to become independent, or to connect itself with some other state. The people of Lyons, it seems, have refused lately to pay taxes. Why should they not? What lawful authority is there left to exact them? The king imposed some of them. The old states, methodized by orders, settled the more ancient. They may say to the Assembly: who are you, that are not our kings, nor the states we have elected, nor sit on the principles on which we have elected you? And who are we, that when we see the gabelles,ᶜˣ which you have ordered to be paid, wholly shaken off, when we see the act of disobedience afterwards ratified by yourselves—who are we, that we are not to judge what taxes we ought or ought not to pay, and are not to avail ourselves of the same powers, the validity of which you have approved in others? To this the answer is, We will send troops. The last reason of kings is always the first with your Assembly. This military aid may serve for a time, whilst the impression of the increase of pay remains, and the vanity of being umpires in all disputes is flattered. But this weapon will snap short, unfaithful to the hand that employs it. The Assembly keep a school where, systematically, and with unremitting perseverance, they teach principles and form regulations destructive to all spirit of subordination, civil and military—and then they expect that they shall hold in obedience an anarchic people by an anarchic army.

The municipal army which, according to the new policy, is to balance this national army, if considered in itself only, is of a constitution much more simple, and in every respect less exceptionable. It is a mere democratic body, unconnected with the crown or the kingdom, armed and trained and officered at the pleasure of the districts to which the corps severally belong, and the personal service of the individuals who compose, or the fine in lieu of personal service, are directed by the same authority.[54] Nothing is more uniform. If, however, considered in any relation to the crown, to the National Assembly, to the public tribunals, or to the other army, or considered in a view to any coherence or connection between its parts, it seems a monster, and can hardly fail to terminate its perplexed movements in some great national calamity. It is a worse preservative of a general constitution than the systasis of Crete,[cxi] or the confederation of Poland, or any other ill-devised corrective which has yet been imagined in the necessities produced by an ill-constructed system of government.

Having concluded my few remarks on the constitution of the supreme power, the executive, the judicature, the military, and on the reciprocal relation of all these establishments, I shall say something of the ability shown by your legislators with regard to the revenue.

IN THEIR PROCEEDINGS relative to this object, if possible, still fewer traces appear of political judgment or financial resource. When the states met, it seemed to be the great object to improve the system of revenue, to enlarge its collection, to cleanse it of oppression and vexation, and to establish it on the most solid footing. Great were the expectations entertained on that head throughout Europe. It was by this grand arrangement that France was to stand or fall; and this became, in my opinion, very properly the test by which the skill and patriotism of those who ruled in that Assembly would be tried. The revenue of the state is the state. In effect, all depends upon it, whether for support or for reformation. The dignity of every occupation wholly depends upon the quantity and the kind of virtue that may be exerted in it. As all great qualities of the mind which operate in

[54] I see by M. Necker's account that the national guards of Paris have received, over and above the money levied within their own city, about £145,000 sterling out of the public treasures. Whether this be an actual payment for the nine months of their existence or an estimate of their yearly charge, I do not clearly perceive. It is of no great importance, as certainly they may take whatever they please.

public, and are not merely suffering and passive, require force for their display, I had almost said for their unequivocal existence, the revenue, which is the spring of all power, becomes in its administration the sphere of every active virtue. Public virtue, being of a nature magnificent and splendid, instituted for great things and conversant about great concerns, requires abundant scope and room and cannot spread and grow under confinement and in circumstances straitened, narrow, and sordid. Through the revenue alone the body politic can act in its true genius and character, and, therefore, it will display just as much of its collective virtue, and as much of that virtue which may characterize those who move it and are, as it were, its life and guiding principle, as it is possessed of a just revenue. For from hence not only magnanimity, and liberality, and beneficence, and fortitude, and providence, and the tutelary protection of all good arts derive their food and the growth of their organs; but continence, and self-denial, and labor, and vigilance, and frugality, and whatever else there is in which the mind shows itself above the appetite, are nowhere more in their proper element than in the provision and distribution of the public wealth. It is, therefore, not without reason that the science of speculative and practical finance, which must take to its aid so many auxiliary branches of knowledge, stands high in the estimation not only of the ordinary sort but of the wisest and best men; and as this science has grown with the progress of its object, the prosperity and improvement of nations has generally increased with the increase of their revenues; and they will both continue to grow and flourish as long as the balance between what is left to strengthen the efforts of individuals and what is collected for the common efforts of the state bear to each other a due reciprocal proportion and are kept in a close correspondence and communication. And perhaps it may be owing to the greatness of revenues and to the urgency of state necessities that old abuses in the constitution of finances are discovered and their true nature and rational theory comes to be more perfectly understood: insomuch, that a smaller revenue might have been more distressing in one period than a far greater is found to be in another, the proportionate wealth even remaining the same. In this state of things, the French Assembly found something in their revenues to preserve, to secure, and wisely to administer, as well as to abrogate and alter. Though their proud assumption might justify the severest tests, yet in trying their abilities on their financial proceedings, I would only consider what is the plain obvious duty of a common finance minister, and try them upon that, and not upon models of ideal perfection.

The objects of a financier are, then, to secure an ample revenue, to impose it with judgment and equality, to employ it economically, and when necessity obliges him to make use of credit, to secure its foundations in that instance, and forever, by the clearness and candor of his proceedings, the exactness of his calculations and the solidity of his funds. On these heads we may take a short and distinct view of the merits and abilities of those in the National Assembly who have taken to themselves the management of this arduous concern. Far from any increase of revenue in their hands, I find, by a report of M. Vernier, from the committee of finances, of the second of August last, that the amount of the national revenue, as compared with its produce before the Revolution, was diminished by the sum of two hundred millions, or *eight millions sterling* of the annual income, considerably more than one-third of the whole.

If this be the result of great ability, never surely was ability displayed in a more distinguished manner or with so powerful an effect. No common folly, no vulgar incapacity, no ordinary official negligence, even no official crime, no corruption, no peculation, hardly any direct hostility which we have seen in the modern world could in so short a time have made so complete an overthrow of the finances and, with them, of the strength of a great kingdom.—*Cedo qui vestram rempublicam tantam amisistis tam cito?*[cxii]

The sophisters and declaimers, as soon as the Assembly met, began with decrying the ancient constitution of the revenue in many of its most essential branches, such as the public monopoly of salt. They charged it, as truly as unwisely, with being ill-contrived, oppressive, and partial. This representation they were not satisfied to make use of in speeches preliminary to some plan of reform; they declared it in a solemn resolution or public sentence, as it were judicially passed upon it; and this they dispersed throughout the nation. At the time they passed the decree, with the same gravity they ordered the same absurd, oppressive, and partial tax to be paid until they could find a revenue to replace it. The consequence was inevitable. The provinces which had been always exempted from this salt monopoly, some of whom were charged with other contributions, perhaps equivalent, were totally disinclined to bear any part of the burden which by an equal distribution was to redeem the others. As to the Assembly, occupied as it was with the declaration and violation of the rights of men, and with their arrangements for general confusion, it had neither leisure nor capacity to contrive, nor authority to enforce, any plan of any kind relative to the replacing the tax or equalizing it, or compensating the provinces, or for conducting their minds to any scheme of accommodation with other districts which were to be relieved.

The people of the salt provinces, impatient under taxes, damned by the authority which had directed their payment, very soon found their patience exhausted. They thought themselves as skillful in demolishing as the Assembly could be. They relieved themselves by throwing off the whole burden. Animated by this example, each district, or part of a district, judging of its own grievance by its own feeling, and of its remedy by its own opinion, did as it pleased with other taxes.

We are next to see how they have conducted themselves in contriving equal impositions, proportioned to the means of the citizens, and the least likely to lean heavy on the active capital employed in the generation of that private wealth from whence the public fortune must be derived. By suffering the several districts, and several of the individuals in each district, to judge of what part of the old revenue they might withhold, instead of better principles of equality, a new inequality was introduced of the most oppressive kind. Payments were regulated by dispositions. The parts of the kingdom which were the most submissive, the most orderly, or the most affectionate to the commonwealth bore the whole burden of the state. Nothing turns out to be so oppressive and unjust as a feeble government. To fill up all the deficiencies in the old impositions and the new deficiencies of every kind which were to be expected—what remained to a state without authority? The National Assembly called for a voluntary benevolence: for a fourth part of the income of all the citizens, to be estimated on the honor of those who were to pay. They obtained something more than could be rationally calculated, but what was far indeed from answerable to their real necessities, and much less to their fond expectations. Rational people could have hoped for little from this their tax in the disguise of a benevolence—a tax weak, ineffective, and unequal; a tax by which luxury, avarice, and selfishness were screened, and the load thrown upon productive capital, upon integrity, generosity, and public spirit; a tax of regulation upon virtue. At length the mask is thrown off, and they are now trying means (with little success) of exacting their benevolence by force.

This benevolence, the rickety offspring of weakness, was to be supported by another resource, the twin brother of the same prolific imbecility. The patriotic donations were to make good the failure of the patriotic contribution. John Doe was to become security for Richard Roe. By this scheme they took things of much price from the giver, comparatively of small value to the receiver; they ruined several trades; they pillaged the crown of its ornaments, the churches of their plate, and the people of their personal decorations. The invention of these juvenile pretenders to liberty was in reality nothing more than a servile imitation of one of the poorest resources of doting despotism. They took an old, huge, fullbottomed periwig out of the wardrobe of the antiquated frippery of Louis the Fourteenth to cover the premature baldness of the National Assembly. They produced this old-fashioned formal folly, though it had been so abundantly exposed in the Memoirs of the Duke de St. Simon, if to reasonable men it had wanted any arguments to display its mischief and insufficiency. A device of the same kind was tried, in my memory, by Louis the Fifteenth, but it answered at no time. However, the necessities of ruinous wars were some excuse for desperate projects. The deliberations of calamity are rarely wise. But here was a season for disposition and providence. It was in a time of profound peace, then enjoyed for five years, and promising a much longer continuance, that they had recourse to this desperate trifling. They were sure to lose more reputation by sporting, in their serious situation, with these toys and playthings of finance, which have filled half their journals, than could possibly be compensated by the poor temporary supply which they afforded. It seemed as if those who adopted such projects were wholly ignorant of their circumstances or wholly unequal to their necessities. Whatever virtue may be in these devices, it is obvious that neither the patriotic gifts, nor the patriotic contribution, can ever be resorted to again. The resources of public folly are soon exhausted. The whole, indeed, of their scheme of revenue is to make, by any artifice, an appearance of a full reservoir for the hour, whilst at the same time they cut off the springs and living fountains of perennial supply. The account not long since furnished by M. Necker was meant, without question, to be favorable. He gives a flattering view of the means of getting through the year, but he expresses, as it is natural he should, some apprehension for that which was to succeed. On this last prognostic, instead of entering into the grounds of this apprehension in order, by a proper foresight, to prevent the prognosticated evil, M. Necker receives a sort of friendly reprimand from the president of the Assembly.

As to their other schemes of taxation, it is impossible to say anything of them with certainty, because they have not yet had their operation; but nobody is so sanguine as to imagine they will fill up any perceptible part of the wide gaping breach which their incapacity had made in their revenues. At present the state of their treasury sinks every day more and more in cash, and swells more and more in fictitious representation. When so little within or without is now found but paper, the representative not of opulence but of want, the creature not of credit but of power, they imagine that our flourishing state in England is owing to that bank-paper, and not the bank-paper to the flourishing condition of our commerce, to the solidity of our credit, and to the total exclusion of all idea of power from any part of the transaction. They forget that, in England, not one shilling of paper money of any description is received but of choice; that the whole has had its origin in cash actually deposited; and that it is convertible at pleasure, in an instant and without the smallest loss, into cash again. Our paper is of value in commerce, because in law it is of none. It is powerful on 'Change,[cxiii] because in Westminster Hall it is impotent. In payment of a debt of twenty shillings, a creditor may refuse all the paper of the Bank of England. Nor is there amongst us a single public security, of any quality or nature whatsoever, that is enforced by authority. In fact, it might be easily shown that our paper wealth, instead of lessening the real coin, has a tendency to increase it; instead of being a substitute for money, it only facilitates its entry, its exit, and its circulation; that it is the symbol of prosperity, and not the badge of distress. Never was a scarcity of cash and an exuberance of paper a subject of complaint in this nation.

Well! but a lessening of prodigal expenses, and the economy which has been introduced by the virtuous and sapient Assembly, make amends for the losses sustained in the receipt of revenue. In this at least they have fulfilled the duty of a financier. Have those who say so looked at the expenses of the National Assembly itself, of the municipalities, of the city of Paris, of the increased pay of the two armies, of the new police, of the new judicatures? Have they even carefully compared the present pension list with the former? These politicians have been cruel, not economical. Comparing the expense of the former prodigal government and its relation to the then revenues with the expenses of this new system as opposed to the state of its new treasury, I believe the present will be found beyond all comparison more chargeable.[55]

It remains only to consider the proofs of financial ability furnished by the present French managers when they are to raise supplies on credit. Here I am a little at a stand, for credit, properly speaking, they have none. The credit of the ancient government was not indeed the best, but they could always, on some terms, command money, not only at home, but from most of the countries of Europe where a surplus capital was accumulated; and the credit of that government was improving daily. The establishment of a system of liberty would of course be supposed to give it new strength; and so it would actually have done if a system of liberty had been established. What offers has their government of pretended liberty had from Holland, from Hamburg, from Switzerland, from Genoa, from England for a dealing in their paper? Why should these nations of commerce and economy enter into any pecuniary dealings with a people who attempt to reverse the very nature of things, amongst whom they see the debtor prescribing at the point of the bayonet the medium of his solvency to the creditor, discharging one of his engagements with another, turning his very penury into his resource and paying his interest with his rags?

Their fanatical confidence in the omnipotence of church plunder has induced these philosophers to overlook all care of the public estate, just as the dream of the philosopher's stone induces dupes, under the

---

[55] The reader will observe that I have but lightly touched (my plan demanded nothing more) on the condition of the French finances, as connected with the demands upon them. If I had intended to do otherwise, the materials in my hands for such a task are not altogether perfect. On this subject I refer the reader to M. de Calonne's work; and the tremendous display that he has made of the havoc and devastation in the public estate, and in all the affairs of France, caused by the presumptuous good intentions of ignorance and incapacity. Such effects those causes will always produce. Looking over that account with a pretty strict eye, and, with perhaps too much rigor, deducting everything which may be placed to the account of a financier out of place, who might be supposed by his enemies desirous of making the most of his cause, I believe it will be found that a more salutary lesson of caution against the daring spirit of innovators than what has been supplied at the expense of France never was at any time furnished to mankind.

more plausible delusion of the hermetic art, to neglect all rational means of improving their fortunes. With these philosophic financiers, this universal medicine made of church mummy is to cure all the evils of the state. These gentlemen perhaps do not believe a great deal in the miracles of piety, but it cannot be questioned that they have an undoubting faith in the prodigies of sacrilege. Is there a debt which presses them?—Issue *assignats*. Are compensations to be made or a maintenance decreed to those whom they have robbed of their freehold in their office, or expelled from their profession?—*Assignats*. Is a fleet to be fitted out?—*Assignats*. If sixteen millions sterling of these *assignats*, forced on the people, leave the wants of the state as urgent as ever—issue, says one, thirty millions sterling of *assignats*—says another, issue fourscore millions more of *assignats*. The only difference among their financial factions is on the greater or the lesser quantity of *assignats* to be imposed on the public sufferance. They are all professors of *assignats*. Even those whose natural good sense and knowledge of commerce, not obliterated by philosophy, furnish decisive arguments against this delusion conclude their arguments by proposing the emission of *assignats*. I suppose they must talk of *assignats*, as no other language would be understood. All experience of their inefficiency does not in the least discourage them. Are the old *assignats* depreciated at market?—What is the remedy? Issue new *assignats*.—*Mais si maladia, opiniatria, non vult se garire, quid illi facere? assignare—postea assignare; ensuita assignare.*[cxiv] The word is a trifle altered. The Latin of your present doctors may be better than that of your old comedy; their wisdom and the variety of their resources are the same. They have not more notes in their song than the cuckoo, though, far from the softness of that harbinger of summer and plenty, their voice is as harsh and as ominous as that of the raven.

Who but the most desperate adventurers in philosophy and finance could at all have thought of destroying the settled revenue of the state, the sole security for the public credit, in the hope of rebuilding it with the materials of confiscated property? If, however, an excessive zeal for the state should have led a pious and venerable prelate (by anticipation a father of the church[56]) to pillage his own order and, for the good of the church and people, to take upon himself the place of grand financier of confiscation and comptroller-

---

[56] La Bruyère of Bossuet.[cxv]

general of sacrilege, he and his coadjutors were in my opinion bound to show by their subsequent conduct that they knew something of the office they assumed. When they had resolved to appropriate to the *Fisc* a certain portion of the landed property of their conquered country, it was their business to render their bank a real fund of credit, as far as such a bank was capable of becoming so.

To establish a current circulating credit upon any *Land-bank,* under any circumstances whatsoever, has hitherto proved difficult at the very least. The attempt has commonly ended in bankruptcy.[cxvi] But when the Assembly were led, through a contempt of moral, to a defiance of economical principles, it might at least have been expected that nothing would be omitted on their part to lessen this difficulty, to prevent any aggravation of this bankruptcy. It might be expected that to render your land-bank tolerable, every means would be adopted that could display openness and candor in the statement of the security—everything which could aid the recovery of the demand. To take things in their most favorable point of view, your condition was that of a man of a large landed estate which he wished to dispose of for the discharge of a debt and the supply of certain services. Not being able instantly to sell, you wished to mortgage. What would a man of fair intentions and a commonly clear understanding do in such circumstances? Ought he not first to ascertain the gross value of the estate, the charges of its management and disposition, the encumbrances perpetual and temporary of all kinds that affect it, then, striking a net surplus, to calculate the just value of the security? When that surplus (the only security to the creditor) had been clearly ascertained and properly vested in the hands of trustees, then he would indicate the parcels to be sold, and the time and conditions of sale; after this, he would admit the public creditor, if he chose it, to subscribe his stock into this new fund, or he might receive proposals for an *assignat* from those who would advance money to purchase this species of security.

This would be to proceed like men of business, methodically and rationally, and on the only principles of public and private credit that have an existence. The dealer would then know exactly what he purchased; and the only doubt which could hang upon his mind would be the dread of the resumption of the spoil, which one day might be made (perhaps with an addition of punishment) from the sacrilegious gripe of those execrable wretches who could become

207

purchasers at the auction of their innocent fellow citizens.

AN open and exact statement of the clear value of the property and of the time, the circumstances, and the place of sale were all necessary to efface as much as possible the stigma that has hitherto been branded on every kind of land-bank. It became necessary on another principle, that is, on account of a pledge of faith previously given on that subject, that their future fidelity in a slippery concern might be established by their adherence to their first engagement. When they had finally determined on a state resource from church booty, they came, on the 14th of April, 1790, to a solemn resolution on the subject, and pledged themselves to their country, "that in the statement of the public charges for each year, there should be brought to account a sum sufficient for defraying the expenses of the R. C. A. religion,[cxvii] the support of the ministers at the altars, the relief of the poor, the pensions to the ecclesiastics, secular as well as regular, of the one and of the other sex, *in order that the estates and goods which are at the disposal of the nation may be disengaged of all charges and employed by the representatives, or the legislative body, to the great and most pressing exigencies of the state".* They further engaged, on the same day, that the sum necessary for the year 1791 should be forthwith determined.

In this resolution they admit it their duty to show distinctly the expense of the above objects which, by other resolutions, they had before engaged should be first in the order of provision. They admit that they ought to show the estate clear and disengaged of all charges, and that they should show it immediately. Have they done this immediately, or at any time? Have they ever furnished a rent-roll of the immovable estates, or given in an inventory of the movable effects which they confiscate to their *assignats?* In what manner they can fulfill their engagements of holding out to public service "an estate disengaged of all charges" without authenticating the value of the estate or the quantum of the charges, I leave it to their English admirers to explain. Instantly upon this assurance, and previously to any one step toward making it good, they issue, on the credit of so handsome a declaration, sixteen millions sterling of their paper. This was manly. Who, after this masterly stroke, can doubt of their abilities in finance? But then, before any other emission of these financial *indulgences,* they took care at least to make good their original promise!—If such estimate either of the value of the estate or the amount of the encumbrances has been made, it has escaped me. I never heard of it.

At length they have spoken out, and they have made a full discovery of their abominable fraud in holding out the church lands as a security for any debts, or any service whatsoever. They rob only to enable them to cheat, but in a very short time they defeat the ends both of the robbery and the fraud by making out accounts for other purposes which blow up their whole apparatus of force and of deception. I am obliged to M. de Calonne for his reference to the document which proves this extraordinary fact; it had by some means escaped me. Indeed it was not necessary to make out my assertion as to the breach of faith on the declaration of the 14th of April, 1790. By a report of their committee it now appears that the charge of keeping up the reduced ecclesiastical establishments and other expenses attendant on religion, and maintaining the religious of both sexes, retained or pensioned, and the other concomitant expenses of the same nature which they have brought upon themselves by this convulsion in property, exceeds the income of the estates acquired by it in the enormous sum of two millions sterling annually, besides a debt of seven millions and upwards. These are the calculating powers of imposture! This is the finance of philosophy! This is the result of all the delusions held out to engage a miserable people in rebellion, murder, and sacrilege, and to make them prompt and zealous instruments in the ruin of their country! Never did a state, in any case, enrich itself by the confiscations of the citizens. This new experiment has succeeded like all the rest. Every honest mind, every true lover of liberty and humanity, must rejoice to find that injustice is not always good policy, nor rapine the high road to riches. I subjoin with pleasure, in a note, the able and spirited observations of M. de Calonne on this subject.[57]

---

[57] "Ce n'est point à l'assemblée entière que je m'adresse ici; je ne parle qu'à ceux qui l'égarent, en lui cachant sous des gazes séduisantes le but où ils l'entraînent. C'est à eux que je dis: votre objet, vous n'en disconviendrez pas, c'est d'ôter tout espoir au clergé, & de consommer sa ruine; c'est-la, en ne vous soupçonnant d'aucune combinaison de cupidité, d'aucun regard sur le jeu des effets publics, c'est-là ce qu'on doit croire que vous avez en vue dans la terrible opération que vous proposez; c'est ce qui doit en être le fruit. Mais le peuple que vous y intéressez, quel avantage peut-il y trouver? En vous servant sans cesse de lui, que faites vous pour lui? Rien, absolu-

In order to persuade the world of the bottomless resource of ecclesiastical confiscation, the Assembly have proceeded to other confiscations of estates in offices, which could not be done with any common color without being compensated out of this grand confiscation of landed property. They have thrown upon this fund, which was to show a surplus disengaged of all charges, a new charge—namely, the compensation to the whole body of the disbanded judicature, and of all suppressed offices and estates, a charge which I cannot ascertain, but which unquestionably amounts to many French millions. Another of the new charges is an annuity of four hundred and eighty thousand pounds sterling, to be paid (if they choose to keep faith) by daily payments, for the interest of the first assignats. Have they even given themselves the trouble to state fairly the expense of the management of the church lands in the hands of the municipalities to whose care, skill, and diligence, and that of their legion of unknown underagents, they have chosen to commit the charge of the forfeited estates, the consequence of which had been so ably pointed out by the bishop of Nancy?

But it is unnecessary to dwell on these obvious heads of encumbrance. Have they made out any clear state of the grand encumbrance of all, I mean the whole of the general and municipal establishments of all sorts, and compared it with the regular income by revenue? Every deficiency in these becomes a charge on the confiscated estate before the creditor can plant his cabbages on an acre of church property. There is no other prop than this confiscation to keep the whole state from tumbling to the ground. In this situation they have purposely covered all that they ought industriously to have cleared with a thick fog, and then, blindfold themselves, like bulls that shut their eyes when they push, they drive, by the point of the

---

ment rien; &, au contraire, vous faites ce qui ne conduit qu'à l'accabler de nouvelles charges. Vous avez rejeté, à son prejudice, une offre de 400 millions, dont l'acceptation pouvoit devenir un moyen de soulagement en sa faveur; & à cette ressource, aussi profitable que legitime, vous avez substitué une injustice ruineuse, qui, de votre propre aveu, charge le trésor public, & par conséquent le peuple, d'un surcroît de depense annuelle de 50 millions au moins, & d'un remboursement de 150 millions.

"Malheureux peuple, voilà ce que vous vaut en dernier résultat l'expropriation de l'Eglise, & la dureté des décrets taxateurs du traitement des ministres d'une religion bienfaisante; & deformais ils seront à votre charge: leurs charités soulageoient les pauvres; & vous allez être imposés pour subvenir à leur entretien!"[cxviii]—*De l'Etat de la France,* p. 81. See also p. 92, and the following pages.

bayonets, their slaves, blindfolded indeed no worse than their lords, to take their fictions for currencies and to swallow down paper pills by thirty-four millions sterling at a dose. Then they proudly lay in their claim to a future credit, on failure of all their past engagements, and at a time when (if in such a matter anything can be clear) it is clear that the surplus estates will never answer even the first of their mortgages, I mean that of the four hundred millions (or sixteen millions sterling) of *assignats*. In all this procedure I can discern neither the solid sense of plain dealing nor the subtle dexterity of ingenious fraud. The objections within the Assembly to pulling up the floodgates for this inundation of fraud are unanswered, but they are thoroughly refuted by a hundred thousand financiers in the street. These are the numbers by which the metaphysic arithmeticians compute. These are the grand calculations on which a philosophical public credit is founded in France. They cannot raise supplies, but they can raise mobs. Let them rejoice in the applauses of the club at Dundee for their wisdom and patriotism in having thus applied the plunder of the citizens to the service of the state. I hear of no address upon this subject from the directors of the Bank of England, though their approbation would be of a *little* more weight in the scale of credit than that of the club at Dundee. But, to do justice to the club, I believe the gentlemen who compose it to be wiser than they appear; that they will be less liberal of their money than of their addresses; and that they would not give a dog's ear of their most rumpled and ragged Scotch paper for twenty of your fairest assignats.

Early in this year the Assembly issued paper to the amount of sixteen millions sterling; what must have been the state into which the Assembly has brought your affairs, that the relief afforded by so vast a supply has been hardly perceptible? This paper also felt an almost immediate depreciation of five per cent, which in a little time came to about seven. The effect of these assignats on the receipt of the revenue is remarkable. M. Necker found that the collectors of the revenue who received in coin paid the treasury in *assignats*. The collectors made seven per cent by thus receiving in money and accounting in depreciated paper. It was not very difficult to foresee that this must be inevitable. It was, however, not the less embarrassing. M. Necker was obliged (I believe, for a considerable part, in the market of London) to buy gold and silver for the mint, which amounted to about twelve thousand pounds above the value of the commodity gained. That minister was of opinion that, whatever their secret nutritive virtue might be, the state could not live upon *assignats* alone, that some real silver was necessary, particularly for the satisfaction of those who, having iron in their hands, were not likely to distinguish themselves for patience when they should perceive that, whilst an increase of pay was held out to them in real money, it was again to be fraudulently drawn back by depreciated paper. The minister, in this very natural distress, applied to the Assembly that they should order the collectors to pay in specie what in specie they had received. It could not escape him that if the treasury paid three per cent for the use of a currency which should be returned seven per cent worse than the minister issued it, such a dealing could not very greatly tend to enrich the public. The Assembly took no notice of this recommendation. They were in this dilemma: if they continued to receive the *assignats,* cash must become an alien to their treasury; if the treasury should refuse those paper *amulets* or should discountenance them in any degree, they must destroy the credit of their sole resource. They seem then to have made their option, and to have given some sort of credit to their paper by taking it themselves; at the same time in their speeches they made a sort of swaggering declaration, something, I rather think, above legislative competence; that is, that there is no difference in value between metallic money and their *assignats.* This was a good, stout, proof article of faith, pronounced under an anathema by the venerable fathers of this philosophic synod. *Credat* who will—certainly not *Judaeus Apella.*^{cxix}

A noble indignation rises in the minds of your popular leaders on hearing the magic lantern in their show of finance compared to the fraudulent exhibitions of Mr. Law. They cannot bear to hear the sands of his Mississippi compared with the rock of the church on which they build their system. Pray let them suppress this glorious spirit until they show to the world what piece of solid ground there is for their *assignats* which they have not preoccupied by other charges. They do injustice to that great mother fraud to compare it with their degenerate imitation. It is not true that Law built solely on a speculation concerning the Mississippi. He added the East India trade; he added the African trade; he added the farms of all the farmed revenue of France. All these together unquestionably could not support the structure which the public enthusiasm, not he, chose to build upon these bases. But these were, however, in comparison generous delusions. They supposed, and they aimed at, an increase of the commerce of France. They opened to it the whole range of the two hemispheres. They did not think of feeding France from its own substance. A grand imagination found in this flight of commerce something to captivate. It was wherewithal to dazzle the eye of an eagle. It was not made to entice the smell of a mole nuzzling and burying himself in his mother earth, as yours is. Men were not then quite shrunk from their natural dimensions by a degrading and sordid philosophy, and fitted for low and vulgar deceptions. Above all, remember that in imposing on the imagination the then managers of the system made a compliment to the freedom of men. In their fraud there was no mixture of force. This was reserved to our time, to quench the little glimmerings of reason which might break in upon the solid darkness of this enlightened age.

On recollection, I have said nothing of a scheme of finance which may be urged in favor of the abilities of these gentlemen, and which has been introduced with great pomp, though not yet finally adopted, in the National Assembly. It comes with something solid in aid of the credit of the paper circulation; and much has been said of its utility and its elegance. I mean the project for coining into money the bells of the suppressed churches. This is their alchemy. There are some follies which baffle argument, which go beyond ridicule, and which excite no feeling in us but disgust; and therefore I say no more upon it.

It is as little worth remarking any further upon all their drawing and re-drawing on their circulation for putting off the evil day, on the play between the treasury and the *Caisse d'Escompte,* and on all these old, exploded contrivances of mercantile fraud now exalted into policy of state. The revenue will not be trifled with. The prattling about the rights of men will not be accepted in payment for a biscuit or a pound of gunpowder. Here then the metaphysicians descend from their airy speculations and faithfully follow examples. What examples? The examples of bankrupts. But defeated, baffled, disgraced, when their breath, their strength, their inventions, their fancies desert them, their confidence still maintains its ground. In the manifest failure of their abilities, they take credit for their benevolence. When the revenue disappears in their hands, they have the presumption, in some of their late proceedings, to value *themselves* on the relief given to the people. They did not relieve the people. If they entertained such intentions, why did they order the obnoxious taxes to be paid? The people relieved themselves in spite of the Assembly.

213

But waiving all discussion on the parties who may claim the merit of this fallacious relief, has there been, in effect, any relief to the people in any form? Mr. Bailly, one of the grand agents of paper circulation, lets you into the nature of this relief. His speech to the National Assembly contained a high and labored panegyric on the inhabitants of Paris for the constancy and unbroken resolution with which they have borne their distress and misery. A fine picture of public felicity! What great courage and unconquerable firmness of mind to endure benefits and sustain redress! One would think from the speech of this learned lord mayor that the Parisians, for this twelvemonth past, had been suffering the straits of some dreadful blockade, that Henry the Fourth had been stopping up the avenues to their supply, and Sully thundering with his ordnance at the gates of Paris, when in reality they are besieged by no other enemies than their own madness and folly, their own credulity and perverseness. But Mr. Bailly will sooner thaw the eternal ice of his Atlantic regions than restore the central heat to Paris whilst it remains "smitten with the cold, dry, petrific mace" of a false and unfeeling philosophy. Some time after this speech, that is, on the thirteenth of last August, the same magistrate, giving an account of his government at the bar of the same Assembly, expresses himself as follows:

> In the month of July, 1789, (the period of everlasting commemoration) the finances of the city of Paris were *yet* in good order; the expenditure was counterbalanced by the receipt; and she had at that time a million (forty thousand pounds sterling) in bank. The expenses which she has been constrained to incur, *subsequent to the Revolution,* amount to 2,500,000 livres. From these expenses, and the great falling off in the product of *the free gifts,* not only a momentary, but a *total,* want of money has taken place.

This is the Paris upon whose nourishment, in the course of the last year, such immense sums, drawn from the vitals of all France, have been expended. As long as Paris stands in the place of ancient Rome, so long she will be maintained by the subject provinces. It is an evil inevitably attendant on the dominion of sovereign democratic republics. As it happened in Rome, it may survive that republican domination which gave rise to it. In that case despotism itself must submit to the vices of popularity. Rome, under her emperors, united the evils of both systems; and this unnatural combination was one great cause of her ruin.

TO tell the people that they are relieved by the dilapidation of their public estate is a cruel and insolent imposition. Statesmen, before they valued themselves on the relief given to the people by the destruction of their revenue, ought first to have carefully attended to the solution of this problem—whether it be more advantageous to the people to pay considerably and to gain in proportion, or to gain little or nothing and to be disburdened of all contribution? My mind is made up to decide in favor of the first proposition. Experience is with me, and, I believe, the best opinions also. To keep a balance between the power of acquisition on the part of the subject and the demands he is to answer on the part of the state is the fundamental part of the skill of a true politician. The means of acquisition are prior in time and in arrangement. Good order is the foundation of all good things. To be enabled to acquire, the people, without being servile, must be tractable and obedient. The magistrate must have his reverence, the laws their authority. The body of the people must not find the principles of natural subordination by art rooted out of their minds. They must respect that property of which they cannot partake. They must labor to obtain what by labor can be obtained; and when they find, as they commonly do, the success disproportioned to the endeavor, they must be taught their consolation in the final proportions of eternal justice. Of this consolation, whoever deprives them deadens their industry and strikes at the root of all acquisition as of all conservation. He that does this is the cruel oppressor, the merciless enemy of the poor and wretched, at the same time that by his wicked speculations he exposes the fruits of successful industry and the accumulations of fortune to the plunder of the negligent, the disappointed, and the unprosperous.

Too many of the financiers by profession are apt to see nothing in revenue but banks, and circulations, and annuities on lives, and tontines, and perpetual rents, and all the small wares of the shop. In a settled order of the state, these things are not to be slighted, nor is the skill in them to be held of trivial estimation. They are good, but then only good when they assume the effects of that settled order and are built upon it. But when men think that these beggarly contrivances may supply a resource for the evils which result from breaking up the foundations of public order, and from causing or suffering the principles of property to be subverted, they will, in the ruin of their country, leave a melancholy and lasting monument of the effect of preposterous politics and presumptuous, short-sighted, narrow-minded wisdom.

The effects of the incapacity shown by the popular leaders in all the great members of the commonwealth are to be covered with the "all-atoning name" of liberty. In some people I see great liberty indeed; in many, if not in the most, an oppressive, degrading servitude. But what is liberty without wisdom and without virtue? It is the greatest of all possible evils; for it is folly, vice, and madness, without tuition or restraint. Those who know what virtuous liberty is cannot bear to see it disgraced by incapable heads on account of their having high-sounding words in their mouths. Grand, swelling sentiments of liberty I am sure I do not despise. They warm the heart; they enlarge and liberalize our minds; they animate our courage in a time of conflict. Old as I am, I read the fine raptures of Lucan and Corneille with pleasure. Neither do I wholly condemn the little arts and devices of popularity. They facilitate the carrying of many points of moment; they keep the people together; they refresh the mind in its exertions; and they diffuse occasional gaiety over the severe brow of moral freedom. Every politician ought to sacrifice to the graces, and to join compliance with reason. But in such an undertaking as that in France, all these subsidiary sentiments and artifices are of little avail. To make a government requires no great prudence. Settle the seat of power, teach obedience, and the work is done. To give freedom is still more easy. It is not necessary to guide; it only requires to let go the rein. But to form a *free government,* that is, to temper together these opposite elements of liberty and restraint in one consistent work, requires much thought, deep reflection, a sagacious, powerful, and combining mind. This I do not find in those who take the lead in the National Assembly. Perhaps they are not so miserably deficient as they appear. I rather believe it. It would put them below the common level of human understanding. But when the leaders choose to make themselves bidders at an auction of popularity, their talents, in the construction of the state, will be of no service. They will become flatterers instead of legislators, the instruments, not the guides, of the people. If any of them should happen to propose a scheme of liberty, soberly limited and defined with proper qualifications, he will be immediately outbid by his competitors who will produce something more splendidly popular. Suspicions will be raised of his fidelity to his cause. Moderation will be stigmatized as the virtue of cowards, and compromise as the prudence of traitors, until, in hopes of preserving the credit which may enable him to temper and moderate, on some occasions, the popular leader is obliged to become active in propagating doctrines and establishing powers that will afterwards defeat any sober purpose at which he ultimately might have aimed.

But am I so unreasonable as to see nothing at all that deserves commendation in the indefatigable labors of this Assembly? I do not deny that, among an infinite number of acts of violence and folly, some good may have been done. They who destroy everything certainly will remove some grievance. They who make everything new have a chance that they may establish something beneficial. To give them credit for what they have done in virtue of the authority they have usurped, or which can excuse them in the crimes by which that authority has been acquired, it must appear that the same things could not have been accomplished without producing such a revolution. Most assuredly they might, because almost every one of the regulations made by them which is not very equivocal was either in the cession of the king, voluntarily made at the meeting of the states, or in the concurrent instructions to the orders. Some usages have been abolished on just grounds, but they were such that if they had stood as they were to all eternity, they would little detract from the happiness and prosperity of any state. The improvements of the National Assembly are superficial, their errors fundamental.

Whatever they are, I wish my countrymen rather to recommend to our neighbors the example of the British constitution than to take models from them for the improvement of our own. In the former, they have got an invaluable treasure. They are not, I think, without some causes of apprehension and complaint, but these they do not owe to their constitution but to their own conduct. I think our happy situation owing to our constitution, but owing to the whole of it, and not to any part singly, owing in a great measure to what we have left standing in our several reviews and reformations as well as to what we have altered or superadded. Our people will find employment enough for a truly patriotic, free, and independent spirit in guarding what they possess from violation. I would not exclude alteration neither, but even when I changed, it should be to preserve. I should be led to my remedy by a great grievance. In what I did, I should follow the example of our ancestors. I would make the reparation as nearly as possible in the style of the building. A politic caution, a guarded circumspection, a moral rather than a complexional timidity

217

were among the ruling principles of our forefathers in their most decided conduct. Not being illuminated with the light of which the gentlemen of France tell us they have got so abundant a share, they acted under a strong impression of the ignorance and fallibility of mankind. He that had made them thus fallible rewarded them for having in their conduct attended to their nature. Let us imitate their caution if we wish to deserve their fortune or to retain their bequests. Let us add, if we please, but let us preserve what they have left; and, standing on the firm ground of the British constitution, let us be satisfied to admire rather than attempt to follow in their desperate flights the aeronauts of France.

I have told you candidly my sentiments. I think they are not likely to alter yours. I do not know that they ought. You are young; you cannot guide but must follow the fortune of your country. But hereafter they may be of some use to you, in some future form which your commonwealth may take. In the present it can hardly remain; but before its final settlement it may be obliged to pass, as one of our poets says, "through great varieties of untried being",[cx] and in all its transmigrations to be purified by fire and blood.

I have little to recommend my opinions but long observation and much impartiality. They come from one who has been no tool of power, no flatterer of greatness; and who in his last acts does not wish to belie the tenor of his life. They come from one almost the whole of whose public exertion has been a struggle for the liberty of others; from one in whose breast no anger, durable or vehement, has ever been kindled but by what he considered as tyranny; and who snatches from his share in the endeavors which are used by good men to discredit opulent oppression the hours he has employed on your affairs; and who in so doing persuades himself he has not departed from his usual office; they come from one who desires honors, distinctions, and emoluments but little, and who expects them not at all; who has no contempt for fame, and no fear of obloquy; who shuns contention, though he will hazard an opinion; from one who wishes to preserve consistency, but who would preserve consistency by varying his means to secure the unity of his end, and, when the equipoise of the vessel in which he sails may be endangered by overloading it upon one side, is desirous of carrying the small weight of his reasons to that which may preserve its equipoise.

Editor's Notes
to the Text

ⁱ The reference is to Cervantes's *Don Quixote*, who set free some condemned criminals and was beaten up and robbed by them.

ⁱⁱ Shakespeare's *Macbeth*, act IV, scene 1:
> Add thereto a tiger's chaudron
> For the ingredients of our cauldron.

Price is concocting a witches' brew, and the Revolutionaries are the tiger.

ⁱⁱⁱ The allusions are: (1) to Hugh Peter, a radical clergyman from New England, who preached at the execution of Charles I in 1649 (1648 by the old calendar) and was horribly executed at the Restoration of 1660 (see also, pp. 57–58); (2) to the Holy League in France, 1584–93, a militant Catholic organisation formed to oppose King Henri III and prevent the succession of the Huguenot Henri IV; (3) to the Solemn League and Covenant of 1643, which brought the Scottish army to the aid of Parliament in the English Civil War. Burke is hinting at the old charge that extreme Catholics and extreme Calvinists join together against monarchy.

^{iv} The Seekers were a radical sect of the mid-seventeenth century, at once mystical and sceptical, who sought after God without attempting to define his nature or commands. The allusions to Price's "noble" supporters are to aristocratic advocates of the relaxation of civil penalties for anti-Trinitarian Christians and deists. The lay divine high in university office may be the Duke of Grafton, then Chancellor of the University of Cambridge. The passage which follows should be compared with that on "the dissidence of dissent" in Burke's *Speech on Conciliation with America.*

219

[v] A "dry garden" or collection of dried plants.

[vi] An old term for priests: "mass Johns".

[vii] Juvenal, *Satires,* IV, 150–51. "Would that he had devoted to trifles all the time he spent in violence".

[viii] Again note the equation of democratic theory with Catholicism, an argument as old as James I.

[ix] Horace, *Epistles,* I, 1, 12: "I concoct and compound what soon I may bring forth".

[x] See Lois G. Schwoerer, *The Declaration of Rights, 1689* (Johns Hopkins University Press, 1981).

[xi] "A privilege does not become a precedent".

[xii] An echo of the language of the Athanasian Creed: "neither confounding the substance nor dividing the persons".

[xiii] "By the common volition of the commonwealth".

[xiv] This could be read as a repudiation of Locke's *Second Treatise.*

[xv] The allusion is to a contested succession at the death of Henry I (1135). The heir *per capita* would be the deceased king's nearest male relative; the heir *per stirpes* the heir of the males next in line at the deceased's accession.

[xvi] Virgil, *Georgics,* IV, 208–09. "Through many years stands the fortune of the house, and the grandfathers of grandfathers are counted in the line".

[xvii] Ancient and fundamental statutes, according to the constitutional beliefs of the time. The statute *de tallagio* was said to have been passed in 1340; the Petition of Right of 1628 was said to have been a statute; the Habeas Corpus Act was passed in 1679. All statutes required the royal signature and were enacted by the king with the authority of parliament.

[xviii] The Act of Succession, 1700. Paine, replying to Burke, was indignant at the suggestion that parliament might bind the people in the future; but there is no other way of establishing a hereditary monarchy, and it was to this that Paine was opposed.

[xix] Terence, *The Woman of Andros,* I, 1. "This reminder is a bit of a rebuke".

[xx] Presumably an allusion to the confusion of tongues at the fall of the Tower of Babel; but the Law of Israel might be held to have become corrupted in Babylon, during either the Captivity or the Diaspora.

[xxi] Livy, *History of Rome,* IX, 1: "Wars are just when they are necessary". This is a remarkable passage, since it may allude (1) to Locke's doctrine that governments are dissolved by an "appeal to heaven" and a drawing of the sword; (2) to the Tory doctrine that the Revolution was justified

by necessity; (3) to the doctrine, too strong for all Whigs and most Tories, that William III had obtained the crown by a just conquest. It was not usual to describe his bloodless march to London as a "war".

xxii To place under the best auspices.

xxiii "Mortmain" (literally, "dead hand") was a legal device to render possession perpetual in a corporation; to render it perpetual in a family might be done by means of "entail".

xxiv This may refer to the provincial assembles or "estates" in some parts of the kingdom of France, or to the Estates General as they were constituted when they last met in 1614, or in 1789 before their procedures were altered.

xxv Maroons were communities of escaped slaves in Jamaica.

xxvi I.e., gold and silver specie.

xxvii An allusion to Warren Hastings and the parliamentary influence of the East India Company.

xxviii Henry Rich, Earl of Holland (1590–1649). Burke is probably thinking of the account of him given in Clarendon's *History of the Rebellion.*

xxix Edmund Waller, *Panegyric to my Lord Protector* (*Works,* 1730, p. 119).

xxx The French Wars of Religion, c. 1560–1598, in which the men named above were leaders.

xxxi Election to office by drawing lots (one of the original meanings of the term "ballot") was common in both ancient and medieval city republics.

xxxii Victims of lynch law in the early French Revolution were sometimes hanged from a lamp-post or *lanterne.*

xxxiii Note the absence of any reference to the United States.

xxxiv Roman generals used to present such donatives to the legions which had made them emperors. This led to disorder, civil war, and the sale of the empire to the highest bidder.

xxxv Joseph Priestley, *History of the Corruptions of Christianity* (Birmingham, 1782), vol. II, p. 484. The last word should be "event".

xxxvi Virgil, *Aeneid,* I, 140-41. "Let Aeolus bluster in that hall, and reign in the closed prison of the winds". Aeolus was a wind god, and the winds were imagined as shut up until released. A Levanter was a strong gale from the east.

xxxvii This passage is Lockean enough.

xxxviii Horace, *Ars Poetica,* 465–66. "Poets are permitted to perish . . . In cold blood he jumped into burning Etna"; a reference to the suicide of Empedocles, supposed to have thrown himself into a volcano, where his sandals alone survived.

xxxix Juvenal, *Satires,* VII, 151: "When the numerous class destroys the cruel tyrants".

xl Note that Burke does not like to be called one.

xli I.e., friends and associates in politics.

xlii He was hanged, drawn, and quartered.

xliii Leaders of conspiracy and rebellion at Rome. Catiline was the type of the nobleman turned traitor to his class.

xliv Lucan, *Pharsalia,* IX, 207: "Neither the appearance of authority nor the look of a senate".

xlv The prison chaplain who ministered to criminals about to be hanged.

xlvi *Lèse-majesté*—the old definition of treason against the king—was now being termed treason against the nation.

xlvii *Macbeth,* Act II, scene ii; the balm is sleep.

xlviii Richard Burke later wrote to his father that he had met this soldier alive and well at Strasbourg; *Correspondence,* VI, p. 372.

xlix The implication is that Price is an enthusiast and antinomian, raised above ordinary morality by a pretended gift of the Holy Spirit. The parallel with Hugh Peter is being drawn again.

l Let us speak of the part which I have played; it is firmly justified in my conscience. Neither this guilty city, nor this assembly yet more guilty, deserve to hear my justification; but it is near to my heart that you, and those who think like you, should not condemn me. My health, I assure you, made it impossible for me to discharge my duties; but even had I put them aside, it was beyond my powers to endure any longer the horror I felt at the blood, the heads, the almost murdered queen, the king led in slavery, entering Paris surrounded by murderers and preceded by the heads of their unhappy guards. The perfidious janissaries, the assassins, the cannibal women, the cry of 'All the bishops to the lamp-post', at the moment when the king was entering his capital with two bishops of his council in his carriage. The gunshot I saw fired into one of the queen's coaches. M. Bailly saying it was 'a great day'. The assembly having icily declared, that morning, that it was beneath its dignity to adjourn to escort the king. M. Mirabeau saying with impunity in the assembly that the ship of state would not be arrested in its course, but would advance more rapidly than ever towards its regeneration. M. Barnave laughing with him, when rivers of blood were running around us. The virtuous Mounier escaped by a miracle from twenty assassins, seeking his head for one trophy the more.

Behold what has made me swear to set foot no longer in this cave of man-eaters, where I had no longer the power to raise my voice, and for six weeks had raised it in vain. Mounier, I, and all honest men, must strain every resource to be able to quit it. No thought of fear has come to me; I should blush to defend myself on that account. On the road I have received, from that part of the people less guilty than those drunk with fury, praise and applause which would have flattered others but have made me tremble. It is to the indignation, the horror, the physical revulsion suffered at the sight of blood, that I have given way. One risks one's own death; one risks it many times, when it may be of use. But no

222

power under heaven, no opinion public or private, has the right to condemn me to suffer a thousand tortures uselessly every minute, to perish of rage and despair, among the triumphs of a crime I have been unable to prevent. They will proscribe me; they will confiscate my property. I shall till the soil and see them no more. Such is my justification. You may read it, show it, let it be copied. So much the worse for those who do not understand it. The fault will not be mine for having given it them.

The word "étoit", in the second sentence of the second paragraph, should probably be "état".

li The feminist comment on this remark is just and obvious.

lii Burke seems to imagine Marie Antoinette committing suicide like Lucretia, to save herself from rape. She was in fact guillotined.

liii Horace, *Ars Poetica,* 99: "It is not enough that poems be beautiful; they must also be tender".

liv Burke may not have meant that *the* multitude—i.e., the poor—were swinish; only that there were always plenty of swine to be found.

lv Virgil, *Aeneid,* III, 105: "The cradle of our race". (The Latin is *cunabula.*)

lvi I.e., enlisted.

lvii Allusions to various rulers guilty of murder or unlawful execution.

lviii French emigrés had been spreading scandal about Marie Antoinette.

lix A lunatic nobleman, imprisoned after the great London riot of 1780. He had recently announced his conversion to Judaism, and Burke seems to include him among the French queen's libellers.

lx Price was an authority on compound interest. The allusion to 1790 years (inaccurately, the period since Judas betrayed Christ) is an anti-semitic joke. Burke is exploiting the circumstance that Price preached at the "Old Jewry", a chapel on the site of a former ghetto.

lxi English deists of the period 1690–1750. Bolingbroke's writings on religion were posthumously published in 1754.

lxii This awkwardly complicated sentence means that the people in a democracy ought not to dictate to those who hold office in their name.

lxiii Cicero, *De Republica,* VI, 13: "That nothing indeed of the events which occur on earth is more pleasing to that supreme and prepotent God who rules this entire universe than those societies and associations of men, cemented by laws, which are called states".

lxiv This should be compared with the indictment of Oxford as monkish and lazy, to be found in Edward Gibbon's *Memoirs.*

lxv The Euripus is a strait in the Aegean Sea with a marked rise and fall in the tide. The allusion is to the difference between landed property and paper money.

^{lxvi} A majestic statement of Burke's mixed feelings about the aristocracy.

^{lxvii} The right of repurchase, enjoyed by a seigneur over any lands which had once formed part of his fief.

^{lxviii} His trial for maladministration was cancelled by Louis XV in 1750.

^{lxix} "That cruel spear". The Romans stuck a spear in the ground at public auctions of goods looted from an enemy.

^{lxx} "What a country is this, gentlemen, where, without taxes and with a few simple and previously unnoticed objectives, one can make a deficit disappear which has made such a stir in Europe".

^{lxxi} The Nairs were a warrior caste in India, supposedly given to banditry.

^{lxxii} Cicero, *Pro Sestio,* IX, 21: "All of us who are good are the friends of nobility".

^{lxxiii} Spenser, *The Faerie Queene,* II, 7, 14.

^{lxxiv} Gilbert Burnet (1643–1715, Bishop of Salisbury), *History of His Own Times* (1734).

^{lxxv} Burke is citing Jean Domat (1625–96), author of *Les Lois Civiles dans leur Ordre Naturel* (1689). See Paul Lucas, "On Edmund Burke's doctrine of prescription; or an appeal from the new to the old lawyers", *Historical Journal,* XI, 1 (1968), pp. 35–63.

^{lxxvi} In the present revolution they have resisted all the attractions of bigotry, all the persecutions and annoyance by the enemies of the revolution. Forgetting their principal interests to give homage to the views of general order which have decided the National Assembly, without complaining, they see done away with that swarm of ecclesiastical establishments by which they lived; and even, losing their episcopal seat, the only one of all these resources which could, or rather which should, in all equity be preserved to them; condemned to the most terrifying misery, without having been, nor having been able to be, heard, they do not grumble, they remain faithful to the principles of the purest patriotism; they are still ready to shed their blood for the maintenance of the constitution, which will reduce their city to the most deplorable nullity.

^{lxxvii} Cicero, *De Officiis* II, 79–80:

If those to whom property has been wrongfully given are more numerous than those from whom it has been unjustly taken, are they, for that reason, also more influential? For these matters are not judged by number, but by weight. And how can it be fair that a man who owned no land should now possess that which was owned for many years, or even generations, previously, and that the man who owned it should now lose it? Indeed, it was because of this type of wrongdoing that the Lacedaemonians banished their ephor Lysander and put to death their king Agis—something which had never before happened among them. And from that time on, civil strife ensued so fierce that tyrants arose, the nobles were exiled, and the state, excellently constituted as it was, fell apart. Not only did it fall, but, by the contagion of evils which, starting in Lacedaemon, spread far and wide, it dragged down also the rest of Greece . . .

II, 83:

This is the right way to deal with fellow citizens; not, as we have seen done twice already, to set the spear in the forum and to subject the property of citizens to the cry of the auctioneer. But that Greek, as befitted a wise and excellent man, thought that he had to consider the good of all. And this is the supreme judgment and wisdom of a good citizen, not to tear apart the common interests of citizens, but to bind all his fellows together by a common fairness.

lxxviii "Sparta is your lot; now adorn it". I.e., make the most of where you were born.

lxxix A plain criticism of Tudor policy at the dissolution of the monasteries.

lxxx "The gifts of the earth".

lxxxi See F. P. Lock, *Burke's Reflections on the Revolution in France* (London, 1985), pp. 58–60, on Burke's progress and possible delays in completing the *Reflections*. At this point Oskar Piest thought it possible to divide the work into two parts.

lxxxii No work of Burke's exists which can be said to carry out this intention.

lxxxiii We may think of the Declaration of Independence and its opening reference to "a decent respect for the opinion of mankind". Whether Burke thought of it is another matter.

lxxxiv Virgil, *Georgics*, I, 120: "Jove himself decreed that the cultivator's way should not be easy".

lxxxv All the establishments in France crown the unhappiness of the people: to make them happy they must be renewed, their ideas, their laws, their customs must be changed; . . . men changed, things changed, words changed . . . destroy everything; yes, destroy everything; since everything is to be recreated.

The Quinze-vingt was a hospital for the blind, the Petit Maisons for the insane.

lxxxvi Four-handed, meaning monkey-like.

lxxxvii Horace, *Epistles*, I, 19, 12–13: "Cato by the bare foot". Cato went barefooted as a philosopher; fools pretended to be like him by doing the same.

lxxxviii All critics of Burke point out that this is incorrect; departments were not geometrically constructed.

lxxxix Pope, *Moral Essays*, IV, 129.

xc "They know not man".

xci For no longer were entire legions led off, as once they were, with their tribunes, and centurions, and soldiers grouped in their own distinct centuries, in order to constitute a state by their concord and mutual affection; but, strangers to each other, were brought in of different companies, without a leader, without mutual attachment, suddenly gathered together, as if from any other class of men, a crowd rather than a colony.

xcii "The Hippocratic face"—i.e., the facial appearance from which the Greek physician Hippocrates predicted the death of the patient.

xciii Quality, relation, action, passion, place, time, situation, condition; further categories in Aristotelian philosophy.

xciv "The limbo of the fathers"—i.e., the resting place of just men who died before the coming of Christ. Burke's adaptation of the term is not very happy.

xcv Virgil, *Aeneid,* III, 75: "around the coasts and shores". The floating island of Delos was fixed by Zeus so that Latona might give birth there.

xcvi Cicero, *De Senectute,* VII, 25: "I sow for the immortal gods".

xcvii Horace, *Epode* 2, 67–70. "When the moneylender Alphius had said this, being all eagerness to become a farmer, he collected all his money in the middle of the month, but when the first comes around, he seeks to invest it again". *Beatus ille qui procul negotiis . . .* (happy is the man who, far from business cares) were famous words in praise of rural life. Burke is restoring them to context.

xcviii The Mississippi Company, promoted in France by John Law, and the South Seas Company in England, were colonial trade schemes which led to wildcat investment fevers, followed by disastrous slumps.

xcix A most curious remark from a man who knew English county politics.

c Petty police officers and debt collectors.

ci The Dauphin was the title of the heir to the French throne.

cii Juvenal, *Satires,* 284–85. "But many cities and public resolutions triumphed".

ciii Decrees or votes of the Athenian assembly.

civ "Can you keep from laughing?" (Burke's insertion).

cv *Comitia* were various popular assemblies at Rome, some in military formation.

cvi "Taken with the most imposing solemnity".

cvii As his majesty has recognized in them, not a system of private associations, but a union of the wills of all Frenchmen toward the common liberty and prosperity as well as for the maintenance of the public good; he thinks that it would be proper that each regiment should take a part in these civic festivals to multiply the relationships and tighten the bonds of union between the citizens and the troops.

cviii Cicero, *De Senectute,* XIII, 83. "But if the gods should grant me as a boon that I should become young again and cry in *their* cradle, I would vehemently refuse". Burke's quotation is slightly changed. The text has "in *my* cradle".

cix Burke is following the argument of Sieyès and others, who alleged that the French nobility were the heirs of the Frankish invaders of Roman Gaul and feudal dues the effects of their conquest.

cx Salt taxes, very important in the old French fiscal system.

cxi An insecure confederation of cities in ancient Greece.

cxii This is a quotation from the Roman dramatist Naevius, preserved in Cicero, *De Senectute* VI, 20. "Tell me, how did you lose a common-wealth as great as yours so quickly?" The reply is "Through foolish young men making speeches".

cxiii The Royal Exchange in the City of London, where financial dealings went on.

cxiv Burke is inventing a dog-Latin verb, *assignare,* from the French *assignats,* and punning on the dog-Latin of Molière's *Le Malade Imaginaire,* in which the candidate for a degree gives, as the treatment for every disease, *assaignare* (to bleed).

cxv This note is unclear; La Bruyère was an essayist and Bossuet a great churchman in the reign of Louis XIV, but the "prelate" in the text is the notoriously irreligious Talleyrand (Bishop of Autun).

cxvi The allusion is to the Tory failure to set up a land-bank in 1696, in reply to the Whig Bank of England.

cxvii "Religion Catholique et Apostolique". The *ancien règime* term for Protestantism was "Religion Pretendue Reformée" (R.P.R.): "the so-called reformed religion".

cxviii I do not speak here to the assembly as a whole; I speak only to those who mislead it, by hiding under flattering veils the end to which they drag it. To them I say: your object, as you will not deny, is to rob the clergy of all hope and to complete its ruin; and this—without raising any suspicion of other greedy conspiracies, or of intending any gamble with the public resources—this is what we must believe you have in view in the terrible operation you have proposed; for this must be the fruit of it. But the people, whom you involve in it: what advantage can they find? In making such incessant use of their name, what are you doing for them? Nothing, nothing at all; on the contrary, your policy can only load them with new expenses. You have rejected, to their loss, an offer of four hundred million pounds, to accept which might have done much to lighten their burden; and for this relief, both legitimate and profitable, you have substituted an act of ruinous injustice, which, on your own showing, charges the public treasury, and in consequence the people, with an increase of annual expenditure totalling at least fifty million, and a subvention of one hundred and fifty million more.

Unhappy people, this is what the expropriation of the Church will bring you at last; this, and the harshness of those decrees which impose such taxes on the ministers of a benevolent religion. Their charity once relieved the poor, and you will be taxed to contribute to their maintenance!

cxix Horace, *Satires,* 5, 100: "let the Jew Apella believe it". Horace's joke was about an alleged Jewish superstition; Burke's is about Jewish understanding of finance, i.e., about what Apella would *not* believe.

cxx Addison, *Cato,* act V, scene 1.

APPENDIX I

Reprintings of the *Reflections*
during the period of the Revolutionary Wars
Supplied by W. R. E. Velema,
Johns Hopkins University

I. FRANCE

Burke's contacts with Charles-François Depont, the "very young gentleman at Paris" to whom he addressed the *Reflections,* have been described by Forster. The only thing that needs mention here is that Depont's last letter to Burke, written in December 1790, was published as a pamphlet in England under the title *Answer to the Reflections of the Right Hon. Edmund Burke, by M. De Pont with the Original Notes* (London: Debrett, Piccadilly, 1791).

More important is the story of the French translation and publication of the *Reflections.* P. G. Dupont (c. 1759–1817), *conseiller* of the Parlement of Paris, had been in England in 1788 or 1789 to study the jury system. He met Burke, probably through his son Richard. Dupont started working on his French translation of the *Reflections* in the last week of October 1790 (i.e., even before it was published in England). He incorporated the revisions and additions of the third English edition (16 November) and his translation was published on 29 November 1790 by Laurent (Paris), who had just published Calonne's *De l'état de la France, présent et à venir* in October. The day after the French publication Dupont writes to Burke: "2500 Exemplaires de la traduction ont été vendus depuis deux Jours" (30 November 1790, *Corr.*, VI, 183). He also mentions attempts to pirate the translation and the fact that it has been placed under the protection of J. S. Bailly, mayor of Paris since July 1789. The book clearly is a success. By 13 December a second impression is out and Dupont writes to Burke: "Vous inspirés à tout le monde de désir d'apprendre l'Anglais; on ne parle que de vous; on veut vous connaître—j'ai vû des lettres écrites du fonds de nos Provinces, et ce sentiment y est le même" (13 December 1790, *Corr.*, VI, 191). In an interesting letter in February 1791 Dupont writes:

> The demand, with us, is not at all abated, as you think it is. It still goes on, but not so fast as with the original, and perhaps it depends upon me, because many people are waiting for a new Edition much more corrected which has been promised to the public. The bookseller [Laurent] told me [a] few days ago, that the 9th thousand was now in circulation, and his purpose was to print this book again, with new characters and upon a fine white paper. . . . If you calculate the number of copies sold to the public, I dare say—16 thousand in England—10 thousand from Paris—6 thousand from Lyon and Strasbourg, where I know the printsellers have counterfeited Editions for their account upon that of Paris—It is not so much as with you, respecting the number of inhabitants—(28 February 1791, *Corr.*, VI, 227–228).

As Dupont himself admits (e.g., *Corr.*, VI, 261), his original translation was bad. This was also noticed by Calonne in a letter to Burke, where he writes about comparing the English and the French versions:

> J'ai meme fait des comparaisons Si desavantageuses au traducteur que malgré L'estime et L'amitié que je lui ai Vouées depuis longtems, je me suis faché Contre lui, et ne me suis abstenu de lui faire des reproches que dans la crainte de le mortifier trop Sensiblement en lui disant quil vous avoit defiguré en plusieurs endroits. J'en ai noté plus de 30 où ma traduction, que j'ai ecritte en marge de la Sienne, m'a paru rendre Infiniment mieux Votre pensée, et approcher davantage votre Stile (9 February 1791, *Corr.*, VI, 221-222).

Dupont keeps correcting his translation, and in the meantime the situation in Paris deteriorates. In July 1791 he writes to Burke:

> L'assemblée a repris sa férocité en reprenant sa force. Les Clubs Jacobites sont plus furieux et plus Sanguinaires que jamais. Le Malheureux libraire

qui a imprimé votre livre et qui vient de terminer l'impression de La 5e Edition va être obligé de fuir. On a entouré sa maison—on vient l'insulter chaque jour et 3 députés du club sont entrés comme des furieux dans sa boutique, lui ont mis le point sous le nez et lui ont dit que dans 15 Jours il *ferait sa grimace.* Ce qui veut dire qu'il sera pendu (7 July 1791, *Corr.,* VI, 284-285).

The Jacobins did not carry out their threats immediately, however, for on 11 August 1791 Dupont writes: "Cette nouvelle Edition est en pleine vente actuellement, et il y a peu de jours où on n'en demande plusieurs" (*Corr.,* VI, 337). This is his last letter to Burke. Later he appears to be staying in England, although in January 1793 he is back in Paris "to try to save his family property" (*Corr.,* VII, 345). Burke gives him support in trying to find a job in St. Domingo (*Corr.,* VIII, 443) and finally mentions him in May 1794 as "my worthy and unfortunate friend Mr. Dupont" (*Corr.,* IX, 378).

II. GERMANY

The standard monograph here is F. Braune, *Edmund Burke in Deutschland. Ein Beitrag zur Geschichte des historisch-politischen Denkens* (Heidelberg, 1917). This is a superficial book, but it contains useful references and technical information.

There are three German editions of the *Reflections:*

1. *Bemerkungen über die französische Revolution und das Betragen einiger Gesellschaften in London bei diesen Ereignissen. Aus dem Englischen nach der vierten Ausgabe übersetzt.* J. Stahel. Vienna, 1791. Second impression 1793. Translator unknown.

2. *Betrachtungen über die französische Staatsrevolution, aus dem Englischen. Mit des Verfassers Porträt.* Schaumburg und Komp. Vienna, 1793.

3. *Betrachtugën über die französische Revolution. Nach dem Englischen des Herrn Burke neu bearbeitet mit einer Einleitung, Anmerkungen, politischen Abhandlungen, und einem critischen verzeignis der in England erschienenen Schriften von Friedrich Gentz.* 2 vols. Friedrich Vieweg dem Alteren. Berlin, 1793. Second impression 1794, third impression 1838. (As the title suggests, this is a very free translation: Gentz leaves things out, corrects Burke, etc.) The *Reflections,* either in their original form or in German translation, were reviewed in a wide variety

of German periodicals (listed by Braune, 41–78). It is generally agreed that two people, both from Hannover ("the Hannoverian school"), were most important in the pre-Gentz reception of Burke in Germany:

a) Ernst Brandes (Hannover, 1810). Brandes met Burke in 1784/ 1785 and later corresponded with him. Only a small part of this exchange is printed in the *Correspondence* and S. Skalweit, "Edmund Burke, Ernst Brandes, und Hannover", *Niedersächsisches Jahrbuch für Landesgeschichte,* XXVIII (1956) 15–72 should be consulted. Brandes' most important works are "Uber den politischen Geist Englands", *Berlinische Monatschrift,* 1786; *Politische Betrachtungen über die französische Revolution* (Jena, 1790); *Uber einige bisherige Folgen der französischen Revolution mit Rücksicht auf Deutschland* (Hannover, 1793). He reviewed the English version of Burke's *Reflections* in the *Göttingsche Anzeigen von gelehrten Sachen,* 26 November 1791, p. 1897 ff.

b) August Wilhelm Rehberg (Hannover, 1757—Göttingen, 1836) wrote even more than Brandes did, but for our purpose his most important work is *Untersuchungen über die französische Revolution, nebst kritischen Nachrichten von den merksürdigsten Schriften, welche darüber in Frankreich erschienen sind,* 2 vols. (Hannover and Osnabrück, 1793). He reviewed the English text of Burke's *Reflections* in the *Allgemeine Literaturzeitung* (Jena), 4 March 1791, p. 561 ff. The best modern discussion of his work is K. Epstein, *The Genesis of German Conservatism* (Princeton, 1966), Ch. 11 ("Rehberg and the Hannoverian School").

Friedrich Gentz's translation of the *Reflections* is available in a modern edition, edited by L. Iser, with an introduction by D. Henrich (Frankfurt am Main, 1967). A recent discussion of Burke and Gentz is P. Pirler, *Friedrich von Gentzens Auseinandersetzung mit Immanuel Kant* (Frankfurt am Main, 1980), 41–70. Gentz wrote Burke one letter, to inform him of the completion of the German translation (8 February 1793, *Corr.,* VII, 346-347).

III. OTHER

It is almost impossible to obtain information on other translations of the *Reflections.* There seems to have been no published Dutch translation in the eighteenth century (G. K. van Hogendorp translated parts of the book for himself). Todd lists three Italian editions, two of them extracts (1791, 1793). The *Reflections* were published in America by H. Gaine (New York) in 1791 and by D. Humphreys (Philadelphia) in 1792.

APPENDIX II

Some Recent Interpretations of Burke

Boulton, James T.: *The Language of Politics in the Age of Wilkes and Burke* (London, 1963).

Cobban, Alfred: *Edmund Burke and the Revolt Against the Eighteenth Century* (London, 1962).

Dreyer, Frederick: *Burke's Politics: a Study in Whig Orthodoxy* (Waterloo, Ontario, 1979).

Freeman, Michael: *Edmund Burke and the Critique of Political Radicalism* (Oxford, 1980).

Kirk, Russell: *Edmund Burke: a Genius Reconsidered* (New Rochelle, 1967).

Kramnick, Isaac F.: *The Rage of Edmund Burke: Portrait of an Ambivalent Conservative* (New York, 1977).

Lock, F. P.: *Burke's Reflections on the Revolution in France* (London, 1985).

Macpherson, C. B.: *Edmund Burke* (Oxford, 1980).

O'Gorman, Frank: *Edmund Burke: His Political Philosophy* (London, 1973).

Parkin, Charles: *The Moral Basis of Burke's Political Thought* (Cambridge, 1956).

Pocock, J. G. A.: (1) *Politics, Language and Time: Essays on Political Thought and History* (New York, 1971), ch. 6: "Burke and the Ancient Constitution: a Problem in the History of Ideas".

235

(2) *Virtue, Commerce and History: Essays on Political Thought and History, Chiefly in the Eighteenth Century* (Cambridge, 1985), ch. 10: "The Political Economy of Burke's Analysis of the French Revolution".

Reid, Christopher: *Edmund Burke and the Practice of Political Writing* (New York: St. Martin's Press, 1985).

Stanlis, Peter J.: *Edmund Burke and the Natural Law* (Ann Arbor, 1958).

Wilkins, Burleigh Taylor: *The Problem of Burke's Political Philosophy* (Oxford, 1967).

1-112
186-End

Granlibakken   Tahoe City
1 - 916 · 583-4242 O
+ 581-0505 H